Managerial leadership

Leadership is an elusive concept, and has been tackled by theorists with varying degrees of success over the years. Many definitions now exist, and *Managerial Leadership* provides a review of these, from the very earliest view of leadership, which saw it as an attribute which people possessed, through the various theories of leadership behaviour, to the re-emergence of charismatic and 'trait' approaches to leadership.

Wright concentrates on the area of middle manager leadership and aims to help leaders and future leaders to lead more effectively. Covering such topics as the implications for managerial leadership in the new era of 'knowledge-worker' organizations; the new paradigms of managerial leadership that the literature is offering to help with this new agenda; the debunking of the charisma myth and the problem of how we get the kind of commitment we need in circumstances where we are flattening out traditional hierarchies by laying off middle managers with many years of service.

This book reveals that to understand leadership it is first necessary to understand the manager's job as a whole and the place of leadership within it.

Peter L. Wright is Lecturer in Occupational Psychology at the University of Bradford Management Centre.

Elements of Business Series
Series editor: David Weir
University of Bradford Management Centre

This important new series is designed to cover the core topics taught at MBA level with an approach suited to the modular teaching and shorter time frames that apply in the MBA sector. Based on current courses and teaching experience, these texts are tailor-made to the needs of today's MBA student.

Other titles in the series

Business and Society
Edmund Marshall

Management Accounting
Leslie Chadwick

Financial Accounting
Iain Ward-Campbell

Managerial Human Resources
Christopher Molander and Jonathan Winterton

Business and Microeconomics
Christopher Pass and Bryan Lowes

Financial Management
Leslie Chadwick and Donald Kirby

Business and Macroeconomics
Christopher Pass, Bryan Lowes and Andrew Robinson

Managerial Leadership

Peter L. Wright

London and New York

First published 1996
by Routledge
11 New Fetter Lane, London EC4P 4EE

Simultaneously published in the USA and Canada
by Routledge
29 West 35th Street, New York, NY 10001

© 1996 Peter L. Wright

Typeset in Garamond by Pure Tech India Ltd, Pondichery
Printed and bound in Great Britain by Mackays of Chathan PLC, Chatham Kent

British Library Cataloguing in Publication Data
A catalogue record for this book is available from the British Library

Library of Congress Cataloguing in Publication Data
A catalogue record for this book has been requested

ISBN 0-415-11068-8 (hbk)
ISBN 0-415-11069-6 (pbk)

For Barbara

Contents

Figures and tables

FIGURES

TABLES

Acknowledgements

I am grateful to the following for their permission to reproduce various figures and tables, in their original or in amended form:

Robert R. Blake, Jacquelyn Mouton and Asha Jane, for Figure 3.1, first published in Blake and McCanse, *Leadership Dilemmas – Grid Solutions* (Gulf, 1991); the *Harvard Business Review*, for Figure 4.1, from Tannenbaum and Schmidt (1958); Joseph Garcia and Fred Fielder, for Figure 4.3, first published in Fiedler and Garcia, *New Approaches to Effective Leadership* (Wiley, 1987); W.J. Reddin & Associates, for Figure 4.4, first published in Reddin, *Managerial Effectiveness* (McGraw-Hill, Inc., 1970); the University of Michigan Press, for Figure 4.6, first published in Misumi, *The Behavioral Science of Leadership* (1985); W.J. Reddin & Associates, for Figures 4.7 and 4.8, first published in Reddin, *How to Make Your Management Style More Effective* (McGraw-Hill, Inc., 1987); John Wiley & Sons, Inc., for Figure 7.1, first published in Manz and Sims (eds) *Business Without Bosses* (1993); the American Psychological Association, for Figure 7.2, first published in Pallak and Perloff (eds) *Psychology and Work: Productivity, Change and Employment* (1986); Joseph Garcia and Fred Fiedler, for Figure 8.5, first published in Fiedler and Garcia, *New Approaches to Effective Leadership* (Wiley, 1987); Lexington Books, a Division of Simon & Schuster, Inc., for Figure 9.1, first published in Hunt, Baliga, Dachler and Schriesheim, *Emerging Leadership Vistas* (1988); Sage Publications, Inc., for Figure 9.2, first published in Bass and Avolio (eds) *Improving Organizational Effectiveness Through Transformational Leadership* (1994).

Fred Luthans, for Table 2.5, first published in Hunt *et al., Leaders and Managers* (Pergamon, 1984); W.J. Reddin & Associates, for Table 4.2, first published in Reddin, *How to Make Your Management Style More Effective* (McGraw-Hill, Inc., 1987); Prentice Hall, for Table 6.1, first published in Yukl, *Leadership in Organizations* (1994); Joseph Garcia and Fred Fiedler, for Table 8.1, first published in Fiedler and Garcia, *New Approaches to Effective Leadership* (Wiley, 1987).

John Wiley & Sons, Inc., for Exercise 5 (pp. 166-8), reproduced in abridged form from Manz and Sims (eds) *Business Without Bosses* (1993).

While the author and the publishers have made every effort to contact the copyright holders of material used in this volume, they would be grateful to hear from any they were unable to contact.

Chapter 1

Introduction: the meaning and measurement of leadership

INTRODUCTION

Leadership is an elusive concept. Like many complex ideas, it is deceptively easy to use in everyday conversation. We may say that someone is a great leader or used great leadership in a particular situation, and others seem to understand what we mean. Nevertheless, it has proved very difficult to arrive at a precise and agreed definition of leadership. Indeed, Bass (1990) suggests that there are almost as many definitions of leadership as there are persons who have attempted to define the concept.

Admittedly, there is a common theme which runs through most definitions of leadership. Most include the notion that leadership involves influence in one form or another (Yukl 1994). The very idea of leadership presupposes the existence of followers. The activity of leadership cannot be carried out without followers to lead, and what leaders do is to influence the behaviour, beliefs and feelings of other group members in an intended direction (Wright and Taylor 1994).

However, this definition still leaves unanswered several important questions regarding the nature of leadership. Furthermore, leadership theorists often hold different views on these questions, creating a number of areas of controversy or ambiguity within leadership research and theory. Among them are the following.

The role of personality

An early view of leadership was that it was a personality characteristic. Some people were thought to 'have' or 'possess' leadership while others were regarded as lacking in this characteristic. This view was soon discarded and those interested in the relationship between personality and leadership turned their attention to attempting to discover whether the possession of particular personality traits, such as intelligence, extraversion, dominance, and so on, were associated with becoming a leader or being an effective leader. Nevertheless, there is still considerable disagreement among leadership theorists concerning the extent to which personality traits are important in leadership.

The existence of leadership positions

Early leadership researchers and theorists also tended to regard leaders as people who occupied formally recognized positions at the head of particular units or organizations. This gave way to the behavioural view of leadership. That is, leadership came to be regarded as something which people did rather than an attribute of a position. Such a person might have a formally recognized leadership role, that is one in which he or she is expected to be the person who exerts influence over others within a particular group or organization. However, people in such positions need not actually act as a leader. They can be mere figureheads, while someone else who does not occupy a formal leadership position may actually have the major influence on the group. Similarly, in groups where the person occupying a formal position of authority has the major influence on the group, he or she may decide to share the leadership role under certain circumstances. Such a leader may ask for a follower's opinion or welcome suggestions from followers even if they have not specifically been asked for. If a follower suggests a course of action which is accepted and acted upon by the leader and the rest of the group, then the follower can be regarded as contributing to the leadership of the group.

In modern leadership theory there are still some differences of opinion or differences in approach with respect to the role of position in leadership. Some writers, such as Katz and Kahn (1978), would suggest that different types of behaviour and different leadership attributes are required at different levels within organizations, while others find little evidence for this view. Similarly, as we shall see, some leadership theorists concentrate upon the study of 'top' leaders, such as the heads of countries and large organizations, while others are concerned with leadership at any level within an organization.

The role of coercion

Some leadership theorists would exclude from leadership certain forms of influence, such as those involving coercion through the use of force or threats. Others, like Wright and Taylor (1994), take the view that threats are simply one of a number of methods a leader may use to influence followers.

The evaluation of leadership performance

If leadership is defined solely in terms of influence, then leaders who are successful in influencing the behaviour, beliefs, and feelings of their followers could be regarded as effective. However, this creates an anomaly. The leader who is successful in exerting influence over his or her followers may influence them to pursue a disastrous course of action and it seems absurd to describe such a person as an effective leader. As Katz and Kahn (1978) point out, to be wrong and influential is organizationally much worse than being merely wrong. They therefore suggest that the concept of leadership should include the cognitive skills and the technical knowledge to make effective decisions.

Bass (1990) attempts to resolve this dilemma by distinguishing between attempted, successful and effective leadership. Attempted leadership is the expenditure of effort with the intent of changing the behaviour of others. Successful leadership occurs when the leadership attempt results in the other members actually changing their behaviour. Effective leadership is successful influence by the leader which results in goal attainment by the influenced followers. While very convenient, this suggestion does not entirely resolve the dilemma of how leadership performance should be assessed. For one thing, some leadership theorists do not define 'successful leadership' in the same way as Bass does. While Bass defines successful leadership in terms of influence, Luthans et al. (1988) and McClelland and Boyatzis (1982) define leadership success in terms of speed of promotion. More importantly, groups may have multiple objectives, particularly if they are part of larger organizations. The members of each group will have objectives concerning the fulfilment of their own needs, while leaders of the larger organization will also have objectives concerning the group's contribution to its overall objectives. Leadership theorists differ in the emphasis they put on these objectives. Some define leadership effectiveness in terms of the achievement of group goals, some in terms of achievement of organizational objectives and some, like Luthans et al. (1988), employ a composite criterion incorporating both aspects. Under some circumstances, however, these objectives may conflict and it is unlikely that senior management will regard a group leader who fulfils the needs of his or her group members at the expense of those of the larger organization as being effective. Thus, when leadership theorists use the term 'effective leadership', they may mean quite different things.

The measurement of leadership and its effects

This brings us to another related problem in the study of leadership. Not only do leadership researchers define it in different ways, they also measure leadership and its effects in different ways. The most common measure of leadership behaviour is a questionnaire administered to the leaders themselves, their superiors, their subordinates or their peers. Inevitably, there are a great many potential sources of bias in such descriptions. They rely on memory, and what managers and others think they usually do may differ significantly from what they actually do (see Chapter 2). A salient recent event may distort peoples' whole perception of a manager's behaviour. Managers may consciously or unconsciously slant their self-descriptions to give what they believe to be a favourable impression of themselves. Subordinates may be consciously or unconsciously influenced to give favourable or unfavourable impressions of their bosses because they like or dislike them, rather than because they actually behave in the ways described. Not surprisingly, therefore, descriptions of leadership behaviour given by the managers themselves, and their superiors, peers and subordinates do not always agree. One way of avoiding this problem is to use direct observation of leader behaviour by impartial observers, and some examples of this approach are given in Chapter 6. However, this is an extremely time-consuming method and is used comparatively rarely.

Similarly, there are differences in the way the effects of leadership are measured. Once again, the questionnaire is commonly used. In some cases, this may be entirely justified, despite its limitations. When the effects being studied relate to inner psychological states, such as subordinates' job satisfaction or commitment, questionnaires represent the most direct method of obtaining data about the variables concerned. On the other hand, when the effects being studied relate to the subordinates' overt behaviour or work performance, then other, more objective sources of data may be available, such as direct observation, output data, labour turnover and absenteeism figures, grievance rates, profitability, and so on. However, it is often very difficult to obtain direct measures of work performance, particularly where the employees' output does not take the form of discrete, quantifiable units and/or is influenced by factors not under their control. Thus, less direct measures may be used, such as performance appraisal data, speed of promotion, and rankings or ratings by superiors, peers or subordinates. All of these, directly or indirectly, represent other people's opinions about the leader's effectiveness, and thus are subject to the sources of bias already mentioned.

The establishment of causal relations between leadership variables and their hypothesized effects

There exist a number of different research methods which can be used to establish causal relationships between leadership variables and their hypothesized effects on subordinates' beliefs, feelings and behaviour. Qualitative research methods may be used. For example, researchers may study the biographies of leaders or carry out unstructured interviews with leaders and come to their own opinions concerning the reasons why such leaders produced the effects on followers which they did. When quantitative information is collected (e.g. from questionnaires or structured observation), it is possible to analyse such data statistically, allowing greater objectivity in the interpretation of findings. However, when information concerning the behaviour or characteristics of leaders is collected at the same time as data concerning their hypothesized effects on subordinates, it is impossible to draw firm conclusions with respect to causality. Thus, as noted in Chapter 3, if it is found that considerate leaders have subordinates with greater productivity, this correlation could arise because consideration leads to greater productivity or because greater productivity leads managers to behave more considerately. The standard method of establishing causality is to carry out an experiment. In the case of leadership, this would involve actually varying specific characteristics or behaviour of leaders, keeping everything else constant, and observing the effects of such differing characteristics or behaviours on the subsequent beliefs, feelings or behaviours of subordinates. It is often extremely difficult to control all the variables involved in real-life settings, and this in turn may make it less certain that true causal relationships have been established. In laboratory studies, on the other hand, it is easier to control the variables involved, but the artificiality of the situation makes it less certain that people would behave in the same way in a real-life situation. In leadership studies, the results obtained sometimes depend on the research methodology used. As we shall see in Chapter 3, for example, researchers have tended to find a positive relationship between participation and productivity in field studies but a negative one in laboratory studies.

The generality of leadership research and theory

For many years, leadership researchers and theorists appeared to assume that their work had wide generality. Given the concentration of leadership research and theory in North America, and the cultural norms which prevailed at the time, this meant that statements concerning the characteristics, behaviour, success and effectiveness of leaders tended to be based on research on white, male, North American subjects. More recently, as we shall see in Chapter 5, it has become apparent that the effects of different leader characteristics and behaviour on follower beliefs, feelings and behaviour may vary according to the gender, ethnic background, nationality and so on of both leaders and followers. Thus, when assessing the practical implications of leadership research and theories, it is worth bearing in mind that prescriptions which are valid for one group, nationality or culture may not be valid for another.

For all the above reasons, care must be taken when interpreting the findings of leadership research. In their publications, leadership researchers typically define leadership and describe their methods of measurement carefully at the beginning of their books and articles. However, it would be tedious to use these in full thereafter, and terms such as leadership, effective leadership and successful leadership are used without qualification. Similarly, in secondary sources, such as the standard texts, such terms may be used without stipulating how the researchers concerned defined and measured them. For this reason, taken out of context, many statements about leadership could be misleading to the unwary. For example, as we have seen, successful leaders could be those who are able to exert influence over followers in one study and those who are promoted rapidly in another. In this book, therefore, I have attempted as far as possible to make it clear exactly what criteria of leadership performance were used in the studies described.

The fact that the results obtained in leadership research may depend on the method used and the population studied means that the results of single studies may be suspect. For this reason, it is useful to have several studies of the same topic, preferably carried out by different research methods, before coming to firm conclusions concerning what has been found. I have therefore attempted to quote large-scale reviews of research where these are available in order to give the overall picture as far as possible. Where such reviews are not available, I have usually quoted several studies, rather than relying on isolated findings.

Inevitably, I have my own preferences with regard to both the definition and methods of study of leadership. For example, I would prefer to define leadership solely in terms of influence, despite the contradictions this involves, because extending the definition of leadership to include other aspects such as decision-making could make the term redundant by making it synonymous with management (Wright and Taylor 1994). Mintzberg (1973, 1975), for example, regards leadership as only one of ten managerial roles. Apart from leadership, he identifies two other interpersonal roles, three informational roles and four decisional roles (see Chapter 2). My own preference is also for studying detailed examples of leader behaviour, using direct observation and sequential methods of analysis which allow the establishment of causality (Callaghan and Wright 1992, 1994). However, this is a general leadership text and I shall attempt to be as impartial as possible in what is included and how it is evaluated. Having revealed my own biases, readers will be able to judge for themselves how successful I have been.

Because this is a general text, I shall take a relatively broad view of leadership. The emphasis will be on managerial leadership: that is, the main concern will be with the characteristics and behaviour of those occupying leadership roles within formal organizations. However, no attempt will be made to restrict the definition of leadership to particular types of behaviour or the measurement of leadership to particular methods, although I shall as far as possible make clear the position of the leadership theorists and researchers whose work I describe with regard to these issues.

In Chapter 2 the nature of managerial work will be reviewed in order to put the study of leadership into context. In Chapter 3 early approaches to the study of leadership will be examined. Two strands can be discerned in the early approaches to the study of leadership. First, there were studies of single personality traits which were assumed to be associated with leadership success and effectiveness irrespective of the situation. Second, there were studies and theories which attempted to identify broad classes of leadership behaviour (leadership styles) which were associated with leadership effectiveness in all situations. Both approaches produced disappointing results and have now largely been abandoned. Chapter 4 will describe and evaluate theories which argue that different leadership styles (e.g. participative, directive, task oriented, person centred, and so on) are appropriate in different leadership situations. Apart from evaluating individual situational style theories, it is possible to assess the utility of the approach as a whole. Chapter 5 examines how well situational style theories in general have coped with a number of common issues, including the extent to which leaders are able to adapt their behaviour to changing circumstances, whether leaders should adapt their style to individual followers or the group, the importance of cultural differences, the high level of abstraction of situational style theories, and the increasing complexity of these theories. It will be argued that while situational style theories represent an advance on the earlier, simplistic behavioural theories, they still give limited advice to practising managers on how to perform the leadership role effectively.

In Chapter 6 alternative approaches to the study of leadership behaviour are considered. These include leadership theories based on operant conditioning, the skills approach to leadership, the leader–member exchange (vertical–dyad linkage) theory of leadership, an explanation of leader behaviour in terms of attribution processes, the event management model of leadership and the study of substitutes for leadership. Chapter 7 reviews a comparatively recent development in leadership theory, the growing interest in self-management. Topics covered in this chapter include individual self-management, self-managing teams, empowerment, the theoretical underpinning of self-management concepts, organizational and individual costs and benefits of self-management, the issue of authority and the implications for leadership. Chapter 8 examines the re-emergence of the trait approach to leadership. First, it considers the argument that earlier research revealed a stronger relationship between personality characteristics and the probability of becoming a leader than was realized at the time. It then reviews newer and more sophisticated theories concerning the relationship between personality characteristics and leadership effectiveness, which take into account both combinations of traits and situational factors. The chapter concludes with a discussion of the effects of implicit leadership theories on follower perceptions of leaders' personality characteristics. Chapter 9 reviews recent developments in the study of charismatic and related inspirational forms of leadership within organizations. Finally, Chapter 10 draws together the main themes to emerge from the book, both theoretical and practical, and suggests areas where further development would be of greatest benefit to the practising manager.

Chapter 2

The work of management and the management of work

INTRODUCTION

The aim of this chapter is to set the scene for the remainder of the book by examining the nature of managerial work. Leadership, as we have defined it, is an important aspect of a manager's job. However, managers have many other responsibilities apart from leadership and the sum total of these responsibilities provides the context within which managers perform their leadership role. Furthermore, such factors as the amount and type of responsibilities which managers have, the time available to perform them and the relative importance attached to these responsibilities by both managers and their organizations can have a marked influence on the type of relationship which managers have with their subordinates and others within the organization. To understand leadership, therefore, it is first necessary to understand the manager's job as a whole and the place of leadership within it. In order to provide an overall impression of the work which managers do, this chapter will examine three main aspects of the manager's job:

1 The context of managerial work – how managers spend their time.
2 The content of managerial work – what managers are attempting to achieve through the expenditure of their time and effort. Martinko and Gardner (1985) refer to the study of this aspect of managerial behaviour as going beyond the 'what' to the 'why' of functions of managerial work.
3 The relationship between what managers do and their managerial effectiveness and success.

HOW MANAGERS SPEND THEIR TIME

The first systematic study of how managers spend their time was carried out by Carlson (1951). He used what has since come to be known as the 'diary method' of data collection. The daily activities of nine Swedish managing directors were recorded for him over a period of four weeks by the directors themselves and others such as their private secretaries or personal assistants using a precoded pad designed by Carlson. He found that the managing directors worked long hours, but had little time alone, because of continual interruptions from visitors and telephone calls. Total time alone during a 'normal' weekday varied from less than half an hour to as much as an hour and a half. However, this tended to be made up of very brief periods. For example, one chief executive had an average total time of 1 hour 28 minutes working alone in his office during a normal weekday. However, this was mainly composed of short intervals of 10 to 15 minutes, many of which were further split up by phone calls. Only 12 times in 35 days did the chief executive work undisturbed in his office during intervals of 23 minutes or more.

When asked which aspect of their duties the executives themselves felt they neglected, almost without exception they identified the long-term planning of their business. The common excuse was the increasing amount of outside activities and the difficulty in getting enough time undisturbed by visitors. Carlson states that before he carried out his study he thought of the chief executive as the conductor of an orchestra standing aloof on his platform. Having completed it, however, he was more inclined to see him as a puppet in a puppet show with hundreds of people pulling the strings and forcing him to act in one way or another.

Similar results were found by Stewart (1967), who studied 160 British managers for four weeks, using the diary method. She found that they spent an average of about 34 per cent of their time alone. However, this did not take into account fleeting contacts lasting five minutes or less, which occurred at an average of about 12 per day. During the four-week period, the managers had an average of nineteen periods of half an hour or longer which were broken by fleeting contacts and only nine such periods without interruption. Excluding fleeting contacts, the managers recorded an average of 13 different activities per day.

Mintzberg (1973) carried out an observational study of five American chief executives for five days in each case. He found that they averaged 36 written and 16 verbal contacts each day, almost every one dealing with a distinct issue. Half their observed activities were completed in less than nine minutes and only one tenth took more than an hour. Replications of Mintzberg's study have produced similar results. Kurke and Aldrich (1983) observed four 'top managers' for five days each and found that the proportion of activities lasting less than nine minutes was 63 per cent, while those lasting more than one hour only accounted for 5 per cent of the manager's time. An even more extreme distribution was found in Choran's (1969) study of three presidents of small companies over a total of six days. Their activities lasted less than nine minutes in 90 per cent of cases, while only 0.02 per cent lasted longer than an hour.

These studies represent only a small part of the research which has been carried out into how managers spend their time. McCall et al. (1978) included some forty studies of how managers spend their time in their review, and many more studies have been carried out since then (see Martinko and Gardner 1985). Nevertheless, they are representative of the work in the area. Inevitably, there are variations in how managers spend their time. Mintzberg (1973) suggests that the work managers do is influenced by an enormous number of variables, including the size of the organization, the type of organization, the manager's level and function within the organization, the manager's personality and preferred style of working, and changes over time, such as how long the manager has been with the organization, seasonal variations, temporary threats, and so on. He notes, for example, that the characteristics of brevity and fragmentation in managerial jobs becomes much more pronounced in lower level jobs. His chief executives averaged 22 minutes per activity, while the foremen studied by Guest (1956) averaged 48 seconds.

However, there are also common patterns. On the basis of their review McCall *et al.* (1978) drew the following conclusions concerning the nature of managerial work. Managers work long hours. Their working day typically consists of a large number of brief, varied and fragmented activities, which follow each other at a rapid pace, with significant and trivial matters interspersed in no particular pattern. Such brevity and fragmentation is partly a consequence of the large number of activities which managers carry out, but is also due to the high level of interruptions which disrupt planned and ongoing activities and leave little time for reflective thought. A similar pattern emerges from Martinko and Gardner's (1985) review of studies of managerial work. Although there are exceptions, most of the more recent studies confirm that managers carry out a large number of activities per day and that their work is characterized by variety, brevity and fragmentation.

Apart from the characteristics already noted, there is another aspect of managerial work which is of particular relevance from our point of view and worth discussing in more detail. Most of the many and varied activities carried out by managers involve interacting with other people. Burns (1954) studied the work of four middle managers over five weeks using the diary method and found that they spent 80 per cent of their time in conversation. The managers studied by Stewart (1967) spent an average of 60 per cent of their time in discussion, 34 per cent in informal discussions and the remainder in committees, telephoning and social activities. Mintzberg found that verbal interaction accounted for 78 per cent of his five managers' time. In the studies of Kurke and Aldrich (1983) and Choran (1969), the corresponding figures were 73 per cent and 65 per cent (see Table 2.1).

A similar pattern was found in Lawrence's (1984) observational study of 16 German and 25 British managers (see Table 2.2). It is less easy to say precisely how much time is spent in verbal interaction than in Mintzberg's study because Lawrence does not quantify the activities involved in 'time spent in works'. However, he does say that these tours of works are frequently rather chatty affairs, with greetings and snappy instructions alternating with ad hoc discussions, and suggests (p. 15) that the tours of works could be parodied as 'the

Table 2.1 Distribution of time spent on different work activities by senior managers in three American studies

	Proportion of time spent on different activities (%)		
	Mintzberg	*Kurke and Aldrich*	*Choran*
Desk work	22	26	35
Telephone calls	6	8	17
Scheduled meetings	59	50	21
Unscheduled meetings	10	12	15
Tours	3	3	12

Sources: Mintzberg 1973; Kurke and Aldrich 1983; Choran 1969

continuation of meetings by other means'. Broadly speaking, Lawrence suggests (p. 15) that the tours provide 'an opportunity for managers to show their face, greet workers and colleagues, pass on instructions and information, gather impressions, check what is happening, and exercise general surveillance'. Thus, the pattern is again one of the majority of the manager's time being spent in verbal interaction.

Oshagbemi's (1988) diary study of 12 British and 26 Nigerian academic leaders (heads of departments, directors, deans, vice chancellors) makes an interesting comparison with earlier studies which had largely been concerned with industrial managers. It might be expected that academic life would afford more time for solitary contemplation than the more pressured existence of industrial managers. To some extent Oshagbemi's findings bear this out. The academic leaders in his sample spent more time on desk work (see Table 2.3), they carried out fewer activities per day, between nine and ten on average, and their activities were not as brief, averaging slightly above one hour per activity. Nevertheless, they spent approximately one-third of their time in scheduled and

Table 2.2 Distribution of time spent on different work activities by German and British managers

Activity type	*Proportion of observed time spent on activity (%)*	
	German Managers	*British Managers*
1a Formal scheduled recurrent meetings	9.78	15.50
1b Convened special purpose meetings	12.62	14.46
1c Ad hoc discussions	20.07	17.93
2 Time spent in the works	16.87	17.35
3 Telephoning	10.66	7.23
4 Office work	11.56	11.16
4 Explanations to researcher	10.45	12.08
Total time accounted for	91.98	95.92

Source: Lawrence 1984

Table 2.3 Distribution of time spent on different work activities by British and Nigerian academic leaders

	Proportion of time spent on different activities (%)	
	British academic leaders	*Nigerian academic leaders*
Desk work	43.42	44.04
Scheduled meetings	25.25	28.62
Unscheduled meetings	6.83	10.50
Telephoning	0.75	0.69
Total	76.25[1]	83.85[1]

Note:

[1] Oshagbemi's data do not include such things as practicals, computing, travelling, lunch, tea and coffee breaks.

Source: Oshagbemi 1988

unscheduled meetings (British academics 32 per cent and Nigerian academics 38 per cent). Their 'time alone' was interrupted by 'fleeting contacts', which are not included in Table 2.3, and occurred at the rate of about eleven or twelve per day. Taking into account fleeting contacts, Oshagbemi estimates that the academic leaders in his sample averaged less than 18 per cent of their time alone.

Not surprisingly, managers often resent the constant pressure and the constant interruptions, which they see as preventing them from getting on with their 'real job'. This feeling was well described by Calkins:

> If administrators are asked to nominate the aspects of the task that are most time-consuming and frustrating to the exercise of their responsibilities, they will agree that they are preoccupied with distractions; with inconsequential little things that push themselves ahead of important issues; with the tyranny of the telephone; with the relentless flitting from one issue to another; with the ceaseless procession of interviews and ceremonials; with the pressure of circumstance and deadlines; and the absence of time to collect one's wits, much less to think or reflect.

> (Calkins 1952: 20)

Only a superb or a hard-boiled administrator, Calkins concludes, can cut through this daily morass to concentrate on the important responsibilities that cannot be shirked. On the other hand, Sayles (1979) suggests that, far from preventing managers from doing their real job, the distractions often are the reality. Management, in large measure, is dealing with the unexpected that interferes with expectations and routines, with unanticipated crises and petty little problems that require much more time than they are really worth.

Furthermore, although managers may complain about the constant interruptions which prevent them from doing their 'real work', according to Mintzberg (1973), there are indications that managers actually prefer brevity and interruptions in their work. He suggests various reasons why this should be so. One is that managers tolerate interruptions because they do not wish to interrupt the flow of current information, particularly the 'hot' which flows frequently and informally by telephone and unscheduled meetings. Another is that managers may become accustomed to variety in their work and find that boredom develops easily. He argues, however, that a more significant reason might be that managers become conditioned by their workload, the ever-present assortment of obligations associated with the job.

> In effect, the manager is encouraged by the realities of his work to develop a particular personality – to overload himself with work, to do things abruptly, to avoid wasting time, to participate only when the value of participation is tangible, to avoid too great an involvement with any one issue. To be superficial is, no doubt, an occupational hazard of managerial work. In order to succeed, the manager must, presumably, become proficient in his superficiality.
>
> (Mintzberg 1973: 35)

One other finding revealed by studies of how managers spend their time is worth noting and that is the fact that managers do not appear to know how they spend their time. The studies reported in this section employed relatively direct methods of data collection, in that information concerning the managers' activities was recorded at the time either by an observer or by the managers themselves in a diary. When this information is compared with what managers say they do in interview or questionnaire surveys, significant differences have been found. According to Carlson (1951), his subjects' perceptions of how they spent their time was strongly influenced by wishful thinking. When asked how they spent their time, they did not describe what they actually did. Rather they described what they believed they did under 'normal' conditions, completely unaware that such 'normal' conditions had not existed for a very long time.

Similarly, Oshagbemi (1988) gained the impression from his pilot study that it was only after participating in his diary study that his subjects realized how they actually spent their time. McCall *et al.* (1978) reviewed the data from studies which compared managers' responses to an interview or questionnaire with the results from systematic observation conducted soon thereafter. They found that managers consistently overestimated the time they spent on production, reading and writing, telephone calls and thinking and consistently underestimated the time spent on meetings and/or formal discussion. They conclude that 'All that can be counted on is that managers make errors – sometimes large errors – when they try to estimate how they spend their time.'

THE CONTENT OF MANAGERIAL JOBS

Studies of how managers spend their time provide us with an impression of the context within which managers do their work. However, they do not tell us what managers actually do or what they are trying to achieve while they are

Table 2.4 Mintzberg's ten managerial roles

	Interpersonal roles
Figurehead	Carrying out ceremonial duties (e.g. greeting touring dignitaries, attending weddings, etc.).
Leader	Responsibility for the work of subordinates (e.g. hiring, training, motivating, encouraging).
Liaison	Contacts outside the vertical chain of command (e.g. with clients, suppliers, business associates, other managers, government officials, etc.).
	Informational roles
Monitor	Seeking information in order to detect changes, to identify problems and opportunities, to build up knowledge about his or her milieu, and to be informed when information must be disseminated and decisions made.
Disseminator	Passing on information directly to subordinates.
Spokesperson	Transmitting information and expressing value statements to those outside the manager's own work unit.
	Decisional roles
Entrepreneur	Introducing controlled change to improve the manager's own work unit, to adapt it to changing conditions in the environment.
Disturbance handler	Dealing with sudden crises which cannot be ignored (e.g. loss of a key subordinate, a fire, a strike, etc.).
Resource allocator	Deciding who within the manager's unit will receive resources such as money, manpower, material, equipment and services.
Negotiator	Representing his or her own unit in negotiations with individuals or groups, both within and outside the organization (e.g. pay negotiations, handling grievance cases, arranging finance, agreeing contracts with customers and suppliers, etc.).

Adapted from: Mintzberg 1973, 1975.

working. A number of studies have attempted to answer these questions. On the basis of his study of chief executives, Mintzberg (1973, 1975) suggested that the manager's job could be described in terms of ten 'roles', or organized sets of behaviours identified with a position. According to Mintzberg, there are three interpersonal roles – figurehead, liaison and leader – which arise directly from the manager's formal authority. By virtue of these interpersonal contacts, both with subordinates and others, the manager emerges as the nerve centre of his or her organizational unit. Thus the interpersonal roles in turn give rise to three informational roles – monitor of information, disseminator of information and spokesperson. Finally, the interpersonal and information roles enable the manager to play four decisional roles – entrepreneur, resource allocator, negotiator and disturbance handler. Brief descriptions of these roles are given in Table 2.4.

While Mintzberg believes that the ten roles are common to the work of all managers, he also takes the view that the extent to which they perform these roles varies, due to the influence of the same set of variables which influence how managers spend their time (see previous section). For example, he suggests that at lower levels, the work is more focused, more short-term in outlook and the figurehead role becomes less significant, while the disturbance handler and negotiator roles become more important.

One particular source of variation in managerial work, the manager's preferred working style, has been studied in depth by Stewart (1982). Based on a series of studies of managerial work, she suggests that it is helpful to look at managerial jobs and behaviour in terms of demands, constraints and choices. Demands are what anyone in a particular job has to do. Constraints are factors internal or external to the organization that limit what the jobholder can do. Finally, choices are activities that the jobholder can do but does not have to do. They are opportunities for one jobholder to do different work from another and to do it in different ways.

Such demands, constraints and choices, Stewart argues, exist in a wide variety of areas. Examples include:

- the amount and type of work managers delegate to subordinates;
- the extent to which they emphasize the administrative or technical aspects of a job;
- the amount of time spent on supervision (e.g. monitoring performance, training, development or welfare);
- the extent to which they undertake the liaison role of establishing cooperative relations with other people inside and outside the organization;
- the interest they take in innovation as opposed to maintenance;
- the extent to which they develop a special expertise in one aspect of the job or use their expertise for purposes other than those which are demanded by the job, and so on.

Stewart suggests that not only do jobs differ in the amount and nature of the actual demands, constraints and choices they involve, but also managers may differ in their perceptions of them. Thus, they may not realize that what they perceive as demands are actually choices. Furthermore, most of the managers studied said that they were normally unaware of choosing what actions they took, or what decisions they made. They were carried along by the momentum of what happened. However, even managers who said that they were not usually conscious of making a choice could describe what aspects of a job and of its situation would give them a choice. For most of them this was when other people did not tell them what to do, especially if they had their own defined area of responsibility within which they were free to manage as they thought best.

Kotter (1982) studied the work behaviour of fifteen general managers using observation, questionnaires and interviews. From these data he identified two sets of job demands which, albeit with some variation, described the jobs of all the general managers in the study:

1 *Challenges and dilemmas associated with responsibilities*

- Setting basic goals, policies and strategies despite great uncertainties.
- Achieving a delicate balance in the allocation of scarce resources among a diverse set of functional and business needs. Not allowing short-run concerns to dominate long-run ones, or marketing issues to stifle production needs.
- Keeping on top of a very large and diverse set of activities. Being able to identify problems ('fires') that are out of control and solve them quickly.

2 *Challenges and dilemmas associated with relationships*

- Getting the information, cooperation and support from bosses to do the job. Being demanding without being perceived as uncooperative.
- Getting corporate staff, other relevant departments or divisions, and other important external groups (e.g. big unions or customers or suppliers) to cooperate despite the lack of any formal authority over them; getting things done despite resistance, red tape, and the like.
- Motivating and controlling a large and diverse group of subordinates. Dealing with inadequate performance, interdepartmental conflict and the like.

Kotter notes that although the general managers in his study shared the same six basic demands, there was considerable variation among them in terms of the overall intensity of these demands, the relative importance of the six problem areas, and the exact nature of each demand. These differences, he suggests, arise partly because there are different types of GM job (e.g. Corporate CEO, Group GM, Operations GM, etc.) and partly from differences in business and corporate settings, particularly the size, age and performance of the organization concerned.

Despite these differences, however, Kotter found that the general managers in his study behaved in remarkably similar ways. He identified three work behaviours which were common to all fifteen general managers:

1 Agenda setting: developing a set of loosely connected goals and plans which addressed their long-, medium- and short-term responsibilities.
2 Network building: developing a network of cooperative relations to and among those people who they felt were actually needed to accomplish their emerging agendas.
3 Implementing the agendas: using their networks along with their interpersonal skills, budgetary resources, and information to influence people and events in a variety of direct and indirect ways.

Kotter suggests that these common work behaviours arise directly from the six dilemmas outlined above. General managers must make and implement decisions despite uncertainty, great diversity, an enormous quantity of potentially relevant information, and the need to influence a large and diverse group of people over whom they have relatively little direct control. They therefore simply cannot go about the work of planning, organizing, staffing, directing and controlling in a simple, straightforward and formal way that focuses on formal plans, the structure of subordinate roles and the like. In Kotter's view, they probably have to adopt an approach somewhat like the general managers in his study or fail. However, Kotter also noted changes in these behaviours over time. His managers tended to concentrate on agenda setting and network building in the first six months to a year in a new job. Thereafter, they continued to update their agendas and networks, but tended to shift their attention more towards implementation.

A major observational study of managers was carried out by Luthans and his colleagues (see Luthans *et al.* 1988). Trained observers recorded in detail the behaviours and activities of 44 managers, studied in their natural setting. The managers came from all levels (lower, middle and upper) and all types of organizations (e.g. manufacturing plants, retail stores, hospitals, corporate headquarters, a railroad, insurance companies, a newspaper office, and financial institutions). They were observed in a completely unstructured format for a varied hour each day over a two-week period. From these data, twelve categories of managerial behaviour were identified (see Table 2.5). For ease of presentation and to synthesize managerial activities, these 12 categories were then collapsed into the four comprehensive activities shown in Table 2.6. In a follow-up interview survey, more intensive descriptions of and qualitative data on managerial activities were obtained by asking subordinates of a further 165 managers to provide specific examples of their immediate boss's behaviour for each of the 12 categories of managerial work.

Having developed a classification scheme for the categorization of managerial activities, the next stage of the study was to observe a further 248 managers to establish the relative frequency of these activities. To gather these data, trained observers filled out a checklist of managerial activities, based on Table 2.5, for 80 times over a two-week period. The observations took place during a predetermined, random, ten-minute period of each working hour. The proportion of time spent on the activities included in the two categorization systems is shown in Table 2.6.

However, there were differences according to the manager's level within the organization. For example, top-level, chief executive officer (CEO) managers interact with outsiders about as often as middle-level managers, but nearly three times as often as first-level managers. Conversely, middle-and first-level managers socialize and politick nearly three times as often as the top-level managers. Luthans *et al.* suggest that the reason for this is that socializing and politicking may have been necessary to get to the top, but once there it is no longer a necessary activity.

Table 2.5 Twelve-fold categorization system for managerial activities

1   Planning/coordinating
- setting goals and objectives
- defining tasks needed to accomplish goals
- scheduling employees, timetables
- assigning tasks and providing routine instructions
- coordinating activities of different subordinates to keep work running smoothly
- organizing the work

2   Staffing
- developing job descriptions for position openings
- reviewing applications
- interviewing applicants
- hiring
- contacting applicants to inform them of hiring decision
- 'filling in' where needed

3   Training/developing
- orienting employees, arranging for training seminars, etc.
- clarifying roles, duties, job descriptions
- coaching, mentoring, walking subordinates through task
- helping subordinate with personal development plans

4   Decision-making/problem-sloving
- defining problems
- choosing between two or more alternatives or strategies
- handling day-to-day operational crises as they arise
- weighing the trade-offs; cost/benefit analysis
- making the decision
- developing new procedures to increase efficiency

5   Handling paperwork
- processing mail
- reading reports, in-box
- writing reports, memos, letters, etc.
- doing routine financial reporting and bookkeeping
- doing general desk work

6   Exchanging routine information
- answering routine procedural questions
- receiving and disseminating requested information
- conveying results of meetings
- giving or receiving routine information over the phone
- holding staff meetings of an informational nature (e.g. status updates, new company policies, etc.)

7   Monitoring/controlling performance
- inspecting work
- walking around
- monitoring performance data (e.g. computer printouts, production, financial reports)
- practising preventative maintenance

8   Monitoring/reinforcing
- allocating formal organizational rewards
- asking for input, participation
- conveying appreciation, compliments
- giving credit where due
- listening to suggestions
- giving positive performance feedback
- increasing job challenge
- delegating responsibility and authority
- letting subordinates determine how to do their own work
- supporting the group before superiors and others, backing a subordinate

9   Disciplining/punishing
- enforcing rules and policies
- glaring, non-verbal harassing
- demoting, firing, laying off employee
- issuing any formal organizational reprimand or notice
- 'chewing out' a subordinate, criticising
- giving negative performance feedback

10   Interacting with outsiders
- public relations
- contacts with customers
- contacts with suppliers, vendors
- external meetings
- community service activities

11   Managing conflict
- managing interpersonal conflict between subordinates or others
- appealing to higher authority to resolve a dispute
- appealing to third-party negotiators
- seeking cooperation or consensus between conflicting parties
- attempting to resolve conflicts between subordiantes and self

12   Socializing/politicking
- engaging in non-work-related chitchat (e.g. family or personal matters)
- 'joking around'
- discussing rumours, hearsay, grapevine
- complaining, griping, downgrading others
- politicking, gamesmanship

Source: Luthans and Lockwood, 1984

Table 2.6 Categorization system for managerial activities, showing the relative frequency of each activity

	% Frequency	
	Major categories	Sub-categories
Routine communication	29	
• Exchanging routine information		15
• Handling paperwork		14
Traditional management	32*	
• Planning		13
• Decision-making		11
• Controlling		6
Networking	19	
• Interacting with outsiders		10
• Socializing/politicking		9
Human resource management	20	
• Motivating/reinforcing		5
• Disciplining/punishing		–
• Managing conflict		4
• Staffing		5
• Training/developing		6

Note:

*The data concerning the relative frequency of managerial activities were derived from two different figures in Luthans *et al.* (1998) and the individual frequencies for planning, decision-making and controlling in one figure do not add up to the total for traditional management given in the other.

Source: Luthans *et al.* 1988

It should also be noted that no data for disciplining/punishing are shown in Table 2.6. This activity was deleted from the later survey and the analysis of the relative frequencies of the managerial activities because the observers were unable to observe it directly. Luthans *et al.* (1988) say that they know from their interview data that this activity was done and therefore infer that most disciplining/punishing was done rarely and in private.

A large-scale questionnaire survey concerning managerial work was carried out by Kraut *et al.* (1989). They asked a sample of 1,412 managers to rate the importance of 57 various managerial activities to their jobs. On the basis of these ratings, they identified the following groups of management tasks:

● managing individual performance;
● instructing subordinates;
● planning and allocating resources;
● coordinating interdependent groups;
● managing group performance;
● monitoring the business environment;
● representing one's staff.

The researchers found that the relative importance of these activities varied with the level of management. Managing individual performance and instructing subordinates were more important to first-line supervisors, while activities involving linking groups (the third, fourth and fifth activities above) were more important to middle managers, and monitoring the business environment was more important to executive-level managers than the other two groups. The 'ambassador' role of representing one's staff, on the other hand, was ranked equally high by all levels of management. Furthermore, while some differences in the rated importance of the different activities were found between the marketing, manufacturing and administration functions, the overall pattern of ratings across these functions was remarkably similar.

It will be apparent that there are considerable similarities between the findings of the various studies of the content of managerial jobs. The importance of such activities as obtaining, monitoring and disseminating information, the management of conflict, 'firefighting', motivating subordinates and allocating resources were common themes. However, there were also differences. Luthans *et al.* (1988) include socializing/politicking in their list of managerial activities and Kotter (1982) identifies networking as a common activity, neither of which is included in the lists of Mintzberg (1973) or Kraut *et al.* (1989). Similarly, Kotter, Luthans *et al.* and Kraut *et al.* include planning in their lists, while Mintzberg does not. In fact, Mintzberg specifically states that during working hours, it was rare to see a chief executive participating in abstract discussion or carrying out general planning. The pressure of the managerial environment, he argues, does not encourage the development of reflective planners.

A number of factors may have given rise to such discrepancies. First, there may have been genuine differences between the jobs of the managers concerned. For example, Mintzberg's (1973) subjects were all chief executives and Kotter's (1982) subjects were all senior managers, while the studies of Luthans *et al.* (1988) and Kraut *et al.* (1989) not only covered a wider range of status levels but also revealed differences in the content of managerial jobs between these different status levels. Another difference between studies may have been the amount of time managers had been in their jobs. Mintzberg excluded from his study managers who had been recently appointed to their positions because of the possibility that their activities might not yet have stabilized, while Kotter observes that managers concentrate on agenda setting and network building during the first six months to a year after a new appointment.

Second, there is the question of the number of managers whose jobs were studied. Mintzberg (1973) studied only five managers and there is therefore the possibility that his findings were unduly influenced by one or more atypical subjects. Stewart's (1982) finding that managers' choices can have a major influence on how they do their jobs suggests that this could quite easily happen.

Finally, there is the question of the method of study. The main methods used to study the content of managerial jobs have been observational studies, interviews and questionnaire surveys. Each has advantages and limitations. The manager who is under observation by an outsider may behave differently from the way he or she would under normal circumstances. An example is the lack of opportunity to observe disciplining/punishing reported by Luthans *et al.* (1988). However, the manager who provides information in a questionnaire or interview survey may not only deliberately distort his or her answers in order to appear more admirable in some way, but may also be genuinely mistaken about the relative frequencies or importance of the various activities he or she undertakes. We have already seen that this happens in the case of studies of how managers spend their time and Stewart's (1982) assertion that many managers are unable to distinguish between demands and choices in their jobs suggests that similar errors may occur when attempting to describe the content of their jobs. On the other hand, as Martinko and Gardner (1985) point out, direct observation of overt behaviour does not necessarily provide all the information necessary to provide a comprehensive description of what managers do. In particular, unless the manager chooses to express his or her thoughts out loud, it does not tell us what the manager is thinking, and this information could be vitally necessary in order to interpret managerial behaviour accurately. For example, a manager sitting back, staring at the ceiling for fifteen minutes could be planning, decision-making or simply daydreaming. Similarly, a manager apparently engaged in socializing could be deliberately gleaning information which could make a significant difference to a promotion decision a year later. Martinko and Gardner therefore suggest that interviews should be used in addition to observational studies in order to capture such cognitive processes.

Taking all these points into account, it seems likely that more valid results concerning the content of managerial jobs will be obtained using large samples, covering different managerial levels within organizations and employing a combination of both direct methods of data collection such as observation and diary studies and indirect methods such as interview or questionnaire surveys. So far, the study which most closely approaches these requirements is that of Luthans *et al.* (1988), but it should be noted that even they did not interview the managers concerned in order to obtain an interpretation of their behaviour at the time it occurred.

MANAGERIAL EFFECTIVENESS AND SUCCESS

Although there have been a great many studies of how managers spend their time and a number concerned with the nature of managerial work, surprisingly few have examined the relationship between the relative frequency of managerial activities and managerial effectiveness and success. During the 1950s there were four studies of the work of industrial foremen which included a measure of effectiveness. However, Martinko and Gardner (1985) conclude that it is difficult to make conclusive statements regarding effective supervisory or managerial behaviour on the basis of these early studies because of a variety of problems, including the technical adequacy of their reports, inappropriate interpretation of statistical tests, differences in observational procedures and the relatively small number of samples studied. One finding with regard to effectiveness which was somewhat consistent was that high-performing managers engaged in less frequent events with longer durations than low-performing managers. Martinko and Gardner regard this as evidence that effective managers are better able to control their time and spend a larger proportion of it on long-range strategic issues. Equally, however, it could mean that high-performing managers had less demanding jobs which did not require them to move as quickly from one problem to another.

Unlike these early studies, Mintzberg (1973) concentrated solely on what managers do and ignored the question of what effective as opposed to ineffective managers do. This approach has been followed by the majority of subsequent studies. However, there are some notable exceptions. Kotter (1982) assessed the performance of his general managers on the basis of both hard measures such as sales and profits, and soft measures such as peer, subordinate and boss judgements. Although he does not present any quantitative data to support his conclusions, Kotter suggests that the behaviour of the better performing general managers in his study differed from the lesser performing ones in the following ways:

- They developed agendas based on more explicit business strategies that addressed longer time frames and included a wider range of business issues.
- They developed such agendas by seeking information from others (including 'bad news') more aggressively, by asking questions more skilfully and by more successfully finding programmes and projects that could help to accomplish multiple objectives at once.
- They created networks with many talented people in them and stronger ties to and among their subordinates.
- They developed such networks more aggressively, using a wider variety of methods with greater skill.
- They tended to mobilize more people to get things done using a wider range of influence tactics with greater skill. They asked, encouraged, cajoled, praised, rewarded, demanded, manipulated, and generally motivated others with great skill in face-to-face situations. They also made greater use of indirect methods of influence, such as getting one member of their network to influence another or setting up a meeting and influencing others through the selection of participants and the choice of an agenda. However, the better performing managers spent somewhat less time on execution of their agendas than did the others. There was less to do, because their networks

automatically accomplished much and the managers themselves were more effective and efficient at getting things done.

Martinko and Gardner (1984a) carried out an observational study of the work behaviour of 41 school principals. The mean observation period was 6.7 days per principal and the sample was subdivided into 22 high and 19 moderate performers based on student performance in exams and on achievement tests and superintendent's rankings of schools and principals. In earlier reports of this work Martinko and Gardner (1984b, 1985) suggested that it provided some evidence of differences in the work behaviour of high- and low-performing school principals in a limited number of areas. On the basis of a later profile analysis of the data, however, Martinko and Gardner (1990) concluded that the study provided no evidence that managerial behaviour was related to performance level. More effective managers did not devote significantly more time or events to the particular activities recorded in their study than did less effective managers. On the other hand, various aspects of managerial behaviour were related to differences in demographic and environmental variables, such as grade level, staff size, geographic location and relative urbanization.

Luthans *et al.* (1988) studied the relationship between managers' work behaviour and both managerial success and effectiveness. For this part of their research, they analysed data from samples of managers (52 in the case of success and 178 in the case of effectiveness) drawn from the 248 managers in their main study. Managerial success was measured in terms of speed of promotion (level in the organization divided by tenure in the organization). The measure of managerial effectiveness was derived from the combined score on three questionnaires filled in by the manager's subordinates concerning the quality and quantity of their unit's performance, their job satisfaction and their organizational commitment.

The distribution of activities for successful and effective managers was quite different, as can be seen in Table 2.7. The activity with the strongest relationship to effective management was routine communication, followed in turn by human resource and traditional management, with networking having the weakest relationship. Successful managers, on the other hand, did significantly more networking than any other activity, with routine communication coming second and traditional and human resource management taking up a much smaller proportion of their time. The close relationship between networking and managerial success was clearly shown in a separate analysis which compared the distribution of activities of the most successful and least successful managers (those who came in the top one-third and bottom one-third respectively on the managerial success index). This showed that, compared with the least successful managers, the most successful managers did 70 per cent more networking and 10 per cent more routine communication, but 25 per cent less human resource activities and 40 per cent less traditional management activities.

Another analysis showed that there was very little overlap between successful and effective managers. From their sample of 178 managers, Luthans *et al.*

Table 2.7 Distribution of activities of successful and effective managers

Activity	Successful managers (n = 52)	Effective managers (n = 178)	Successful and effective (n = 15)	All managers (n = 248)
Traditional management	13	19	34	32
Routine communication	28	44	31	29
Networking	48	11	20	19
Human resource management	11	26	20	20

Source: Luthans *et al.* 1988

(1988) identified the 60 most effective and the 60 most successful managers and found that there were only 15 who were in both the successful and effective groups. The breakdown of activities for these fifteen managers is also given in Table 2.7. It will be seen that the distribution of activities for managers who were both successful and effective is remarkably similar to that for the total sample. Luthans *et al.* therefore conclude that the few managers in their sample who were both successful and effective were not really distinctive from managers in general. They used a fairly balanced approach to their activities, which Luthans *et al.* take as an indication that to be both successful and effective, none of them can be ignored.

However, before leaving the work of Luthans *et al.* (1988), it should be noted that their ratings of success and effectiveness were, in effect, based on the views of different people. The measure of effectiveness was based upon subordinate ratings, while their measure of success was based on how fast the manager was promoted, which one might expect to be based at least in part on superiors' assessment of how effective the manager would be in a higher level job. Thus, the fact that there was little overlap between successful and effective managers may have resulted in part from the fact that superiors and subordinates used different criteria when assessing effectiveness. In future research, therefore, it would be useful to have comparative data from more objective measures of managerial effectiveness, such as output, labour turnover and absenteeism figures, as well as questionnaire data. In this context, it is worth noting that Kotter (1982), who used a composite measure of managerial performance based on both objective and subjective data, found that one of the characteristics of his better performing managers was that they developed better networks and used them more aggressively than the lesser performing managers. Nevertheless, Luthans *et al.* (1988) remains a very rich source of information and speculation concerning the nature of managerial work and its relationships to managerial effectiveness and success.

CONCLUSIONS: IMPLICATIONS OF RESEARCH INTO THE NATURE OF MANAGERIAL WORK

Having come to the end of this review of the nature of managerial work and its relationship to managerial success and effectiveness, what conclusions can we draw? To my mind, two main characteristics of managerial work stand out. First, managers work under considerable pressure. They perform many different activities during their working day, and what little free time they have is frequently interrupted by telephone calls and visitors. This in turn means that activities which are important but less pressing, such as tours and long-term planning, tend to be put off and ultimately neglected. What steps can managers take, therefore, in order to cope more effectively with the pressures under which they work? I would suggest the following:

1 Establish what they actually do at present. In order to develop realistic plans concerning ways in which they can perform their jobs more effectively, managers need to have a clear idea of what they currently do. If they do not know with any degree of accuracy how much time they spend on different activities, how can they come to any realistic conclusions concerning whether to increase or decrease the frequency of such activities and if so by how much? As we have seen, the research evidence suggests that managers in fact do not have an accurate impression of how they spend their time. I am no exception in that respect. I was one of Oshagbemi's subjects in his pilot survey and found that what I thought I did and what I actually did differed in a number of significant respects. In order to obtain more systematic data concerning the way in which they spend their time, therefore, it would be a useful exercise for managers to carry out their own diary study. A diary format which could be used for this purpose is described in Exercise I at the end of this chapter.

2 Decide what activities the job should entail and what emphasis should be given to them. As Stewart (1982) points out, managers not only do not necessarily have a correct idea of how they spend their time, they also tend not to be aware of the actual nature of the demands, constraints and choices their jobs entail. They tend to exaggerate the demands and constraints and thus restrict the opportunities for choice. Stewart therefore suggests that managers should take a strategic view of their jobs. That is, they should stand back from the job and attempt to see it as an outsider might in order to obtain a more accurate perception of its demands and constraints. Then, in much the way that top management need to decide what business the organization should be in, the individual manager needs to decide which activities, within the demands and constraints of the job, should be performed in order to do the job effectively and to develop his or her career. This strategic review of the job can then be compared with what the manager currently does in order to decide what changes in the distribution of activities need to be made to achieve either or both of these objectives.

3 Having decided which activities the manager would like to increase or decrease in frequency, various actions can be taken to change the distribution of current activities. Among them are the following:

- Eliminate unnecessary activities. If activities are not demands – no one would miss them if they were not done and they do not contribute to effectiveness or career development, nor are they enjoyable for their own sake – then stop doing them. If they are demands, but do not fulfil the other requirements, then try to persuade the person making the demands that they are unnecessary. In bureaucratic organizations, or those subject to the demands of other bureaucratic organizations, this may be extremely difficult, if not impossible. It can also be damaging to career prospects, as drawing attention too forcefully to the pointlessness of demands made by people who are unwilling or unable to give them up can be extremely annoying to them. In that case:
- Develop strategic superficiality. As far as possible, spend no more time on an activity than it is worth. In many cases, managers are merely required to perform a certain activity rather than perform it well. In one organization in which I worked, all managers were required to provide information concerning the amount of time their subordinates spent on different projects. This was then collated and issued in summary form in the organization's management information system. At first, conscientious managers attempted to collect accurate information, but as it became obvious that no one actually used it for anything, increasingly rough estimates were given with no apparent consequences. One senior manager went so far as to provide the same information each month and he was only found out when he absentmindedly went on including data for a subordinate for three months after he had left the company.
- Delegate activities which can beneficially be performed by subordinates. This suggestion has two aspects. If there are job demands which can be performed by subordinates, then delegating such activities will generate free time which the manager can more usefully spend on other things. Even if the subordinate does not perform them as well as the manager, there may still be a net gain to the organization if the manager is able to spend more time on a task where his or her expertise is more crucial. Furthermore, such delegation may help to develop the subordinate concerned by broadening his or her experience. On the other hand, many subordinates have become very cynical about the phrase 'good for your career development' and regard it simply as a euphemism for off-loading unwanted, unrewarded and unrewarding jobs on to someone who is already overloaded with such work. If this is how delegation is seen, the resulting loss of motivation and commitment on the part of the subordinate may well outweigh any gains from the free time such delegation generates.
- Schedule important but not immediately pressing activities. Mintzberg (1975) suggests that many managers suffer from a diary complex. What does not get scheduled does not get done. Thus merely deciding that time must be found for activities which are not immediately pressing, such as tours, reflective thinking or long-range planning, will not have the desired effect. Rather, Mintzberg suggests, managers should schedule such activities and enter into

an obligation to do them, for example by initiating a project and involving others who will report back to them or by committing themselves to a tour at a specific time so that others will expect them to be there. As Carlson (1951) notes, the converse of this for others who have to deal with such managers and want them to do something is that mere promises to do it when they have some free time have a much lower probability of producing the desired result than getting it into their diaries with a specific date and time attached.

- The disruptive effects of interruptions can be reduced by the way in which managers schedule their working day. Carlson (1951) suggests that chief executives can be protected against unnecessary interruptions by the introduction of fixed reception hours for certain types of visitors or telephone calls. Similarly, Stewart (1967) suggests that managers can arrange with subordinates that they are available between certain set times, but should not be disturbed at other times except for emergencies.

However, care must be taken that such techniques do not cut the manager off from important information and personal contacts. Kotter (1982) argues that to be successful, general managers must centre their whole approach around the development and use of a network of relationships. It is therefore hardly surprising that they spend almost all of their time each day with other people. Under these circumstances, he states, even a pattern such as engaging in frequent, short, disjointed conversations can be seen as understandable, efficient and effective.

4 Improve managerial skills. The above techniques have as their objective changing what managers do. An alternative approach is to change how well they do it. By carrying out certain tasks more skilfully, managers may be able to do the same work in less time or more work in the same time. For example, as we have seen, Kotter (1982) suggests that better performing managers spent less time on execution because there was less to do since their networks automatically accomplished much and because they were more effective and more efficient in getting things done. Similarly, Luthans *et al.* state that:

planning seems to be a skill that is not equally well developed among all managers. Such qualitative differences among managers as planners mean that the frequency (amount) of doing planning activity does not distinguish the successful (best) from the less successful (mediocre) manager. . . . Less successful managers may be spending more time preparing ineffective plans, planning the wrong things or substituting planning for real performance.

(Luthans *et al.* 1988: 51)

Areas in which skill development might lead to more effective performance include the following:

- Formal communication (e.g. letters, memos, presentations, talks, etc.).
- Administration (e.g. more effective handling of paperwork).

- Planning, problem-solving and decision-making.
- Stress management.
- Managing relationships with others.

This brings us to the second major characteristic of managerial work. Managers get things done through people. As Mintzberg (1973: 44) puts it: 'Unlike other workers, the manager does not leave the telephone or the meeting to get back to work. Rather, these contacts *are* his work.' Similarly, Kotter states that the general managers he studied:

> typically spent the vast majority of their time with other people, discussing a wide variety of topics. In these conversations the GMs usually asked numerous questions, yet they very rarely could be seen making big decisions. These conversations often contained a considerable amount of joking and non-work-related issues. Indeed, in many of these discussions the substantive issue involved was relatively unimportant to the business. The GMs rarely gave orders, but they often tried to influence others. Their time was seldom planned in advance in any detail and was usually characterized by brief and disjointed conversations. All of this took a little less than sixty hours per week.
>
> (Kotter 1982: 127)

Thus, to be both successful and effective, managers need to be able to handle other people well. Undoubtedly, other abilities are also required. These include specialist knowledge in particular areas, a clear conception of the goals of their organization, the ability to assess the relevance and importance of the information they receive, the ability to make effective decisions, which will enhance the organization's achievement of its goals, and so on. Nevertheless, to use these abilities effectively more often than not requires interacting with other people. Information is obtained from and imparted to other people, decisions are implemented by other people, and how well the organization is able to achieve its goals will depend upon the actions of a great many people, both inside and outside the organization.

In order to handle other people effectively in the many different types of relationships in which managers are involved, a number of more specific skills are required. Among them are the following:

- Leadership skills – the ability to influence the behaviour, beliefs and feelings of subordinates.
- Skills of persuasion – the ability to influence others over whom one has no direct authority, such as outsiders, peers within the organization and superiors, including one's own boss.
- Skills relating to the acquisition and use of power within organizations.
- Political skills.
- Networking skills.
- Conflict-resolution skills.

Many of these skills, of course, overlap. For example, often it may be more effective to use persuasion rather than direct orders even with people over whom one has direct authority. However, this is hardly surprising. Permeating all these skills is the underlying theme of what have variously been termed interpersonal, interactive or social skills. For example, Luthans *et al.* (1988) comment that they found social skills to be a more important ingredient in networking than even the dynamics of the informal organization and power. In a sense then, the above groups of skills can be regarded as overlapping subsets of skills drawn from a larger, more general pool of skills involved in influencing peoples' behaviour, beliefs and feelings. The question of interpersonal skills will be taken up again in Chapter 6.

EXERCISE 1: TIME MANAGEMENT

Step One

Make up a Time Management Diary. Run off photocopies of Figure 2.1, either from this book, page 31, or from a typed A4 version, if more convenient. At least 14 copies will be required, and further copies may be needed if your daily activities fill more than one page.

Step Two

Fill in the diary over a two-week period, starting each day on a new page. For each activity lasting more than five minutes, provide the following information. Try to fill in the diary as near as possible to the time when the activity took place.

Time Note the start time of the activity. Except for fleeting contacts (described below), enter a new start time every time you begin a new activity.

Activity Note the nature of the activity. How precisely activities are defined will depend upon your needs. If you wish merely to assess your distribution of time across broad classes of activities, then a relatively coarse classification system such as that used by Lawrence (see Table 2.2, p. 11) will suffice. If, on the other hand, you wish to assess the time spent on more specific aspects of these broad categories (e.g. types of desk work), then a more fine-grained classification system will be required. Inevitably, however, the more fine-grained the system, the longer the data will take to collate at the end of each week. To help with this process, therefore, it would be useful to develop a preliminary classification system for your activities before starting the exercise, so that similar activities can be classified under the same heading.

With whom   Note who is present when the activity takes place or enter 'alone' if it does not involve anyone else.

Also note:

Contacts   The last two columns in Figure 2.1 are intended for fleeting contacts lasting five minutes or less, either on the telephone or in person. Again, the detail with which these contacts are recorded will depend upon your needs. If you merely want to know how many such fleeting contacts occur, then a tick in the appropriate column for each contact will suffice. If you are concerned about interruptions, then it could be useful to differentiate between calls in (mark I) and calls out (mark O). A similar system could be used for personal contacts, where 'I' would be contacts initiated by other people and 'O' fleeting contacts initiated by yourself. If it is important to know who is the greatest source of fleeting contacts, then the name of the person could be entered in the 'with whom' column.

Step Three

At the end of each week, collate the data in the Daily Time Logs and enter in the Weekly Time Distribution Chart (Figure 2.2, p. 32). Enter each activity, the total time spent on this activity, the percentage of the total time spent on all activities which this represents and the number of interruptions for each activity. Also provide a rating of:

(a) Importance: assess how much the activity contributes towards the achievement of your work and personal objectives.
(b) Choice: the amount of choice you have about whether you or someone who reports to you perform(s) this activity.
(c) The potential for delegating this activity: take into account whether you would be permitted to delegate this activity to someone else, how much of the activity could be delegated (all or only part), how much training the person to whom the task is delegated would need in order to be able to perform it satisfactorily, how acceptable the task would be to the person to whom it is delegated.

Step Four

Ask and attempt to answer the following questions:
1 Is the activity important enough to warrant the amount of time and effort I spend on it? If not:
   (a) Can I drop it?
   (b) Can I delegate all or part of it?
   (c) Can I reduce the amount of time the activity requires by reducing the quality of work produced, without adversely affecting my effectiveness and without anyone noticing?

Daily Time Log				
Time	Activity	With whom	Contacts	
			Phone	In person

Figure 2.1 Daily Time Log

Weekly Time Distribution Chart							
Activity	Total	% of total	Interruptions		Import-ance	Choice	Del-egation
			Phone	In person			

Figure 2.2 Weekly Time Distribution Chart

Notes:

Ratings	Importance	Choice	Delegation
1	Makes vital contribution	Activity is obligatory	No possibility of delegation
2	Makes valuable contribution	Very little choice	Difficult to delegate
3	Makes moderate contribution	Some choice	Moderately difficult to delegate
4	Makes little contribution	A great deal of choice	Relatively easy to delegate
5	Makes no contribution	Complete choice	Could easily be delegated

2 Is the number of interruptions preventing me from performing activities effectively? If so:
  (a) Can I reduce the amount of interruptions without cutting myself off from important information sources?
  (b) Can I reschedule the activity to a time when there is less likelihood of interruptions?
3 Am I interrupting myself (i.e. finding less important things to do when I become bored or hit a snag with some important longer term activity)? See self-management techniques, Chapter 7.
4 Are important tasks taking too long because I lack certain skills which would help me to perform them more effectively? If so, what are they and how might I develop them?
5 Are there any activities which would contribute to my effectiveness/personal development which I am not doing? If so, what are they and how can I ensure that they are given the attention which they deserve?
6 Are my phone calls/personal contacts interrupting other people's work patterns? Is there any way in which I could make them less intrusive?

Chapter 3

Early approaches to the study of leadership
Traits and styles

EARLY TRAIT THEORIES OF LEADERSHIP

Early research into leadership was mainly concerned with the personality characteristics of leaders. Most studies attempted to identify the personality characteristics which would distinguish leaders from followers, while a much smaller number attempted to differentiate between more effective and less effective leaders. In general, the results of this research were disappointing.

The problem was not the fact that the research failed to find any relationship between personality and leadership, but that the relationships found were inconsistent. Major reviews of this research by Stogdill (1948) and Mann (1959) show that many research studies identified personality characteristics which differentiated leaders from followers. However, others found no difference between leaders and followers with respect to these characteristics, or even found that people who possessed them were less likely to become leaders. For example, Mann found 91 results in which there was a significant positive relationship between leadership status and intelligence, but there were also 90 results in which the relationship was non-significant, and one in which there was a significant negative correlation. Stogdill's review also produced inconsistent results. For example, leaders were found to be more extroverted in five studies, more introverted in two studies and no difference was found in two studies. Similarly, leaders were found to be more dominant in eleven studies, while bossy, domineering persons were rejected as leaders in four studies and no difference was found in two studies. Furthermore, Stogdill found nineteen studies in which patterns of leadership traits differed with the situation. These studies, he concluded (p. 63), were evidence that: 'The qualities, characteristics, and skills required in a leader are determined to a large extent by the demands of the situation in which he is to function as a leader.'

The results of research into the personality traits associated with leadership effectiveness were also disappointing. Heslin's (1964) review of research into group effectiveness suggested (p. 255) that certain characteristics, namely intelligence, ability and adjustment, appeared 'to be fairly consistently related to group performance measures'. However, he described the relationship between personality characteristics and group performance as being generally weak for predictive purposes. He suggested that this was due in part to situational factors, in particular, the nature of the task and the characteristics of the group members. Similarly, Korman (1968) reviewed research into the prediction of managerial performance and found that, in general, the results of objective personality tests were not associated with subsequent managerial performance, and while tests of ability were a fair predictor of first-line supervisory performance, they showed little usefulness for predicting managerial performance above this level. On the basis of this evidence, Howell (1976) concluded that, at the very best, such traits 'probably account for less than 10 percent of the observed differences in managerial effectiveness' (p. 81).

In a later review, Stogdill (1974) suggested that his original survey had been to some extent misinterpreted by other writers. It did not show that situational factors alone determined leadership status, but that both personality and the demands of the situation were involved. On the basis of his original survey of leadership research up to 1947 and subsequent studies between 1948 and 1970, Stogdill concluded that:

> The leader is characterized by a strong drive for responsibility and task completion, vigor and persistence in pursuit of goals, venturesomeness and originality in problem solving, drive to exercise initiative in social situations, self-confidence and a sense of personal identity, willingness to accept consequences of decision and action, readiness to absorb interpersonal stress, willingness to tolerate frustration and delay, ability to influence other persons' behavior, and capacity to structure social interaction systems to the purpose at hand.
>
> (Stogdill 1974: 81)

These clusters of characteristics, Stogdill claims, differentiate leaders from followers, effective from ineffective leaders and higher echelon from lower echelon leaders. Like Korman (1968), however, Stogdill states that tests designed to measure different aspects of personality have not proved very predictive or useful for the selection of leaders. Considered singly, he argues, the personality characteristics described above hold little diagnostic or predictive significance. Rather, they appear to interact in combination to give an advantage to the person seeking the responsibilities of leadership.

Stogdill's view seems to have some justification. In retrospect, it appears that early leadership researchers were overly optimistic. They expected to be able to identify personality characteristics which clearly and consistently differentiate leaders from the ordinary mass of followers, and became disillusioned when this did not happen. However, this does not necessarily mean that personality has no effect. If a large number of different characteristics are advantageous then it is not surprising that any one of them should correlate at a low level with leadership status or leadership effectiveness. A leader might possess one of the desirable characteristics in abundance, but still fail as a leader because he or she lacks other desirable characteristics. Thus, it would make more sense to search for a combination of characteristics related to leadership rather than examining each characteristic singly.

Similarly, the finding that the traits required for leadership varied in different situations was not a particularly damning result. It simply meant that it would be necessary to identify the different types of leadership situations which existed and the types of personality traits which were desirable in them.

Both these challenges were taken up by later leadership theorists, as we shall see in Chapter 8. However, the immediate effect of the reviews by writers such as Stogdill and Mann was considerably to reduce the level of interest in discovering the personality traits associated with leadership and during the 1950s the main thrust of leadership research and theory turned to the study of leadership behaviour.

EARLY BEHAVIOURAL THEORIES OF LEADERSHIP

Instead of attempting to explain leadership in terms of the leader's personal characteristics, behavioural leadership theorists turned their attention to what leaders did, and in particular to how they behaved towards subordinates. Such behaviour was typically described in terms of the leadership or managerial style adopted by the leader. Sometimes the styles were represented as discrete types of leadership, but more commonly they were envisaged as dimensions of leadership behaviour, along which the behaviour of the leader could vary. In general, leadership behaviour was described by any one theorist or researcher in terms of a relatively small number of styles or dimensions. Commonly, there would be two to four styles and only one or two dimensions. However, they were given a wide variety of different names by different leadership theorists. Bass (1990) lists no fewer than twenty-nine different systems for classifying leadership behaviour, and his list is by no means exhaustive. Despite the different names, however, the concepts were often very similar, and in practice the vast majority of work in this area can be described in terms of four main styles.

1 *Concern for task*: the extent to which the leader emphasizes high levels of productivity, organizes and defines group activities in relation to the group's task objectives, and so on. (Also called concern for production, production-centred, task-oriented and task-centred leadership.)
2 *Concern for people*: the extent to which the leader is concerned about his or her subordinates as people – their needs, interests, problems, development, etc. – rather than simply treating them as units of production. (Also called person-centred, person-oriented and employee-centred leadership.)
3 *Directive leadership*: the extent to which the leader makes all the decisions concerning group activities him- or herself and expects subordinates simply to follow instructions. (Also called authoritarian or autocratic leadership.)

4 *Participative leadership*: the extent to which the leader shares decision-making concerning group activities with subordinates. (Also called democratic leadership.)[1]

It is rare to find all four styles included in the same research study or theory. In some cases, only directive and participative leadership are considered, and these are usually represented as discrete types of leadership or as the opposite ends of a single dimension of leadership behaviour. Examples include the experimental study of authoritarian, democratic and *laissez-faire* leadership by Lewin *et al.* (1939), and Tannenbaum and Schmidt's (1958) seven-point continuum of leadership behaviour relating to directive and participative decision-making. Treating participative and directive leadership in this way may be to some extent justified, as leaders will rarely act in a way which is simultaneously highly directive and highly participative. Nevertheless, it is an oversimplification. Some leaders may be highly participative on certain issues but highly directive on others, and this is quite different from being moderately participative on most issues, although the two 'styles' could come at the same point on a single leadership dimension. For example, Pelz and Andrews (1966) found that the correlation between the degree of autonomy and the scientific contribution of scientists in research and development laboratories was highest in departments which were neither very tightly nor very loosely organized. They therefore suggested that scientific performance would be highest under conditions of what they called 'controlled freedom'; that is, when scientists had autonomy within a relatively structured context, rather than one in which they were left completely on their own.

In other cases, concern for task and concern for people are used on their own, and these too are sometimes represented either as discrete types of leadership or as opposite ends of a single leadership dimension. Such an approach was taken in the early studies of leadership styles carried out at the University of Michigan (see, for example, Katz *et al.* 1950 and Katz *et al.* 1951). Dichotomizing concern for task and concern for people in this way is much less justified, as it is quite feasible to show simultaneously high concern for both task and people. This was shown quite clearly by one of the supervisors in the study by Katz *et al.* who listed the following as being the most important aspects of his job:

> keeping the section running smoothly; keeping the clerks happy; keeping production up; making impartial assignments of work; making proper decisions on some difficult cases involving some payments and maybe a premium that hadn't been paid before.
>
> (Katz *et al.* 1950: 21)

This supervisor was classified as being employee centred, despite including 'keeping production up' as one of the most important aspects of his job.

Commonly, the directive and participative dimensions are merged with the concern for task and concern for people dimensions. One example is two famous dimensions called consideration and initiating structure developed on the basis of extensive research into leader behaviour at the Ohio State University (see, for example, Fleishman 1953; Halpin and Winer 1957; Fleishman and Harris 1962). These researchers took a different approach to leadership style from those described above. They regarded consideration and initiating structure as being two independent dimensions. Thus, leaders could be high on one dimension and not the other, but equally could be high on both or low on both. However, the two dimensions contain elements of all four of the leadership styles mentioned earlier. The consideration dimension includes elements of both concern for people and participative leadership, and the initiating structure dimension includes elements of concern for task and directive leadership. Because there are several different scales which are used to measure consideration and initiating structure, it is impossible to say precisely what the balance is between these different elements. However, some idea of the overlap can be obtained by quoting individual items from the questionnaires concerned. Three versions of the scales for consideration include the items 'He does personal favours for group members' and 'He gets group approval on important matters before going ahead'. Similarly, three versions of the initiating structure scales include the items 'He rules with an iron hand' and 'He emphasizes the meeting of deadlines' (see Schriesheim and Kerr 1974). Now it may well be that leaders with a high concern for task also tend to be directive while considerate leaders also tend to be participative, but this need not necessarily be the case. For example, one of the ways in which directive leaders obtain the compliance and sometimes even the commitment of subordinates is by doing them favours. In my experience, such leaders can be very popular with some group members, even though they are never consulted on significant matters, particularly if the favours involve breaking organizational rules or protecting group members from the larger organization.

Finally, some leadership theorists go even further and collapse all four styles into one leadership dimension, with participative, person-centred leadership at one end of a continuum and directive, task-centred leadership at the other. One example is the 'attitude towards men' scale quoted in Likert (1961: 119) which yielded a single score indicating 'the extent to which the manager has a supportive attitude towards his men ... and believes in using group methods of supervision'. Needless to say, such a combination of all the approaches outlined above manages to combine all their disadvantages too.

In early behavioural theories of leadership, this merging of dimensions did not cause a major problem. Such theories tended to be humanistic, claiming that both participative and person-centred leadership yielded greater subordinate satisfaction and better performance than either directive or task-centred leadership. The research evidence available at the time either supported or was interpreted as supporting this viewpoint. For a number of reasons, however, it became apparent that such a position was difficult to maintain.

One problem was that of establishing causality. Most of the research studies on which conclusions regarding the effectiveness of leadership styles were based were static, correlational studies. That is, they took measures of leadership styles and measures of other variables such as subordinate satisfaction, performance, labour turnover, absenteeism, grievances and so on during the same time period and then related the leadership style measures (usually derived from a questionnaire filled in by the leaders themselves, their subordinates or superiors) to one or more of the other measures obtained. Using this method, it is quite possible to establish the extent to which leadership style is related to these other variables, such as satisfaction, performance and so on, but it is impossible to establish the cause or causes of such relationships. For example, in the study by Katz *et al.* (1950) of the leadership behaviour of supervisors of clerical departments, it was found that the heads of high-producing departments were employee centred in six cases and production centred in one, whereas the heads of low-producing sections were employee centred in three cases and production centred in seven. Now, such results could have occurred because employee-centred supervision was more effective than production-centred supervision, and this is the way in which they were usually interpreted. Equally, however, they could have occurred because the performance of the subordinates influenced the way in which their supervisors behaved towards them, with supervisors of low-producing sections feeling that they had to emphasize production because performance was poor and supervisors of high-producing sections responding favourably towards subordinates because their performance was so good. A third possibility is that there was a reciprocal relationship between the supervisors' behaviour and their subordinates' performance, with each influencing the other in a cyclical fashion.

A number of ways of overcoming this problem have been developed, but they tend to be more complex and more time-consuming than questionnaire surveys and are therefore used much less often. The standard method of establishing causality is to carry out an experiment. Unfortunately, early experimental studies of leadership yielded ambiguous results in many cases. One such study is the much-quoted Lewin *et al.* (1939) Boys' Club experiment (see also White and Lippitt 1960). Four clubs for ten-year-old boys were organized on a voluntary basis. The boys carried out a number of craft activities for three successive six-week periods supervised by four adults who played the role of authoritarian, democratic and *laissez-faire* leaders. The adults played different leadership roles with different groups to eliminate the influence of their personal characteristics on the results obtained. Nineteen of the twenty boys liked the leaders who acted in a democratic manner better than those who acted in an autocratic manner. However, they reacted differently to the authoritarian leaders, three groups becoming submissive and one aggressive. The amount of time spent on productive activity also varied. With the leader present, the amount of time spent on productive activity was 74 per cent in the groups which reacted submissively to authoritarian leadership, 52 per cent in the group which reacted aggressively to authoritarian leadership, 50 per cent in the democratic groups and 33 per cent in the *laissez-faire* groups. When the group leader was out of the room, however, time spent on productive activity under authoritarian leadership declined dramatically to 29 per cent in the submissive groups and 16 per cent in the aggressive group. Time spent on productive activity in the democratic groups, on the other hand, dropped only slightly, from 50 per cent to 46 per cent.

This experiment is frequently quoted as providing convincing evidence of the superiority of democratic leadership. Whether it does or not, however, depends on the criteria of success used. If the criteria used to evaluate leadership effectiveness are high morale and willingness to work independently, then democratic leadership was shown to be more effective. On the other hand, if one's sole criterion of effective leadership is time spent in productive activity, then the study, if anything, provides support for the argument that close, authoritarian supervision is the most effective leadership style.

Another experimental study, this time of adult employees in an industrial organization, produced similar results. Morse and Reimer (1956) arranged the introduction of change programmes in four parallel divisions of a department engaged in relatively routine clerical work. An autonomy programme designed to increase rank-and-file decision-making was introduced in two divisions and a hierarchically controlled programme designed to increase the upper management role in decision-making was introduced in the other two. It was predicted that individual satisfaction and productivity would increase under the autonomy programme and decrease under the hierarchically controlled programme. As far as individual satisfaction was concerned, the results were in the expected direction. At the end of a year under the two experimental conditions, the individual satisfactions of the members of the work groups increased significantly in the autonomous programme and decreased significantly in the hierarchically controlled programme. With respect to productivity, the researchers' predictions were only partially fulfilled. Productivity had risen under both decision-making systems and furthermore the productivity increase was significantly greater in the hierarchically controlled programme than that in the autonomy programme. On the other hand, turnover caused by dissatisfaction or employees going to other jobs was much higher under the hierarchically controlled programme, as were unfavourable comments in exit interviews concerning pressure, work standards, and so on. According to Likert (1961), the results give every reason to believe that productivity would have continued to rise under the autonomy programme and eventually declined under the hierarchically controlled programme as the effects of the hostility, resentment and turnover it generated began to make themselves felt. Bass (1990) goes further and states that Morse and Reimer showed that although authoritarian methods contributed more to increased productivity during the first year, a sizeable drop in performance followed in subsequent years because of the adverse impact of the authoritarian approach on human factors. Both these assertions might well have proved correct had the experiment been continued. However, it was terminated after a year and no further data are reported in Morse and Reimer's (1956) paper. Thus any assertions about what might have happened are mere speculation.

A third experimental study was carried out by Coch and French (1948) in a garment factory which had a history of resistance to changes in work methods. Three different methods of introducing forthcoming changes in work methods were employed with four groups of workers. One group was simply told about the changes, another group met and elected representatives who participated in the decisions about the changes, and in the remaining two groups all the operators participated in the decisions about the changes. When the changes were introduced, productivity fell sharply in the group which was simply informed of the changes and did not improve appreciably thereafter. There were also numerous instances of aggression towards management and 17 per cent of the workers quit in the first 40 days following the changes. In the group which participated through representatives, productivity also declined at first, but then improved steadily and after fourteen days surpassed its previous level. None of its members resigned during the 40 days following the changes in work methods and there was only one act of aggression against the supervisor. In the two groups in which all the operators participated in the decisions, productivity returned to its previous level after only four days and by the end of the study was 14 per cent above its previous level. Furthermore, there were no resignations and no instances of aggression towards management. In this study, therefore, the results provided much more clear-cut evidence of the beneficial effects of participation on productivity. Nevertheless, when the study was repeated in Norway (French *et al.* 1960), participation had no effect on productivity and little effect on satisfaction.

This brings us to another major problem with respect to studies of leadership styles. The results tend to be inconsistent between studies. For example, Korman (1966) reviewed 14 studies which presented a total of 70 correlations between consideration, initiating structure and a variety of criterion variables, including group productivity, overall ratings, errors, inter-unit stress, attitudes towards supervision, labour turnover, absenteeism, grievances, accidents and so on. As can be seen in Table 3.1, he found virtually every possible combination of results. In the case of both consideration and initiating structure, the correlations with the criterion variables were sometimes significantly positive, sometimes significantly negative and sometimes non-significant. Sometimes either consideration or initiating structure was significantly correlated with the criterion variable while the other was not, sometimes there was a significant positive correlation in both cases and more often than not neither correlated significantly with the criterion variable. According to Korman (1966), these studies not only show that very little was then known about how consideration and initiating structure predicted work group performance, they did not even enable us to say whether they had any predictive significance at all. To answer

Table 3.1 Correlations between consideration, initiating structure and criterion variables

		Correlation with criterion variable	
Consideration		*Initiating structure*	*No. of Cases*
Significant positive	+	Significant positive	5
Significant positive	+	Significant negative	0
Significant positive	+	Non-significant	5
Significant negative	+	Significant positive	8
Significant negative	+	Significant negative	2
Significant negative	+	Non-significant	1
Non-significant	+	Significant positive	11
Non-significant	+	Significant negative	1
Non-significant	+	Non-significant	37

Source: Korman 1966

these questions, Korman suggested, there was a need for more systematic research which made greater use of experimental methods, took into account situational variables which might moderate the effects of consideration and initiating structure on criterion variables, and examined the possibility of curvilinear relationships between consideration, initiating structure and criterion variables.

A more wide-ranging survey of research into the relationship between leadership styles and follower satisfaction and productivity was carried out by Stogdill (1974). He compared two sets of styles: 'person-oriented' leadership styles (democratic, permissive, participative, follower-oriented and considerate) and 'work-oriented' leadership styles (autocratic, restrictive, task-oriented, distant, directive and structured). Stogdill's survey shows that the follower-oriented styles were more frequently found to be positively related to follower satisfaction than the work-oriented styles. A positive relationship between follower-oriented styles and follower satisfaction occurred in 48 cases and a zero or negative one in only 16, compared with a positive relationship between work-oriented styles and follower satisfaction in 14 cases and a zero or negative one in 19. Conversely, follower-oriented styles were more frequently found to have a negative relationship with group productivity than work-oriented styles. A positive relationship between follower-oriented styles and group productivity occurred in 47 cases and zero or negative relationships in 46, while a positive relationship was found between work-oriented styles and group productivity in 47 cases and a zero or negative one in 33. Thus Stogdill's survey indicated that, under certain circumstances, both person-oriented and work-oriented leadership behaviours may be related positively to group productivity, but equally, under other circumstances, neither may be.

In varying degrees, subsequent reviews of leadership research have continued to produce conflicting results. Kerr and Schriesheim (1974) carried out an update of Korman's (1966) review. They concluded that later research into consideration and initiating structure had yielded more statistically significant relationships than Korman found, and suggested that this probably reflected researchers' increased efforts to conceptualize and measure situational variables relating to leadership behaviour. Nevertheless, not all the studies yielded statistically significant relationships and the six longitudinal and experimental studies reviewed by Kerr and Schriesheim yielded ambiguous evidence concerning the cause and effect relationships between leader behaviour and subordinate satisfaction, morale and performance. In the case of performance, the results suggested that under some conditions subordinate performance causes subsequent leader behaviour while on other occasions such performance is caused by leader behaviour.

More recently, Fisher and Edwards (1988) carried out a meta-analysis of consideration and initiating structure studies. Meta-analysis is a statistical technique which allows the averaging of correlation coefficients from different studies. Fisher and Edwards derived separate mean correlations for three of the scales which are used to measure consideration and initiating structure. As can be seen in Table 3.2, two of the scales produced quite similar results. There were low to moderate positive correlations between both consideration and initiating structure and job performance, high positive correlations between consideration and the satisfaction measuress and moderately positive correlations between initiating structure and the satisfaction measures. The third scale, the Supervisory Behavior Description Questionnaire (SBDQ), yielded similar results to the other two in the case of consideration. However, the results for initiating structure differed markedly, with low negative correlations being found in the case of both the job performance and the two satisfaction measures. Bass (1990) attributes these anomalous results to the fact that the SBDQ has more items referring to punitive methods of supervision than the other two. Bass also notes a number of other factors which can influence the relationship between initiating structure and the satisfaction and productivity of subordinates, including the constraints and goals in the situation and the attitudes, training and motivation of the personnel involved.

A major survey of research into the effects of participative decision-making upon productivity and job satisfaction was carried out by Locke and Schweiger (1979). As can be seen in Table 3.3, the pattern of results in laboratory studies, correlational field studies and experimental field studies was remarkably similar. Most studies found either that participative decision-making made no difference to productivity or that the effect depended on contextual factors such as the knowledge and motivation of participants, task attributes, group characteristics and so on. Where type of leadership did make a difference to productivity, participative leadership was superior to and inferior to directive leadership in an equal number of cases. On the other hand, the results generally favoured participative over directive leadership with respect to satisfaction.

Table 3.2 Mean correlations of consideration and initiating structure with job performance, overall job satisfaction and satisfaction with supervision

	Correlation of consideration with		
	Performance	Overall job satisfaction	Satisfaction with supervision
LBDQ	0.45 (19)	0.65 (21)	0.99 (7)
SBDQ	0.46 (21)	0.83 (8)	0.99 (10)
LBDQXII	0.27 (11)	0.70 (25)	0.95 (19)
	Correlation of initiating structure with		
	Performance	Overall job satisfaction	Satisfaction with supervision
LBDQ	.47 (19)	.51 (21)	.57 (7)
SBDQ	− .06 (21)	− .04 (8)	−.30 (10)
LBDQXII	.22 (11)	.46 (25)	.73 (19)

Notes:
LBDQ = Leader Behaviour Description Questionnaire
SBDQ = Supervisory Behaviour Description Questionnaire
LBDQXII = Leader Behaviour Description Questionnaire XII

Figures in parentheses denote the number of correlations from which the mean correlation is derived in each case.

Source: Fisher and Edwards 1988

Conflicting results of a different kind were found in Miller and Monge's (1986) more recent survey of research into participation, productivity and satisfaction using meta-analysis. Correlations between participation and productivity in nine field studies were all positive and the average correlation was +0.27. On the other hand, correlations between participation and productivity in four laboratory studies were all negative and the average correlation was −0.33. Correlations between participation and satisfaction were positive in all but one of 41 cases and the weighted mean correlation was +0.34.

One response to the conflicting and inconclusive results produced by early research into leadership styles was to suggest that both concern for task and concern for people were necessary for effective leadership. A highly influential theory which took this approach was Blake and Mouton's (1964) Managerial Grid. They suggested that leadership attitudes could be described by integrating two independent dimensions which they called concern for production (later called concern for results) and concern for people. As shown in Figure 3.1, these were represented as forming two nine-point scales at right angles to each other. In theory, therefore, this yielded 81 different leadership styles. In practice, however, Blake and Mouton were mainly concerned with five particular styles, those occurring at the four corners and at the centre of the grid. In a more recent description of Grid styles, Blake and McCanse (1991) identify two additional styles (9 + 9 Paternalism and Opportunism) and a third dimension which they use to explore the positive and negative motivations underlying the

Table 3.3 Summary of results of studies of participative decision-making

Result	Type of study							
	Laboratory		Correlational field		Experimental field		Combined results	
	Production	Satisfaction	Production	Satisfaction	Production	Satisfaction	Production	Satisfaction
PDM superior	4	5	3	13	3	8	10 (22%)	26 (60%)
No difference or contextual	6	0	10	8	10	5	26 (56%)	13 (30%)
PDM inferior	4	2	3	1	3	1	10 (22%)	4 (9%)

Source: Locke and Schweiger 1979

Note: PDM = Participative decision-making

styles. Although the definitions of these styles are expressed in terms of the leader's concerns for production and people, this is yet another theory which confounds these concepts with participative and directive leadership. For example, the 9,1 leader is said to be one who 'feels his responsibilities are to plan, direct and control the actions of his subordinates in whatever way is necessary to reach the production objectives of the enterprise' (p. 19). In Blake and Mouton's model, however, the 1,9 style, with its high concern for people and low concern for production, is not equated with participative leadership. Rather, it seems to be more akin to *laissez-faire*, with people being allowed to set their own goals and standards, producing what Blake and Mouton describe as a pseudo-democratic atmosphere. It is the 9,9 manager who is said to use sound participation, achieving 'the effective integration of people with production ... by involving them and their ideas in determining the conditions and strategies of work' (p. 142). The key to the 9,9 style, according to Blake and Mouton, is the involvement and participation of those responsible for work in

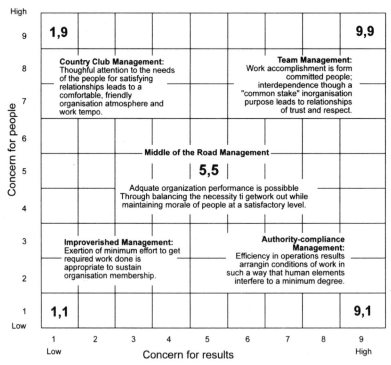

Figure 3.1. The Managerial Grid

Source: The Leadership Grid® figure, from *Leadership Dilemmas—Grid Solutions*, by Robert R. Blake and Anne Adams McCanse. Formerly the Managerial Grid by Robert R. Blake and Jane S. Mouton. Houston: Gulf Publishing Company (Grid Figure: p. 29). Copyright 1991 by Scientific Methods, Inc. Reproduced by permission of the owners.

its planning and execution. This brings about goal commitment through the alignment of individual and organizational goals and the kind of team action that leads to high organizational accomplishment. The 9,9 orientation, Blake and Mouton (1978) argue, is more positively associated with career success, productivity and corporate profitability that any other leadership style.

Blake and Mouton's Managerial Grid is undoubtedly a convenient way of presenting the concern for people and the concern for production/task dimensions of leadership behaviour, and it was taken up by several later leadership theorists. Theirs was also the first of the popular attitudinal behavioural theories of leadership to move away from the early humanist approaches and suggest that a concern for production could be a necessary and legitimate aspect of the leader's role. Nevertheless, they remained committed to the idea that there was one best leadership style, even though it was a different one from that advocated by earlier leadership theorists, and as we have seen the research evidence does not in general support the view that any one leadership style is invariably superior to any other. For example, Korman's (1966) survey showed that, while there were cases in which there was a significant positive correlation between both consideration and initiating structure and the criterion variable, this was only one of many other possible combinations of results. Furthermore, subsequent research has shown that combining consideration and initiating structure and consideration does little if anything to increase their ability to predict performance and satisfaction beyond what each measure can achieve alone (Larson *et al.* 1976; Nystrom 1978).

What seems to have happened is that leadership-style theorists fell into the same trap as trait theorists. They assumed that there would be one set of leadership behaviours which would invariably be associated with successful leadership regardless of the situation. The fact that research studies produced no consistent relationship between leadership styles and work group performance suggested that this was not the case. Unlike the response to the failure of early trait theories, however, this time the reaction was not to try to find yet another way of studying leadership. Instead, a new generation of behavioural leadership theorists attempted to find ways of incorporating the situation into their theories, and from the mid-1960s the majority of major behavioural theories of leadership have been situational theories. This approach to leadership will be taken up in the next chapter.

NOTE

1 Some writers make finer distinctions than the four-fold classification system used in this chapter. For example, Bass (1990) regards participative versus directive leadership as being only one dimension among others which go to make up the authoritarian versus democratic dimension. However, other writers on leadership do not necessarily use these terms in the same way and it was therefore thought that developing a finer classification system would unnecessarily complicate an already complex subject.

Chapter 4

Situational style theories of leadership

INTRODUCTION

Early behavioural theories of leadership were relatively simple. They tended to describe leadership behaviour in terms of one or two dimensions and stated what would be the effects on subordinate behaviour and/or satisfaction of adopting a leadership style corresponding to different positions, usually only high and low, on these dimensions. Including the situation as a variable in such theories made them much more complex. It required, in addition, some system for classifying the situations which a leader is likely to face, and the stipulation of which leadership style was appropriate in each of these situations. What usually did not change, however, were the descriptions of leader behaviour. Typically, these consisted of the same leadership dimensions used by the earlier 'one best way' theorists.

An early example of an attempt to take into account situational factors in identifying the most effective leadership style was the work of Tannenbaum and Schmidt (1958). They suggested that the range of possible leadership behaviours could be represented as a seven-point continuum, as shown in Figure 4.1. Each type of action is related to the degree of authority used by the boss and the amount of freedom available to subordinates in reaching decisions, ranging from the manager making the decision and announcing it on the one hand to the manager permitting subordinates to make decisions within prescribed limits on the other.

Tannenbaum and Schmidt suggest that the manager can permit subordinates greater freedom if the following essential conditions exist. The subordinates have relatively high needs for independence, have a readiness to assume responsibility in decision-making, have a relatively high tolerance for ambiguity, are interested in the problem and feel that it is important, understand and identify with the goals of the organization, have the necessary knowledge and skills to deal with the problem and have learned to expect to share in decision-making. Additionally, they suggest, the manager needs to take into account the type of organization, how well subordinates work together as a group, the complexity of the problem and the pressure of time in selecting an appropriate approach to decision-making.

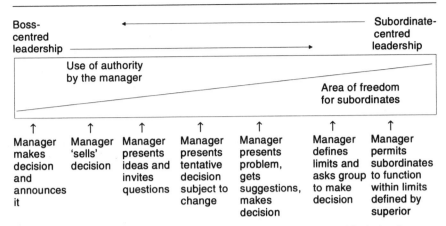

Figure 4.1. Tannenbaum and Schmidt's continuum of leadership behaviour

Many of the situational factors identified by Tannenbaum and Schmidt can be found in later situational leadership theories. Nevertheless, their work does not constitute a fully developed leadership theory. It tells managers what factors to take into account when choosing a leadership pattern, but does not tell them specifically which they should choose. They are merely told that in certain situations a more subordinate-centred approach to decision-making would be appropriate and when such conditions do not exist a more boss-centred approach would presumably be appropriate. However, most real-life managerial situations are likely to be a mixture of the various situational conditions outlined by Tannenbaum and Schmidt and while they describe various situational variables and discuss their significance, they do not develop a typology of situations and stipulate which of their seven decision-making methods would be most appropriate in each type of decision-making situation.

Various other writers on leadership have subsequently produced similar lists that have indicated the situational factors which managers need to take into account when deciding what approach to decision-making should be adopted. Examples include Strauss (1977), Yukl (1981) and Wright and Taylor (1994). From the mid-1960s, however, a number of theorists began to develop models of leadership behaviour and effectiveness that stipulated more precisely the leadership styles which were appropriate in different leadership situations. In this chapter, some of the more prominent of these situational style[1] theories of leadership will be described and evaluated.

FIEDLER'S CONTINGENCY MODEL

The first major situational theory of leadership was Fiedler's (1964, 1967) Contingency Model. Its name derives from the fact that, according to Fiedler, the most effective leadership style is contingent upon the degree to which the situation enables the leader to exert influence over his or her group members. This in turn is said to be dependent upon three factors:

1 The leader's position power – the power the organization confers on the leader for the purpose of getting the task done.
2 The structure of the task – the degree to which the task is clearly spelled out as to goals, methods and standards of performance.
3 The interpersonal relationship between leader and members – the extent to which the leader is able to obtain group members' compliance with minimum effort because he or she is liked and trusted (Fiedler 1967; Fiedler and Garcia 1987).

Fiedler states that situations are favourable for the leader to exert influence over his or her group when position power is high, the task is highly structured and leader–member relations are good, and unfavourable when position power is low, the task unstructured and leader–member relations poor.

On the basis of extensive research, Fiedler (1967) argues that groups under task-oriented leaders tend to perform better when the situation is either favourable or highly unfavourable for the leader to exert influence over the group, but groups under relationship-oriented leaders tend to perform better in certain intermediate situations when the situation is neither favourable nor unfavourable. This view of leadership effectiveness can be represented diagrammatically, as shown in Figure 4.2.

Fiedler uses the three situational variables to generate eight different leadership situations which he refers to as octants. These are shown in Figure 4.2,

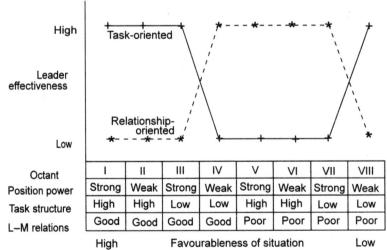

Figure 4.2. Schematic representation of Fiedler's Contingency Model
Source: Fiedler and Garcia 1987

together with the leadership style which is predicted to be most effective in each case. There is some ambiguity with respect to octant 7. Fiedler and Garcia (1987) do not actually stipulate which style would be most effective in this octant, and some versions of Figure 4.2 seem to imply that a task-oriented style would be most appropriate in this situation. In most reports on tests of the model, however, it is assumed that a relationship-oriented style would be most effective in this octant and this is the view which is represented in Figure 4.2.

Fiedler explains his research findings as follows. In favourable situations, where the leader has power, the support of the group, and a straightforward task, the group members expect to be told what to do and consultation is superfluous. In highly unfavourable situations, where a disliked leader with little power has an ambiguous and unclear task, attempts at consultation are unlikely to be met with a constructive response, and it is therefore better for the leader to 'take charge', rather than risk the group falling apart in dissension. On the other hand, in situations of intermediate favourableness, the provision of a non-threatening, permissive environment is necessary if members are to feel free to make suggestions and contribute to the discussion on how to tackle the group's task, and leaders who are diplomatic and indirect in their dealings with group members are more likely to gain their cooperation. In these situations, therefore, a relationship-oriented style is more effective.

It is difficult to assess the validity of Fiedler's Contingency Model with any degree of precision. A large number of validation studies have been carried out. Fiedler and Garcia (1987) provide details of 13 laboratory and 8 field studies published between 1963 and 1984. They note that most validation studies have supported the Contingency Model's predictions, although not always at a statistically significant level. However, it should also be noted that there are a substantial minority of results, some 32 per cent, which are in the opposite direction from the Contingency Model's predictions. These occur particularly in octant 2 (good leader–member relations, high task structure and low position power) where 11 of the results in Fiedler and Garcia's survey are in the expected direction and 7 in the opposition direction.

In general, then, it can be said that the overall pattern of results supports Fiedler's Contingency Model. This can be seen if the results of the original studies on which the model was based and the subsequent validation studies shown in Figure 4.3 are compared with the predicted pattern of results shown in Figure 4.2. However, as we have seen, the closeness of fit between the model's predictions and research findings varies both between octants and between different research studies within the same octant.

It might be thought that meta-analysis, allowing as it does the averaging of results from different studies, would clarify the situation. However, meta-analyses of the findings of contingency model validation studies have also produced mixed results. Strube and Garcia (1981) noted that there were instances in which the theory was not supported within octants, but concluded that as a whole it was overwhelmingly supported. Peters *et al.* (1985) were

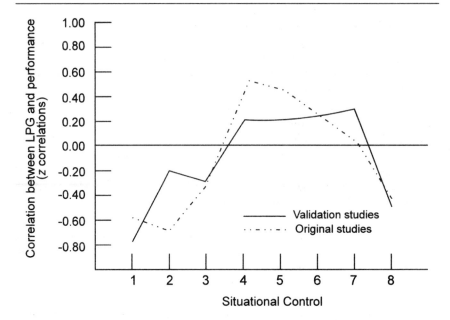

Figure 4.3 Results of research into Fiedler's Contingency Model of Leadership: median correlations between leader LPC and performance for the original studies and validation studies to 1982

Source: Fiedler and Garcia 1987

somewhat less supportive. They state that, taken as a whole, their meta-analyses lead to a generally positive conclusion regarding the validity of contingency theory. However, they also found two areas in which the data did not support the theory. First, in their analysis of laboratory validation studies, the result for octant 2 was in the opposite direction from the model's predictions. Second, in the field validation studies, there was residual variance in octants 1, 3, 4 and 6 which could not be attributed to sampling error, suggesting that additional moderator variables beyond those included in contingency theory need to be specified to account more fully for the results obtained. Peters *et al.* therefore regard the Contingency Model as being incomplete in its present form.

A third meta-analysis, including almost twice as many validation correlations as the previous two, was even less supportive. Nathan *et al.* (1986, quoted Bass 1990) argue that the validity coefficients in each octant vary too much to allow anyone to expect that the model's prediction would be fulfilled. The best that can be said, they conclude, is that the results are as predicted by the theory over half the time.

The inconsistent support for Fiedler's Contingency Model is undoubtedly due in part to flaws in the original development of the theory. Among its more serious limitations are the following:

1 Fiedler's measure of leadership style is inadequate. At the heart of the Contingency Model is an enigmatic personality questionnaire known as the least preferred co-worker (LPC) scale, which asks respondents to describe in terms of a number of dimensions the person with whom they can work least well. Respondents are scored on the extent to which they describe their least preferred co-worker in relatively favourable terms (high LPC) or relatively unfavourable terms (low LPC). An individual's LPC score is interpreted as indicating his or her attitude or emotional response to a person who impedes or frustrates the accomplishment of a task. According to Fiedler and Garcia (1987: 76), the low LPC leader says, in effect, 'Accomplishing a task is so important that you must be totally worthless or despicable if you keep me from getting the job done and I reject everything about you.' A low LPC leader is therefore regarded as having high task motivation. The high LPC leader on the other hand, says, in effect, 'You may be a very poor co-worker, you may be frustrating, inefficient, or lazy. But the co-worker role is just one of many, and that doesn't mean that you might not be quite pleasant or worthwhile in other respects.' A high LPC leader is therefore called relationship motivated.

This explanation of Fiedler's leadership measure may go some way towards explaining why validation studies of the Contingency Model have produced such mixed results. While the Contingency Model is expressed in terms of the relationship between leader behaviour and leadership effectiveness, the validation studies actually attempt to predict leadership effectiveness on the basis of a personality measure, which is assumed also to predict leader behaviour. However, it is notoriously difficult to predict behaviour with any degree of precision on the basis of a measure of personality. Thus validation studies of Fiedler's Contingency Model could fail either because leader behaviour is not associated with leadership effectiveness in the way in which Fiedler says it is or because the LPC scale does not provide a sufficiently precise measure of such behaviour.

Unfortunately, attempts to establish exactly what the LPC scale actually does measure have not produced consistent results. From the outset, there has been little agreement as to what it actually means. More precisely, there is little agreement as to what else a high or low LPC score tells us about the respondent apart from the obvious fact that he or she assesses a least preferred co-worker relatively favourably or unfavourably. Fiedler himself has made three suggestions. He initially proposed that it was a measure of social distance, with low LPC people being more socially or psychologically distant from other group members than high LPC people. Then, in the original (1967) version of the Contingency Model, LPC scores were said to indicate whether leaders were relationship oriented (high LPC score) or task oriented (low LPC score). Finally, in later versions of the Contingency Model (Fiedler 1972; Fiedler and Garcia 1987) the LPC score is interpreted as measuring a motivational hierarchy. That is, Fiedler now takes the view that it indicates the degree to which the individual sets a higher priority or value on task accomplishment (low LPC) or maintaining good interpersonal relationships (high LPC), but this does not mean that individuals will always behave in accordance with these primary goals. When they have achieved their primary goals, high LPC leaders may turn their attention to the task and low LPC leaders may turn to the less important goal (to them) of developing or maintaining good relations with co-workers. Other interpretations of the LPC questionnaire include Hill's (1969) suggestion that it measures cognitive complexity and Rice's (1978) suggestion that it measures attitudes and values. None of these interpretations, however, has been consistently supported by the research evidence. All of them have received support from some research studies, but equally all of them have been contradicted by others (see Bass 1990). Schriesheim and Kerr (1977) aptly described the LPC scale as a 'measure in search of a meaning' (p. 23), and subsequent research has done little to clarify matters. According to Bass (1990), 'Although the contingency model may still appear to be supported by a wide array of studies, the meaning of LPC remains unclear and controversial, and no adequate theoretical explanation of its effects has been presented.' (p. 508).

My own preference would be to regard LPC scores as providing an indication of the subject's tolerance for ambiguity. High LPC managers are able to see good in people whom they dislike, but low LPC managers assess people in a more 'all or nothing' way. Hofstede's (1980) finding that his Uncertainty Avoidance Index had a significant negative correlation ($r = -0.44$) with LPC scores provides some support for this view. Thus Fiedler's results could be interpreted as showing that managers who are intolerant of ambiguity are more effective in situations which are clearly favourable or unfavourable, whereas managers who are tolerant of ambiguity are more effective in situations of mixed favourableness and unfavourableness. A link with leadership style theory could then be maintained on the grounds that intolerance of ambiguity has been regarded as one of the characteristics of the authoritarian personality (Adorno *et al.* 1950).

Nevertheless, this interpretation remains merely one speculative explanation among many. It would appear that the only interpretation of LPC scores that we can be reasonably sure of is that they indicate the extent to which people rate their least preferred co-workers favourably or unfavourably. Thus, the fact that the research results with respect to the way Contingency Model are generally in the predicted direction is not as informative as it might seem, because we do not know what these results mean, except in terms of what they tell us about people with differing LPC scores.

2 There may well be other situational variables in addition to those identified by Fiedler. In particular, the Contingency Model ignores the characteristics of the subordinates – their knowledge and skills and their preferences with respect to the way in which they are led – and these could very well influence the effectiveness of different leadership styles.

3 Fiedler describes leadership behaviour in terms of a single dimension from relationship oriented to task oriented. This is not supported by the research evidence, such as that carried out with respect to consideration and initiating

structure, which suggests that these are two separate dimensions. In many respects, it would make more sense for Fiedler to describe leadership style in terms of a directive vs. participative dimension and it is noticeable that when he attempts to explain his results, he does so in terms of the degree to which consultation would be beneficial in different situations. Whatever the dimension is called, however, a single, bipolar dimension is far too simple to provide an adequate description of leader behaviour.

In summary, Fiedler's Contingency Model served the useful function of stimulating the study of situational factors in leadership and the fact that his results were generally in the predicted direction showed that situational factors do influence leadership effectiveness in a systematic way. However, its major drawback is that, because of the enigmatic nature of his measure of leadership style, we cannot be sure what these results actually mean.

REDDIN'S 3-D LEADERSHIP THEORY

Another early situational style theory of leadership was Reddin's (1966, 1970) 3-D Theory. This theory is, in effect, a situational version of Blake and Mouton's (1964) Managerial Grid. Reddin identifies four basic leadership styles:

- the related style (high on relationships orientation and low on task orientation);
- the dedicated style (high on task orientation and low on relationships orientation);
- the integrated style (high on both task and relationships orientations);
- the separated style (low on both task and relationships orientations).

Unlike Blake and Mouton, however, Reddin does not assume that any one style is necessarily more effective than any other. Each of them, he argues, could be effective in certain situations, but not effective in others.

Reddin therefore turned Blake and Mouton's (1964) Managerial Grid into a three-dimensional model by adding an extra dimension which he called 'effectiveness'. Each basic style, he suggests, can have a more effective and a less effective form, as shown in Figure 4.4. Reddin (1970) defines these eight styles as follows:

Executive   A manager who is using a high task orientation and a high relationships orientation in a situation where such behaviour is appropriate and who is, therefore, more effective; perceived as a good motivating force who sets high standards, treats everyone somewhat differently, and prefers team management.

Compromiser   A manager who is using a high task orientation and a high relationships orientation in a situation that requires a high orientation to only one or neither and who is, therefore, less effective; perceived as being a poor decision-maker, as one who allows various pressures in the situation to influence him or her too much, and as avoiding or minimizing immediate pressures and problems rather than maximizing long-term production.

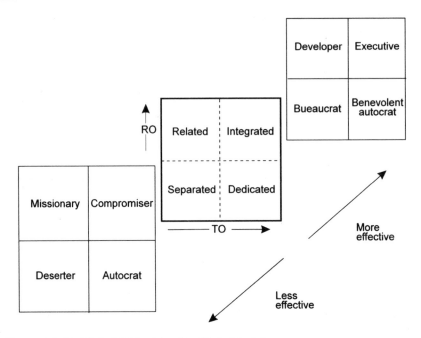

Figure 4.4 Reddin's 3-D Leadership Style Model
Source: Reddin 1970

Benevolent autocrat A manager who is using a high task orientation and a low relationships orientation in a situation where such behaviour is appropriate and who is therefore more effective; perceived as knowing what he or she wants and how to get it without causing resentment.

Autocrat A manager who is using a high task orientation and a low relationships orientation in a situation where such behaviour is inappropriate and who is, therefore, less effective; perceived as having no confidence in others, as unpleasant, and as interested only in the immediate task.

Developer A manager who is using a high relationships orientation and a low task orientation in a situation where such behaviour is appropriate and who is, therefore, more effective; perceived as having implicit trust in people and as being primarily concerned with developing them as individuals.

Missionary A manager who is using a high relationships orientation and a high task orientation in a situation where such behaviour is inappropriate and who is, therefore, less effective; perceived as being primarily interested in harmony.

Bureaucrat A manager who is using a low task orientation and a low relationships orientation in a situation where such behaviour is appropriate and who is, therefore, more effective; perceived as being primarily interested in rules and procedures for their own sake, as wanting to control the situation by their use, and as conscientious.

Deserter   A manager who is using a low task orientation and a low relationships orientation in a situation where such behaviour is inappropriate and who is, therefore, less effective; perceived as uninvolved and passive or negative.

Reddin (1970) argues that managers can move along the third dimension, from a less effective to a more effective style, by matching their basic style to the needs of the situation. It is quite possible and reasonable, he states, for behaviour labelled 'deserter' in one situation to be labelled 'bureaucrat' in another. Managerial style cannot be defined solely with reference to behaviour. It must always be defined with reference to the demands of the situation. Reddin identifies five different elements or aspects of the situation, the organization (its philosophy or culture), the technology (the way the work is done) and the manager's superior, co-workers and subordinates. He then analyses each in detail to show how to assess the demands they make on managerial behaviour. Forty 'demand indicators', ten for each basic style, are listed, in order to enable managers to assess the behaviour which the organization, the technology, their superior, co-workers and subordinates are demanding of them. These demands can then be represented on the basic styles grid to show the behaviour which the manager can and must use if the demands of all the situational elements are to be met.

Reddin (1987) later added a further list of twenty situational elements. These are intended to enable managers to analyse which elements are making the greatest demands on them, which style is most appropriate to deal with these elements and how effectively they are dealing with them.

The major strength of Reddin's approach is that it provides managers with a framework for analysing their own leadership behaviour in order to come to a reasoned judgement concerning the style which would be most appropriate in their particular circumstances. In so doing, it includes more situational variables than most other leadership theories, and yet the basic model is straightforward and easy to understand, making it a useful vehicle for management development. Its main limitation as a scientific theory is that Reddin does not provide a means of measuring situational demands, as opposed to assessing them in general terms. Thus, while measures of leadership styles exist, these cannot be related to effectiveness in different situations in any precise way, because precise measures of such situations do not exist. This makes it difficult to carry out a rigorous validation study of the model and not surprisingly therefore it has generated little research.

HERSEY AND BLANCHARD'S SITUATIONAL LEADERSHIP THEORY

Another situational style theory of leadership based on Blake and Mouton's Managerial Grid was developed by Hersey and Blanchard. Early forms of this theory (e.g. Hersey and Blanchard 1969) were called the Life Cycle Theory of leadership, but it was later retitled more simply, but less informatively, the Situational Leadership Theory (Hersey and Blanchard 1977). In their theory, Hersey and Blanchard identify two dimensions of leadership behaviour, task and relationship. According to Hersey and Blanchard (1982: p. 152), 'task behavior is the extent to which a leader provides direction for people: telling them what to do, when to do it, where to do it, and how to do it. It means setting goals for them and defining their roles.' Relationship behaviour, on the other hand, is 'the extent to which the leader engages in two-way communication with people: providing support, encouragement, "psychological strokes", and facilitating behaviours. It means actively listening to people and supporting their efforts.'

As in Reddin's (1966, 1970) model, categorizing leaders as being either high or low on these dimensions yields four basic leadership styles. Hersey and Blanchard (1982) describe these styles as follows:

- Telling (high task/low relationship behaviour): a style characterized by the leader defining roles and telling people what, how, when and where to do various tasks.
- Selling (high task and relationship behaviour): a style in which most of the direction is still provided by the leader, but through two-way communication and explanation the leader tries to get followers psychologically to 'buy into' desired behaviours.
- Participating (high relationship and low task behaviour): a style in which leader and follower share decision-making, with the main role of the leader being facilitating and communicating.
- Delegating (low relationship and task behaviour): a style in which, although the leader may still identify the problem, the responsibility for carrying out plans is given to followers.

Situational Leadership Theory takes into account the influence of only one situational variable. Hersey and Blanchard (1982) take the view that it would be an impossible task if managers attempted to look at all the possible interacting situational variables every time they had to make a leadership decision. While they recognize the importance of other situational variables, therefore, they concentrate on what they regard as the most important one – the relationship between leader and follower. They justify this decision on the ground that if the follower decides not to follow, it really does not matter what the boss thinks, what the nature of the work is, how much time is involved, or what the other situational variables are.

The specific situational variable identified by Hersey and Blanchard is the maturity of followers in relation to a specific task to be performed. Maturity is defined as the ability and willingness of people to take responsibility for directing their own behaviour. Four levels of maturity are identified:

1 Low maturity (M1): unable and unwilling or insecure.
2 Low to moderate maturity (M2): unable, but willing or confident.
3 Moderate to high maturity (M3): able, but unwilling or insecure.
4 High maturity (M4): able/competent and willing/confident.

According to Situational Leadership Theory, the appropriate leadership style depends on the maturity of the followers. A telling style has the highest probability of being effective with people of low maturity, because they require clear, specific direction and too much supportive behaviour may be seen as permissive, easy, and most importantly, as rewarding poor performance. A selling style is most appropriate with people of low to moderate maturity. It provides directive behaviour, because of their lack of ability, but also supportive behaviour to reinforce their willingness and enthusiasm. A participative style has the highest probability of being effective with people of moderate to high maturity. By allowing two-way communication and active listening, the leader supports the followers' efforts to use the abilities they already have. Finally, a low profile, delegatory style has the highest probability of being effective with people of high maturity, because they know what to do and, being psychologically mature, do not need above average amounts of two-way communication and supportive behaviour. The appropriate style for each situation is shown diagrammatically in Figure 4.5. As noted in Chapter 3, Korman (1966) suggested the possibility of curvilinear relationships between consideration, initiating structure and outcome variables. Hersey and Blanchard (1982) claim that Situational Leadership Theory has identified such a relationship in the bell-shaped curve shown in Figure 4.5.

According to Hersey and Blanchard (1982), it is implicit in Situational Leadership Theory that leaders should not only adopt a leadership style which is appropriate to their followers' level of maturity, but should also help followers to grow in maturity as far as they are willing and able to go. Conversely, if a follower's performance begins to slip and ability or motivation decreases, the leader should reassess the follower's level of maturity and move backwards through the curve shown in Figure 4.5, providing appropriate support and direction.

Intuitively, Situational Leadership Theory makes a certain amount of sense in very general terms. Subordinates who are new in a job may need and appreciate more support and guidance, while those who have been in a job longer and know what they should be doing can more happily be left to get on with it, providing they are still motivated. Beyond this rather obvious statement, however, Situational Leadership Theory has a number of serious shortcomings.

1 The theory has generated very little research. Of the validation studies which have been carried out, some have provided partial, rather weak support, while the others have yielded negative evidence. For example, the results of a study of high-school teachers carried out by Vecchio (1987) suggest that recently hired employees may need and appreciate more task structuring from their

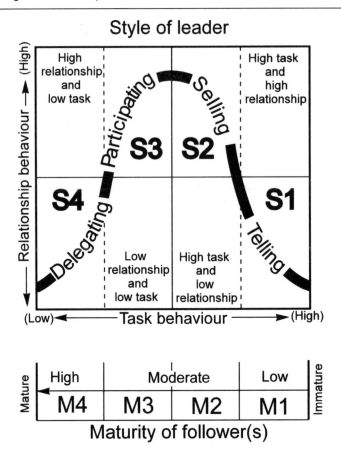

Figure 4.5 Hersey and Blanchard's Situational Leadership Theory
Source: Hersey and Blanchard 1982

superiors. However, the results did not support Situational Leadership Theory in the case of moderate and high maturity subordinates. Vecchio therefore concludes that the theory may only hold for certain types of employees. A later study of university hall directors and resident advisors was carried out by Blank *et al.* (1990). Their results revealed a lack of support for the basic assumptions which underlie Situational Leadership Theory. Blank *et al.* conclude that, given the results of the small amount of research which has so far been carried out, it is difficult to be optimistic about Situational Leadership Theory.

2 The theory is extremely limited in scope. The effectiveness of different leadership styles may depend to some extent on the characteristics of followers. However, the theory ignores a great many other potential situational variables, whose influence on leadership effectiveness could be equally important. As we shall see in relation to the Path–Goal Theory of

Leadership, such variables may interact with each other to produce different effects from those which they would produce on their own. Whether directiveness is an appropriate style, for example, may depend upon the relative task knowledge of the leader and follower, rather than the absolute level of the follower's ability. Even if the follower has low to moderate ability with respect to a particular task, a directive style may not be appropriate if the leader's ability with respect to that task is even lower. However, Situational Leadership Theory seems to assume that leaders are capable of making effective decisions with respect to all areas of their subordinates' jobs, if necessary, and this is a questionable assumption given the complexity of modern work roles.

Furthermore, Situational Leadership Theory does not include all the potential situational variables relating to follower characteristics. In Path–Goal Theory, for example, it is proposed that the subordinate's level of authoritarianism may influence the way he or she responds to different leadership styles. Thus an able, well motivated, but highly authoritarian follower may still prefer a leader who employs a directive style and issues clear-cut instructions.

3 Situational Leadership Theory is yet another leadership theory which confuses task orientation with direction and support with participation. For example, there is no reason why a task-oriented leader should not employ a participative style because he or she believes that this is the most effective way of getting the task done, but this participative style could be performed in a warm, supportive manner or a cold, distant manner.

4 The subordinate maturity scale is quite arbitrary (Graeff 1983). It is assumed that an able but unwilling follower is more mature than an unable but willing one. However, the unable but willing follower could be one who recognizes his or her own shortcomings but tries his or her best because the task is an important one and there is no one else available to do it. Conversely, the able but unwilling follower could be one who petulantly refuses to co-operate because he or she was not allowed to have his or her own way. Under these circumstances, it would seem reasonable to reverse the two mid-points of the scale.

5 Although Korman (1966) suggested that consideration and initiating structure might have curvilinear relationships with other variables such as performance and job satisfaction, Situational Leadership Theory does not suggest such a relationship in relation to task orientation (Graeff 1983). A direct negative relationship is proposed instead. High task orientation is recommended when follower maturity is low or moderately low and low task orientation is recommended when follower maturity is moderately high or high.

Despite the lack of consistent supportive evidence and its many conceptual deficiencies, Situational Leadership Theory has enormous popularity with training directors and personnel managers (Graeff 1983). Bass (1990) suggests that one reason for this may be that its very simplicity gives managers a sense of quick mastery of complex problems. The shortcomings listed above suggest that such a sense of mastery would almost certainly be illusory.

HOUSE'S PATH–GOAL THEORY

House's Path–Goal Theory of Leadership has its origins in the expectancy theories of motivation developed by Georgopoulos *et al.* (1957), Vroom (1964) and others. Essentially, such theories suggest that an individual's motivation to perform a particular task will depend upon the value which he or she places on different outcomes and his or her assessment of the probability of attaining such outcomes by expending effort on the task in question. The more likely that it appears that expenditure of effort will result in the attainment of positive outcomes and the avoidance of negative ones, and the greater the value the individual places on attaining or avoiding such outcomes, then the more motivated he or she will be. These ideas were used to form the basis of a non-situational Path–Goal Theory of Leadership by Evans (1970) and then a situational version developed by House (1971).

The central tenet of the Path–Goal Theory of Leadership is that 'the motivational functions of the leader consist of increasing personal pay-offs to subordinates for work-goal attainment, and making the path to these pay-offs easier to travel by clarifying it, reducing road blocks and pitfalls, and increasing the opportunities for personal satisfaction en route' (House 1971: 324). In more precise terms, Path–Goal Theory is based on two main propositions:

1 Leader behaviour is acceptable and satisfying to subordinates to the extent that the subordinates see such behaviour as either an immediate source of satisfaction or as instrumental to future satisfaction.
2 The leader's behaviour will be motivational i.e. increase effort, to the extent that (a) such behaviour makes satisfaction of subordinates' needs contingent on performance and (b) such behaviour complements the environment of subordinates by providing the coaching, guidance, support and rewards necessary for effective performance.

In Path–Goal Theory, leadership behaviour has been described in a number of different ways. In the original (House 1971) version, hypotheses derived from the theory were expressed in terms of the two Ohio State dimensions of initiating structure and consideration. In a later version of the theory, however, House and Mitchell (1974) identified four kinds of leader behaviour:

1 Directive leadership: characterized by a leader who lets subordinates know what is expected of them, gives specific guidance as to what should be done and how it should be done, makes his or her part in the group understood, schedules work to be done, maintains definite standards of performance, and asks that the group members follow standard rules and procedures. This type

of leadership is also called instrumental leadership in some versions of the theory.

2 Supportive leadership: characterized by a friendly and approachable leader who shows concern for the status, well-being and needs of subordinates, does little things to make their life more pleasant, treats members as equals and is friendly and approachable.

3 Participative leadership: characterized by a leader who consults with subordinates, solicits their suggestions and takes these suggestions seriously into consideration before making a decision.

4 Achievement-oriented leadership: characterized by a leader who sets challenging goals, expects subordinates to perform at their highest levels, continually seeks improvement in performance and shows confidence that subordinates will assume responsibility, put forth effort and accomplish challenging goals.

According to Path–Goal Theory, the most effective leadership style will depend upon two sets of situational factors:

1 The personal characteristics of the subordinates, e.g. their level of authoritarianism, their perception of their own ability with respect to their assigned tasks, and their perceived locus of control (the extent to which they believe that what happens to them is primarily influenced by their own behaviour or external factors such as chance or the actions of other people).

2 The environmental pressures and demands with which subordinates must cope in order to accomplish the work goals and satisfy their needs (e.g. the nature of the subordinates' task, the formal authority structure of the organization and the primary work group).

In summary, then, the Path–Goal Theory of Leadership asserts that: (a) the leader's behaviour will exert a beneficial influence on subordinates' motivation to perform, job satisfaction and acceptance of the leader to the extent that it smooths the path to the achievement of their goals; and (b) the leadership behaviours which perform this function will vary depending on the characteristics of the subordinates and their working environment. As Fiedler and House (1988) put it, the role of the leader is to complement that which 'is missing' with respect to the environment, the task and the competence and motivation of subordinates in order to enhance their motivation, satisfaction and performance.

Based on these underlying principles, a wide variety of hypotheses has been developed concerning what would be the most effective leadership style in different situations. Some of the major ones are as follows:

1 In an unstructured working environment (ambiguous task demands and little policy or procedural guidance), directive leadership will enhance subordinates' performance by providing guidance and reducing role ambiguity (Fiedler and House 1988).

2 In an unstructured working environment, directive leadership will enhance subordinates' performance by increasing role clarity (Fiedler and House 1988).

3 In a structured working environment, directive leadership will enhance subordinates' performance by preventing low motivation from decreasing performance (Fiedler and House 1988).

4 The more structured the working environment, the lower the relationship between directive leadership and subordinate satisfaction, because directiveness is seen as more of a hindrance when tasks are clear (House 1971).

5 The more structured the working environment, the more supportive leadership will enhance subordinates' satisfaction and performance (Fiedler and House 1988). Supportive leadership will have its most positive effect on subordinate satisfaction for subordinates who have stressful, frustrating or dissatisfying tasks (House 1971).

6 Participative leadership will be most effective under conditions where subordinates' tasks are unstructured and subordinates have a preference for internal structure (Fiedler and House 1988).

7 Achievement-oriented leadership will cause subordinates to strive for higher standards of performance and have more confidence in their ability to meet challenging goals (House 1971).

As in the case of Fiedler's contingency theory, Path–Goal Theory has generated a great deal of research and again, while much of it is supportive, there are also a substantial number of conflicting results (see Bass 1990). For example, a meta-analysis of 48 studies designed to test Path–Goal Theory was carried out by Indvik (1986). The results supported hypotheses 1, 3, 4 and 5 above, but not hypothesis 2, in that the effect on performance was minimal when task structure was low, contrary to predictions. On the other hand, the results of a comprehensive study of Path–Goal Theory based on a survey of 467 non-academic staff at a university by Indvik (1988, quoted Bass 1990) were less favourable. Only seven of the seventeen hypotheses concerning the effects of directive, supportive, participative and achievement-oriented leadership were supported.

One reason for the conflicting results found in Path–Goal Theory research, Yukl (1994) suggests, is that the assumptions underlying some of the hypotheses are questionable. For example, it is assumed that role ambiguity is unpleasant to an employee, but some people seem to like a job in which duties and procedures are not specified in detail and there is ample opportunity to define their work role themselves. Yukl also points out that clarification of the subordinate's role sometimes makes it evident that successful task performance and attainment of specific task goals are more difficult than the employee initially believed, thus decreasing rather than increasing motivation.

Another major difficulty in validating the theory is its complexity. Hypotheses derived from the theory tend to be expressed in terms of the effect of a single moderator variable (e.g. task structure), on the relationship between a single kind of leader behaviour and outcome variables, such as performance or satisfaction. However, moderator variables may interact with each other to produce different effects. For example, Dessler (1973, quoted House and Mitchell 1974) found that for subordinates at lower organizational levels who were doing routine, repetitive, unambiguous tasks, directive leadership was preferred by closed-minded, dogmatic, authoritarian subordinates and non-directive leadership was preferred by non-authoritarian, open-minded subordinates. However, for subordinates at higher organizational levels doing non-routine, ambiguous tasks, directive leadership was preferred by both authoritarian and non-authoritarian subordinates. According to House and Mitchell (1974), this study shows that two contingency factors, task ambiguity and the subordinates' degree of authoritarianism, appear to operate simultaneously. When measured in combination, the findings are as predicted by the theory. However, when the subordinate's personality is not taken into account, task ambiguity does not always operate as a contingency variable as predicted by the theory. The inclusion of the moderator variable of subordinate authoritarianism could also help to account for the fact that some employees do not find role ambiguity unpleasant, in that, as we have already noted, intolerance of ambiguity is thought to be an aspect of the authoritarian personality (Adorno *et al.* 1950). Again, however, the increase in explanatory power of the theory is gained at the expense of a corresponding increase in its complexity.

As Filley *et al.* (1976) point out, different kinds of leadership behaviour may also interact. The description of directive leadership, for example, does not stipulate the manner in which this type of leadership is performed. Thus, it could be performed in a cold, distant and domineering manner or, equally, it could be performed with many of the attributes of supportive leadership (e.g. in a friendly manner, showing concern for the needs and well-being of subordinates, doing little things to make the work more pleasant, and so on). Where directive and supportive leadership are predicted to have opposite effects on outcome variables, therefore, the latter combination would ensure that one of the predictions was not supported.

The fact that Path–Goal Theory allows such combinations of leadership styles and moderator variables is admirable in that it reflects the complexities of leadership behaviour and the situations which leaders face. Unfortunately, it also is a theory which is difficult to describe in a concise, readily comprehensible form and one which is even more difficult to test. Indeed, what has tended to happen is that researchers do not even attempt to validate the whole theory, but instead attempt to test specific elements of it. Given the way that the predictions with respect to one part of the theory can be reversed by taking into account elements from other parts of the theory, it is hardly surprising that contradictory results have been obtained. Lawler and Suttle (1973) commented that expectancy theory, on which Path–Goal theory is based, had become so complex that it had exceeded the means which exist to test it. In many respects, the same can be said of Path–Goal theory.

A number of suggestions have been made concerning ways in which Path–Goal Theory predictions might be improved. Johns (1978) criticizes the questionnaire measure used in Path–Goal research. The measure is said to tap the extent to which task characteristics are simple, repetitive and unambiguous. Johns argues that this represents an overly narrow view of the range of task characteristics which might influence the relationship between leader behaviour and employee responses. He suggests using instead the task characteristics from Hackman and Oldham's (1976) Job Characteristics Model. These are the variety of skills required, the extent to which the task requires the completion of a whole and identifiable piece of work, the significance of the task, autonomy and feedback. A study of 232 operatives in a paper products plant provided some support for the moderating effects of these variables on the relationship between initiating structure and subordinate job satisfaction. In each case, the relationship was stronger the higher the level of the moderator variable, although the difference did not reach significance in most cases. On the other hand, there were no consistent moderator effects for the relationships between consideration and job satisfaction.

Schriesheim and DeNisi (1981) also suggest that task structure is only one dimension along which different jobs can be categorized and that other aspects of the task should be considered. They hypothesized that the relationship between instrumental (directive) leadership and subordinate satisfaction with supervision would be moderated by task variety, feedback and the extent to which the job involves dealing with others. It was predicted that the relationship would be:

1 Positive for subordinates perceiving high levels of task variety and negative for subordinates perceiving low levels of task variety.
2 Positive for subordinates receiving low feedback and negative for subordinates receiving high feedback from their jobs.
3 Positive for subordinates with little opportunity to deal with others and zero or negative for subordinates having many such opportunities.

These hypotheses were tested using two samples, one of 110 bank tellers and clerks and the other of 205 non-operative employees in a manufacturing company. The hypotheses concerning task variety and dealing with others were supported at a significant level in both samples, while the feedback hypothesis was supported in the manufacturing sample but not the bank sample.

Finally, Yukl (1981, 1989) criticizes Path–Goal Theory on the grounds that it conceptualizes leadership behaviour at a very abstract level in terms of broad categories which do not relate easily to the intervening (moderator) variables. It is obvious, he states, that only certain aspects of the behaviour within any one category may account for the hypothesized effects. Yukl therefore suggests that we should examine the separate effects of more specific behaviours. For example, instead of looking at the effects of, say, directive leadership, we should examine separately the effects of its constituent aspects, such as clarifying roles, providing instruction, structuring reward contingencies, providing praise and recognition, planning, co-ordinating, and facilitating work.

All these suggestions undoubtedly have some merit. However, they all entail further subdividing the variables considered by the theory. This would make it even more difficult to subject it to a comprehensive test. Thus the theory would become a large set of loosely related hypotheses rather than an integrated leadership theory. This in turn would make Path–Goal Theory even more difficult to present to practising managers in a clear and succinct manner, and further reduce its value as a vehicle for management development.

VROOM, YETTON AND JAGO'S NORMATIVE MODEL

The original version of the normative model of leadership was developed by Vroom and Yetton (1973). It was later revised by Vroom and Jago (1988) in an attempt to overcome some of the limitations of the earlier model. As the later model represents an extension of the earlier version rather than a radical change in approach, only the later version will be described. The model is concerned with the relationship between the amount and form of participation in decision-making which managers allow their subordinates and the effectiveness of such decisions. The model has five main elements.

Decision process

Two sets of decision processes are identified, one concerned with group problems which affect the entire team and one with individual problems which affect only one subordinate. In each case, five alternative methods of allocating the responsibility for decision-making between the manager and his or her subordinates are described. These methods represent steps on a scale of participation or power sharing. As one moves through the list of decision processes there is a progressive increase in the opportunities provided for subordinates to influence the decision.

The five alternative decision methods for group problems are:

1 The leader makes the decision alone, using the information available.
2 The leader makes the decision alone, after obtaining any necessary information from relevant subordinates.
3 The leader makes the decision after obtaining ideas and suggestions from relevant subordinates on an individual basis, but the decision need not necessarily represent their views.
4 The leader makes the decision after obtaining ideas and suggestions from relevant subordinates in a group meeting, but again the decision need not necessarily represent their views.
5 The leader chairs a group meeting on the problem and is willing to accept and implement any solution which has the support of the entire group.

The corresponding decision methods for individual problems are:

1 The leader makes the decision alone, using the information available.
2 The leader makes the decision alone, after obtaining any necessary information from the subordinate in question.
3 The leader makes the decision after obtaining ideas and suggestions from the subordinate in question, but the decision need not necessarily represent his/her views.
4 The leader and subordinate analyse the problem together and arrive at a mutually satisfactory solution in an atmosphere of free and open exchange of information and ideas.
5 The leader delegates the problem to the subordinate in question, giving him/her full authority to solve the problem alone.

Effectiveness equations

The effectiveness of a decision is evaluated in terms of the quality of the decision and the commitment of subordinates to the decision. However, some decisions are made under severe time constraints and in such cases the negative effects of lengthy decision-making processes also need to be taken into account. This yields the following formula for decision effectiveness:

$$\mathbf{D_{Eff}} = \mathbf{D_{Qual}} + \mathbf{D_{Comm}} - \mathbf{D_{TP}} \qquad (1)$$

$$\begin{aligned}
\text{Where } \mathbf{D_{Eff}} &= \textbf{Decision effectiveness} \\
\mathbf{D_{Qual}} &= \textbf{Decision quality} \\
\mathbf{D_{Comm}} &= \textbf{Decision commitment} \\
\mathbf{D_{TP}} &= \textbf{Decision time penalty}
\end{aligned}$$

A more comprehensive criterion, overall effectiveness, is also put forward. This takes into account the fact that decision-making has a cost in terms of the amount of people's time it takes up, but also may have a benefit in terms of increasing insight, teamwork and identification with organizational goals. This yields the formula:

$$\mathbf{O_{Eff}} = \mathbf{D_{Eff}} - \textbf{ Cost} + \textbf{Development} \qquad (2)$$

In general, the more participative the decision-making, the greater the cost, but also the greater the scope for development.

Problem attributes

Twelve attributes of problems are identified. These are shown in Table 4.1. The extent to which a problem has such attributes is assessed by the manager who is faced with the problem. Each attribute is assessed on a five-point scale with the exception of time constraint and geographical dispersion which require simple yes/no answers.

Mathematical functions

The manager's assessment of the extent to which a problem possesses the twelve attributes in Table 4.1 provides the basis for estimating the overall effectiveness of the five degrees of participation. The values given to the twelve attributes are entered into a further, more detailed set of mathematical formulae to obtain separate estimates for each of the four basic criteria – quality, commitment, time and development – for each of the five decision processes. These mathematical functions, Vroom and Jago state, are designed to be consistent with the accumulated research evidence concerning the effects of participation, or to be derivable from theories of individual, group and organizational behaviour which themselves have been thoroughly evaluated in research. The estimates obtained from these formulae are then summed for each decision process, together with any decision-time penalty, in accordance with Equation 2, to yield a prediction of the overall effectiveness of each of the five decision processes. The model's choice of decision process is the one which produces the predicted overall effectiveness (i.e. the largest value for O_{Eff}).

Recommendations concerning the choice of decision process

Vroom and Jago's recommendations concerning the decision process which should be employed in order to make an effective decision are presented in three different forms. First, advice is given on which decision processes to avoid and which to move towards when attempting, respectively, to improve decision quality, improve decision commitment, reduce decision costs and increase subordinate development in relation to both group and individual problems. For example, it is suggested that, when attempting to improve decision quality with respect to a group problem the leader should:

1 Avoid the use of decision process 1 when:
  ● the leader lacks the necessary information.
2 Avoid the use of decision process 5 when:
  ● subordinates do not share the organizational goals; *and/or*
  ● subordinates do not have the necessary information.
3 Avoid the use of decision processes 2 and 5 when:
  ● the leader lacks the necessary information; *and*
  ● the problem is unstructured.
4 Move towards decision process 5 when:
  ● the leader lacks the necessary information; *and*
  ● subordinates share the organizational goals; *and*
  ● there is conflict among subordinates over preferred solutions.

Table 4.1   Problem attributes in the Vroom and Jago normative model

Quality requirement:	How important is the technical quality of the decision?
Commitment requirement:	How important is subordinate commitment to the decision?
Leader information:	Does the manager have sufficient information to make a high-quality decision?
Problem structure:	Is the problem well-structured?
Commitment probability:	If the manager were to make the decision by him/herself, is reasonable certain that his/her subordinates would be committed to the decision?
Goal congruence:	Do the subordinates share the organizational goals to be attained in solving the problem?
Subordinate conflict:	Is conflict among subordinates over preferred solutions likely?
Subordinate information:	Do the subordinates have sufficient information to make a high-quality decision?
Time constraint:	Does a critically severe time constraint limit the manager's ability to involve subordinates?
Geographical dispersion:	Are the costs of bringing together geographically dispersed subordinates prohibitive?
Motivation–time:	How important is it to minimize the time it takes to make the decision?
Motivation–development:	How important is it to maximize the opportunities for subordinate development?

Source: Vroom and Jago 1988

However, Vroom and Jago note that a sacrifice in precision is necessary in order to present the model's prescriptions in this form.

Second, a computer program has been developed into which the data concerning problem attributes can be entered. When all questions have been answered, the screen indicates the model's choice of the decision process and its choice if each of the underlying criteria (quality, commitment, time and development) is considered separately.

Finally, the recommended decision processes for time- and development-driven group and individual problems are presented in four decision trees. These have the advantage that they can be inspected visually and do not require the use of a computer to arrive at the recommended decision process. However, they provide a slightly less sophisticated prediction of the most effective decision process in that two simplifying assumptions are made. The first is that the status of the attribute is clearcut and only yes/no answers exist for all attributes.

The second is that there are no critically severe time constraints and that the subordinates are not geographically dispersed.

One of the major advantages of Vroom and Jago's normative model is its precision. It provides precise descriptions of different leadership styles and situations and identifies, again in precise terms, the most appropriate style to adopt in each situation. This is an area in which previous leadership theories, even some later ones, have often fallen down. There is also some supporting evidence from research studies. Unlike Fiedler's contingency model, Vroom and Yetton's (1973) original normative model generated relatively little research. Such research as has been carried out tends to consist of a global evaluation of the theory, rather than an attempt to validate its separate elements. Vroom and Jago (1988) summarize six studies of successful and unsuccessful managerial decisions. The studies examined a total of 1,545 decisions – 769 successful and 776 unsuccessful. Managers whose behaviour conformed to the Vroom and Yetton normative model made successful decisions in 62 per cent of cases. Those whose behaviour failed to conform to the model made successful decisions in only 37 per cent of cases.

Studies by Margerison and Glube (1979) and Paul and Ebadi (1989) looked at the effects of decision-making style on subordinate performance and satisfaction. Both studies found that managers whose decision-making styles conformed more closely to those recommended by the Vroom and Yetton model in a test, had subordinates who were more productive and more satisfied with supervision than those of managers whose decision-making styles conformed less closely to those recommended by the model.

Little research has yet been carried out on the new model. One example is a laboratory study (reported in Vroom and Jago 1988) which was conducted in order to test the ability of the new model correctly to predict the success of different decision strategies. It was found that the new model predicted decision success at a rate two-and-a-half times that of the original Vroom and Yetton model. The predictions of the new model correlated 0.75 with the actual outcomes in the 80 decisions, whereas the correlation for the original model was 0.29.

Nevertheless, there still remain theoretical and practical difficulties with the normative model.

1 While it encompasses a relatively large number of situational variables, it describes leadership style in terms of a single dimension, from autocratic to participative. It can therefore provide only a partial explanation of leadership effectiveness, as there are undoubtedly other ways in which leaders' behaviour can vary and which can influence their effectiveness. However, as Vroom and Jago (1988) point out, the theory does not profess to deal with all of leadership or of what leaders do. It concentrates only on those aspects bearing on power-sharing by leaders and on participation and influence by those who work for them. Thus it avoids the confusion between degrees of

participation and other aspects of leadership commonly found in earlier theories.

2 Managers may not use a single decision-making method for any one problem. As Vroom (1984) points out, they may initially consult subordinates individually and then hold a group meeting or vice versa. He suggests that these different processes may correspond to different phases of problem-solving – one for defining the problem, the second for generating alternatives and so on.

3 The model is extremely complex, the later version even more so than the original model. It has been described as a method of deciding how to decide (Huber 1975). However, it is far too complex for a manager to remember all the details of the model and work out in his or her head which is the most effective decision process to use. Admittedly, Vroom does not see the model being used in this way. He contends (1984: 28) that 'it is best viewed, not as a programme to be *used*, but rather as a stimulus for people to examine their own behaviour and to consider their own models'. Similarly, with respect to the new model, Vroom and Jago (1988) state that their computer program is not the type of managerial tool they would expect a leader to consult and follow each and every time he or she encountered a decision. However, they suggest that there are three distinct purposes that the computer program can serve. It can be used:

● in difficult leadership situations which requre the degree of precision which the program provides;
● to answer 'what if' questions when the critical features of a situation are ambiguous, unknown, or subject to change;
● as a tool to develop and calibrate the internal 'rules' that govern our habitual responses to situations.

On some occasions, Vroom and Jago state, people may conclude that their own choice of decision process is better than that of the model. They take the view that such disagreement is fine, since their purpose is reflection and thoughtfulness rather than conformity.

MISUMI'S PM LEADERSHIP THEORY

The leadership theories examined so far were all developed within a North American context. The final theory to be discussed in this section, Misumi's PM Theory, was developed in Japan and although it had its beginnings in a replication of North American research, it has since developed along quite different paths. It is not even a conventional situational theory. Nevertheless, it does have situational elements and it is therefore useful to explore its similarities to and differences from North American situational style theories at this point.

Shortly after World War II, Kurt Lewin suggested that a programme of leadership research be begun in Japan to test the generalizability of leadership studies carried out in the USA. One of the early studies inspired by this suggestion was a replication with Japanese school children of the studies by Lewin *et al.* (1939) of autocratic, democratic and *laissez-faire* leadership carried out by Misumi and his colleagues in the early 1950s. The democratic groups in the Japanese study were found to be less clearly superior to the autocratic groups than were their counterparts in the USA (Misumi and Peterson 1985). Democratic guidance was more effective when the task was easy for the children to carry out, but autocratic guidance was more effective when the task was difficult (Misumi 1985).

More important than the particular results of the study, however, were the lessons learned about leadership research. According to Misumi and Peterson (1985), a key lesson was that such heavily value laden and politically meaningful concepts as 'democratic', 'autocratic', and '*laissez-faire*' were both very difficult to represent operationally and very difficult to communicate in a non-emotional manner. A second lesson was that it was possible to train people acting as leaders to give performance pressure or no pressure and to express personal concern or no concern to subjects. This led to the development in the early 1960s of a four-fold classification of leadership types which has been the basis of Misumi's subsequent research and theorizing.

Misumi distinguishes between two leadership functions, performance and maintenance. The performance leadership function involves forming and reaching group goals, while the maintenance function involves preserving group social stability. Any concrete behaviour reflects some degree of emphasis on each function. However, some behaviours may more 'purely' address one function than the other. As conceptualized in the initial studies, the key components of distinctly performance-oriented leader behaviour were emphasizing fast work speed, good quality, high accuracy, high quantity and the observation of rules, while those of distinctly maintenance-oriented leadership behaviour were emphasizing subordinate feelings, comfort, stress reduction and appreciation. A PM leadership pattern includes both kinds of behaviour, while the P-type emphasizes just performance, the M-type emphasizes just maintenance and the pm type emphasizes neither.

According to Misumi and Peterson (1985), a loose conceptual link to the first study was maintained by relating to the PM concepts the more popular, emotionally laden concepts used previously. 'Autocratic' leadership has something to do with primarily P-oriented behaviour, possible combined with distinctly counter-M-oriented behaviour. '*Laissez-faire*' leadership has a rough similarity to pm-type leadership. Different aspects of what might naively be called 'democratic' leadership are reflected by primarily M-oriented behaviour and by behaviour involving a combined P and M emphasis.

At first sight Misumi's approach to leadership may seem almost identical to that adopted by Blake and Mouton (1964). However, there are differences. While Misumi may see his P and M types of leadership as being loosely related to autocratic, democratic and *laissez-faire* leadership, he does not specifically include these aspects of leadership in his definitions of P and M, whereas they are incorporated into Blake and Mouton's definitions of their styles. Furthermore, Misumi's PM-type of leadership does not, as might be thought, correspond to Blake and Mouton's 9,9 style. Observational records of laboratory studies and data from field studies suggest that PM-type leaders may typically be less extreme in P than are P-type leaders and less extreme in M than are M-type leaders. Thus PM-type leadership is somewhat more akin to the 'middle-of-the-road' style of leadership which Blake and Mouton regard as suboptimal.

Having established the four PM leadership types on the basis of laboratory research, the next step was to determine whether they could be identified in the 'real world'. Accordingly, a field survey was carried out of 215 miners from eight work groups in a coalmine. The miners described the leadership of their first- and second-level supervisors. Supervisors were identified as PM-type leaders when their subordinates gave them above average P and M scores and as pm-type leaders when they were given below average P and M scores. P-type and M-type leaders were identified when workers gave above average for one function but not the other. There were consistent differences in leadership descriptions between high-producing and low-producing groups. In three of the four high-producing groups, either the first-level or the second-level supervisor was described as a PM-type supervisor. No P-type supervisors were found at either the first or second level in any of the high-producing groups. In three of the four low-producing groups, both the first- and second-level supervisors were described as P-type leaders.

Further field surveys were carried out in the late 1960s. Eighteen employers, including manufacturing, utility, wholesale, retail and governmental organizations were studied. The typical finding was that the highest levels of performance and the most positive work attitudes were found under PM-type leadership, followed by M-type, P-type and finally pm-type leadership.

Unlike most North American leadership style researchers, Misumi does not confine himself to studying the relationship between leadership styles and outcome variables such as productivity, performance and work attitudes. His research programme has three additional aspects. Misumi distinguishes between the forms of leadership (its morphology) and the dynamics, or causal processes surrounding leadership and the relationships of leadership to other variables. He also distinguishes between general or universal characteristics and specific or situationally contingent aspects of the morphology and dynamics of leadership. This produces a research programme the basic structure of which can be divided into four parts, as shown in Figure 4.6.

The research described so far falls into the general morphology category. Studies in the area of specific morphology have been carried out in order to determine the specific expression of the basic PM types in particular social settings. Misumi (1985) argues that the basic form of leadership behaviour is relatively simple. The complexity in leadership behaviours reflects the complex-

	Situation	
Dimension	General characteristics	Specific situational expressions
Behavioural forms (morphology dimension)	General behavioural morphology	Specific behavioural morphology
Behavioural causes (dynamics dimension)	General behavioural dynamics	Specific behavioural dynamics

Figure 4.6   Misumi's paradigm for the science of leadership behaviour
Source: Misumi 1985

ity of the environment in which the leadership is observed. Leadership appears in varied forms in many varied social situations. For example, the performance-oriented leadership of top managers, middle managers and foremen can differ considerably even within the same business enterprise. Details in the expression of performance-oriented leadership in different organizations and groups are likely to vary even more.

In Misumi's research, therefore, different survey measures are developed for use in different settings (e.g. industry, government, education, sports, etc.). This usually involves consulting practitioners in the fields being studied or collecting open-ended anecdotes and 'critical incidents' describing leadership behaviours, around which questions can be developed. Questionnaires designed for particular settings typically include a relatively small number of broadly applicable items and a larger number of items particularly meaningful in that setting. Factor analysis of the results of specific morphology studies have identified a variety of setting-specific leadership dimensions. For example, in an analysis of leadership in government offices, it was found that an important component of the leadership that section chiefs provided for their subordinates was keeping their section informed about changes in other sections, in part by maintaining personal contacts with other sections. However, this expression of performance-oriented leadership was less important for subsection chiefs and the difference between the expressions of leadership of the two groups is reflected in differences in the factor structure for the questionnaires designed for each group (Misumi 1985).

Studies carried out in a variety of different settings, including production, service and governmental organizations, politics, schools, sports, and the leadership provided for children, indicate that PM-type leadership is typically associated with high values on performance and attitudinal criteria, while pm-type leadership is associated with low levels on these criteria. However, the order of P-type and M-type leadership varies with respect to social, psychological and performance criteria. In a few studies, there are no clear differences in criterion levels between P-type and M-type leadership. Some studies suggest that P-type leadership is more consistent with productivity than is M-type leadership during the initial leader–member exchanges or when group composition changes often, as in engineering project groups. Results from other settings suggest that P-type leadership may be associated with increasingly lower levels of criteria over time relative to M-type leadership, as the resistance of group members increases.

However, Misumi (1985) also notes that the two basic leadership functions may need to be expressed in ways which take into account more specific variables than the task and norms of particular work groups. The personal situation and task situation of individual subordinates may require that different actions be taken to produce the social integration or work coordination of different subordinates. For example, a supervisor's suggestion about how to work more effectively may be experienced as supportive help in learning by a new employee, as harassment or unwanted pressure by an unmotivated employee who has a generally negative relationship with the supervisor, or as personal support and encouragement by an experienced employee having a basically friendly relationship with the supervisor. Similarly, expressing personal concern about an employee's private life may have a different meaning for subordinates who try to integrate their private life and work life than for subordinates who try to divorce the one from the other. Misumi therefore suggests that an important part of leadership in any social context is understanding unique personal and work needs and recognizing how these needs fluctuate, even within a single day, and evolve over time. Effective leadership requires an understanding, not only of the specific leadership morphology associated with a major kind of social context, but also the highly specific morphology of behaviours as they will be experienced and accepted by individual subordinates.

In the area of general dynamics, experimental studies have been carried out in an attempt to identify the causal processes through which the four PM leadership types are associated with productivity and work attitudes. For example, in a study of the effect of set on problem-solving, it was found that P-type leadership induced the greatest tendency to become fixated on one particular problem-solving method, followed by pm-type leadership, then M-type leadership, with PM-type leadership having the least effect. In the case of low-anxiety groups, however, M-type leadership produced the next highest level of set after P-type leadership, with pm-type leadership coming third and PM-type leadership lowest as before. According to Misumi and Peterson, this suggests that M behaviour is only useful for reducing the effects of set when there is either internal tension, such as high initial anxiety level, or high external tension, such as a high level of P leadership. They suggest that these results explain why PM-type leadership is typically most effective in work settings such as engineering groups, scientific groups and even production groups engaged in quality circles, where creativity and innovation are particularly important. Furthermore, in those field studies showing relatively small differences between PM- and M-type leadership, as is sometimes the case, the reduced difference could be due to pressure being experienced from other sources.

Other general dynamics research has included studies of the effects of the four PM leadership types on the facilitation of learning, performance on simple perceptual and motor tasks, physiological arousal and group processes. In general, these studies support the contention that PM-type leadership is typically associated with valued individual and group outcomes in Japan. However, they also show that M-type leadership may be preferred in situations with highly anxious subordinates and in which physiological arousal needs to be minimized. Also P-type leadership may be desired in situations in which a temporary group is being used to accomplish a task that requires quick work but little quality or involving members who have a low achievement orientation. Although PM-type leadership has typically been found to enhance learning, one study showed that the timing of P- and M-oriented behaviour was important. P-oriented behaviour was best timed so that it was provided during the learning periods and M-oriented so that it was provided during breaks.

Misumi and Peterson (1985) suggest that these studies indicate that the general usefulness of the PM type is the result of several processes occurring simultaneously. Over a long period of time in the relationship between a leader and a subordinate group, not one but many of these processes are likely to be significant. Thus, there is evidence that Japanese supervisors should respond in ways that are contingent to particular subordinates or particular settings. For example, leaders are advised to provide a larger proportion of expressly P-oriented leadership while subordinates are engaged in work and more M-oriented while they are at rest. Over time and across situations, in the typical long-term relationship between a Japanese supervisor and subordinate group, however, the PM type of leadership is generally desirable.

Misumi and Peterson (1985) report on two types of research that have been carried out in the area of specific dynamics. The first is concerned with reciprocal relationships between PM leadership types and work attitudes. Data collected a year apart in a bank in Okinawa showed that leadership generally had a stronger effect on a work attitude measure than work attitudes had on leadership. The second area of research is concerned with change programmes based on PM leadership. Currently, such change programmes are based on three processes:

- making people in leadership positions aware of discrepancies between self-perceptions and peer perceptions of their behaviour;
- bringing self-ratings closer to peer ratings;
- moving each leader towards PM-type leadership.

The change programmes appear to be successful in reducing self-perceptions and reports of others of P- and M-oriented behaviours. Mixed success has been found in documenting actual behaviour change. However, when people working for the same employer publicly make commitments about specific behaviour changes to fellow group members, the evidence suggests that the behaviour of Japanese managers can be changed towards the PM type.

In summary, Misumi's PM Theory has a number of admirable qualities. It is well supported by a long-term research programme. It examined in much greater depth than North American theories the underlying psychological processes that explain why different types of leadership behaviour have the effects which they do. It also examines in greater depth than most North American theories the specific behaviours which go to make up each behavioural style.

Nevertheless, the theory has two main limitations as a practical guide to managers wishing to know which types of behaviour to adopt in order to improve their leadership performance. Both arise from the fact that the theory has been developed in a somewhat ad hoc manner in certain respects. The first relates to the situational factors influencing leadership performance. A number of suggestions are made concerning circumstances in which P-type or M-type leadership might be more effective. However, these are presented simply as a list of findings rather than organized into a unified situational model. Thus the manager wishing to know when an alternative to PM-type leadership would be appropriate would have to memorize a list of exceptions rather than refer to a predictive model. The second practical limitation is a consequence of Misumi's fundamental approach to leadership theory. While PM-type leadership has been found to be appropriate in most situations, the actual behaviours which go to make up this leadership style may vary between organizations, between levels within the same organization, and even according to the personality of the individual subordinate concerned. Unless, the particular managerial job in question has been studied by Misumi and his associates, therefore, the manager would have to work out for him- or herself which particular behaviours constitute PM-type leadership in his or her particular job. Thus, for the most part, Misumi's theory can only give general rather than specific guidance concerning appropriate types of leadership behaviour.

It will also be noted that Misumi and Peterson (1985) stipulate from time to time that their conclusions apply specifically to Japanese managers. They suggest that certain characteristics of Japan make the generalizability of Misumi's field research outside Japan uncertain. Management development programmes based on the PM theory have been run in China. However, according to Peterson (1988), a major modification introduced in the Chinese programmes involves adding a moral 'character' (C) dimension to the P and M dimensions. Thus the PM theory is becoming relabelled as CPM in many of the Chinese projects. The rationale for this addition is that many Chinese human resource managers emphasize the moral character of leaders and believe that any leadership perspective which does not do so is incomplete. Items in the character dimension include the following:

- attitude towards workers;
- receptiveness to recommendations and criticisms from workers;

- fairness to all employees;
- commitment to remain within the law and resist temptations for personal gain;
- attitude towards the government party and willingness to follow the party even when personal views conflict with those of the government;
- level of teamwork i.e. sincere belief in the value of co-operation.

With respect to the application of PM leadership theory in the West, Misumi and Peterson (1985) point out that most credible leadership research indicates that the most effective leadership style is contingent on the situation, whereas most PM research in Japan produces a non-contingent conclusion. They suggest that this difference may be explained in terms of what Kerr and Jermier (1978) call 'substitutes for leadership' (see Chapter 6). These are variables in organizational settings that minimize the effect of a particular aspect of leadership or leadership in general. Misumi and Peterson argue that individual and organizational level substitutes for leadership may be less evident in Japan than the USA, thus increasing the need and opportunity for both P and M leadership in a Japanese context.

While this idea may have some validity, it also seems that to some extent Misumi and Peterson (1985) may overstate the differences between the USA and Japan with respect to situational factors in leadership. As we have seen, experimental studies in the area of general dynamics revealed a number of situations in which either P- or M-type leadership may be more desirable. Misumi and Peterson claim that such situations appear to be less common in Japan than they are reported to be in other countries. However, it must be pointed out that Misumi's field research elicits data on what subordinates say that their bosses usually do. Thus, it is possible that leaders who are high in both P and M sometimes emphasize either P or M in specific situations and Misumi's field research would not necessarily indicate how often such situations occurred.

However, this is not to say that cultural differences do not influence the types of leadership which are effective in different countries or with different groups within those countries. There is ample evidence that they do, as we shall see in the next chapter. It is merely being suggested that the differences between Japan and the USA with respect to the influence of situational factors on leadership effectiveness may not be as great as Misumi and Peterson suggest. One final point is worth noting. North American leadership theorists generally make little reference to the effect of cultural differences on the generality of their theories. However, if Misumi is correct in assuming that his conclusions may have limited generality outside Japan, then it would also seem to follow that North American theories may also have limited generality with respect to Japan, and perhaps many other countries too. This issue is discussed in more depth in the next chapter.

SUMMARY

In this chapter, we have described the contributions and limitations of a number of prominent situational style theories of leadership. Such theories have undoubtedly increased our awareness of the wide variety of factors which can influence both leadership success and leadership effectiveness. Nevertheless, it will be apparent that none of these theories has yet provided a comprehensive description of leadership behaviours and situational variables or a completely satisfactory explanation of their relationship with leadership success and effectiveness. For an explanation of why this is so, we may have to look beyond the limitations of individual theories and examine instead the limitations of the approach as a whole. This question will be taken up in the next chapter.

NOTE

1 It is worth noting that writers on leadership are not consistent in the use of the term situational leadership theory. Some writers (e.g. Yukl 1989) use it, as we have, to describe a theory that stipulates which is the most appropriate leadership style in different situations. However, others call such theories contingency theories, after the first major theory of its type developed by Fiedler (1964, 1967), and sometimes (e.g. Howell and Dipboye 1982) the term situational approaches to leadership is used to describe the extreme view that the leader merely reacts to events and has little control over the manner in which the group performs.

EXERCISE 2: THE MANAGEMENT STYLE DIAGNOSTIC TEST

Instructions

1 The individual score sheet, Figure 4.7, has boxes numbered 1 to 56. These are used to record your choice from each pair of statements, also numbered 1 to 56, in the questionnaire.

Look at the 56 pairs of statements in the questionnaire on pp. 83–5. If you think that the first statement of a pair is the one that best applies to you, put an A in the appropriate box. If you think that the second statement is the one that best applies to you, put a B. When you have finished, every box will contain either an A or a B.

Notice that the boxes are numbered in sequence across the page; therefore you should fill in the top line first, the second line next and so on.

2 Total your As in each horizontal row and write the number alongside the row.

3 Total your Bs in each vertical column. Write the total below its column. Transfer the total of the As from step 2 just above the letters A–H.

4 Add each pair of numbers to give eight totals.
5 These eight numbers are your raw scores for the eight styles. (Together they should equal 56.)
6 Then add or subtract the adjustment factors indicated beneath to get eight new totals. These are your adjusted scores.

THE MANAGEMENT STYLE DIAGNOSIS TEST QUESTION-NAIRE

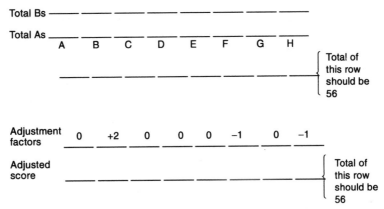

Figure 4.7   Individual score sheet
Source: Reddin 1987

Table 4.2   The management style diagnosis test questionnaire

	A	B
1	I do not show too much interest in maintaining good relationships with those above me.	I overlook violations of any kind if it helps to make things run more smoothly.
2	I do not always show a lot of interest in my subordinates.	I evaluate individuals personally. I frequently point out their good and bad points and criticise where necessary.
3	I believe the value of creativity, change, and innovation is often over-emphasized.	I have some interest in high productivity but it is not always apparent and thus productivity sometimes suffers.
4	I think that the idea of setting overall objectives can be overdone.	I prefer to write out communications with others.
5	I think that planning can be over-emphasized.	When conflict arises I always help those involved to find a basis for agreement.
6	I think that the actual introduction of a change imposed from outside should require only a moderate effort on my part.	I am certain that the best way to eliminate errors is for those making them to have their errors explained to them in detail.
7	I do not seem as interested as I might be in the actual imple-mentation of decisions.	I actively support and promote the team approach to management.
8	I try to avoid disagreements with higher management even though this may lower my own or my subordi-nates' productivity.	I believe that evaluation and review are often overstressed.
9	I treat subordinates with great kindness and consideration.	I seem more interested in day-to-day productivity than in long run productivity.
10	I think that some new ideas lead to disagreement and friction.	While I do try to keep an open channel of communication with others, I am sometimes unsuc-cessful in doing so.
11	I allow subordinates to set their own objectives according to their needs and accept them even if somewhat unsatisfactory.	I respond to disagreement and conflict by referring to rules and procedures.
12	I prefer to let each individual make their own plans as long as they are clear.	I think that most errors arise for a good reason and it is always better to look for the reason than at the error itself.
13	I prefer to introduce change slowly rather than rapidly.	I believe a strong team needs a strong leader who knows what to do.
14	I tolerate deviations in implementing plans if this will avert unpleasant-ness.	If a procedure or control is violated I make sure I concentrate on finding out why.
15	I prefer to do my job with no interference from those above.	I am not too interested in impro-ving productivity just for its own sake.

Table 4.2 (Contd)

A	B
16 I direct the work of my subordinates and discourage deviations from my plans.	I communicate with others so as to maintain a good relationship above all else.
17 I think new ideas from below are sometimes less useful than those from above.	When conflict arises I am always fair and firm.
18 Deviations from the specific objectives I set for others are discouraged.	I believe that errors would be minimal if people simply followed established rules and procedures.
19 I see planning as a one-person job.	I believe in the team approach to the extent that I think all problems are best solved that way.
20 I think a good way to introduce change is to make an announcement and then let people get on with it.	I show that I think tough control techniques are among the most important aids to high productivity.
21 I watch implementation of plans closely, point out errors and criticize where necessary.	I have both methods and output under constant review and changes in them are regularly implemented as needed.
22 I want to improve my relationships with superiors but do not always take the action necessary.	I could supply more useful information to others than I do.
23 When dealing with subordinates I attempt to combine both task and relationships considerations but one or the other often suffers.	At the first sign of conflict I attempt to smooth things over.
24 I sometimes encourage new ideas but do not always follow up on too many of them.	I believe that when an error occurs the person responsible should be reprimanded.
25 While my objectives are usually fairly clear, I allow them to be quite loose so that they are not always a good guide.	I think that the team approach is of use at times but that formal meetings accomplish as much or even more.
26 I make an effort at planning but the plans do not always work out.	I believe that performance data is best fed back to the individual concerned rather than to a superior or a staff unit.
27 I sometimes talk about the problems of introducing change but do not always attempt to deal with these problems.	I keep methods and output under constant review and make changes to ensure high output.
28 I keep an eye on the implementation of plans but do not always take action when it is most needed.	I set high standards for myself and encourage others to set high output standards.
29 I believe that there will be few problems between myself and higher management if proper procedures and channels are followed.	I avoid conflict even when facing it could be useful.

Table 4.2 (Contd)

A	B
30 I think that things go best when subordinates understand and follow the duties in their job descriptions.	I believe that if an error occurs it should be corrected in such a way that no one will be upset.
31 I believe that formal meetings are a perfectly sound way to produce new ideas.	I believe in 'One Person, One Job, Well Done.'
32 The objectives I set are usually fairly clear though somewhat inflexible.	I say that I believe control techniques are useful but I establish few and violate some.
33 I plan with a fine attention to detail.	I encourage others to evaluate their own and my own performance.
34 I introduce changes formally and follow closely any established procedures.	I personally set high output standards for myself and others and work hard to see that they are met.
35 Once plans are made I try to ensure their implementation follows the original plan.	I have an open communication channel with everyone on any matter and others have it with me.
36 I understand and co-operate well with higher level management.	I show little concern about errors and usually do little to correct or reduce them.
37 My relationship with subordinates is excellent and is characterized by mutual trust and respect.	I believe that team meetings are good primarily because they get people to talk together more.
38 I always seek out new and good ideas and motivate others to be as creative as possible.	I sometimes object to what I believe are unnecessary procedures.
39 I successfully motivate others to set their own clear objectives.	I talk about the importance of evaluation and review but do not always get involved with it myself as much as I might.
40 When I am responsible for planning I involve many others.	I believe that the best measure of output is a comparison based on norms previously established.
41 I prepare those affected by change by talking with them well in advance.	I keep everyone fully informed of what I think they need to know in order to do their job better.
42 I am responsive to sound proposals for modifying plans, am open to suggestions, and am always willing to help.	I try to resolve conflict as quickly as possible by uncovering its underlying causes.
43 I work well with higher level management and ensure that they know exactly how I see my job.	I think control procedures can be overdone.
44 I make it quite clear to subordinates what I expect of them. I show that I value efficiency and productivity.	I believe that the proper treatment of people is the best way to get productivity.
45 I both develop and propose many new ideas.	When disagreement arises I usually take a firm but understanding stand.

Table 4.2 (Contd)

A	B
46 I personally set clear objectives that are understood by all those involved.	I like the idea of team work but often am not able to find ways to apply it.
47 I plan well and concentrate primarily on my own good ideas and assign individual responsibilities.	I emphasize regular evaluation, measurement and review of performance.
48 I inform all concerned of the reason for a change.	I maintain open trusting communication channels with everyone.
49 I watch the implementation of plans by individuals and give direct assistance and guidance where needed.	I treat errors primarily as opportunities for everyone to learn and am prepared to look openly at my own errors.
50 I believe higher management is simply another team that should cooperate effectively with teams lower down.	I have a few doubts about the team approach to management but would give it a trial if the situation was appropriate.
51 I consistently obtain high output from my subordinates.	I believe it is sometimes necessary to say that a satisfactory job has been done when it was not really all that was expected.
52 I am constantly on the watch for new, useful and productive ideas from any source and develop many new ideas myself.	I sometimes 'shoot down' the ideas of others.
53 I set objectives with others which are clear and fully agreed to by all those directly involved.	I believe that one can learn from errors and that I should show it more in my behaviour.
54 When I am involved the plans made represent the best thinking of all concerned.	I believe that controls are an important element in obtaining productivity.
55 I inform all concerned well in advance of any possible changes and give them an opportunity to influence the proposed change.	I motivate others to set high output standards and encourage and support them so that these high standards are met.
56 I keep an eye on the implementation of plans and respond quickly to, and solve, any blockages.	When facing disagreement I try to be as persuasive as possible.

Interpreting the questionnaire results

Transfer your adjusted scores from the bottom line of Figure 4.7 to the chart in Figure 4.8. Simply shade in a vertical line to indicate your adjusted score on each of the eight styles. These scores will help you to identify your dominant, supporting and over-rejected styles. Your dominant style is a style which you use a great deal. Some managers have no dominant style, while others have two or three and sometimes even more. The supporting style is one which you make above average use of compared with other managers. An over-rejected style is one which a manager uses far less frequently than the average manager. This style is one you tend to lean away from; it is what you really do not like doing. The combination of the over-rejected style and the dominant style sometimes gives a much clearer indication of the way you prefer to behave than just the dominant style alone. The definitions of the eight styles are given in this chapter on pages 55–7.

Using the results of the test

Having filled in Figure 4.8, consider your management style profile in relation to your current job or the type of job which you are likely to do in the future:

1 How far your dominant style (or styles) match the requirements of the job.
2 Whether different management styles are required in different situations encountered in this job.
3 Whether you have the ability to perform the styles required in these situations well.
4 Whether you have the necessary flexibility to adapt your style to meet the situational requirements.
5 Whether any over-rejected styles really are not required for the job or simply represent styles that you prefer to avoid for personal reasons.
6 Whether it would be beneficial to use particular managerial styles more in this job, or develop your ability to perform them well in order to perform the job more effectively.

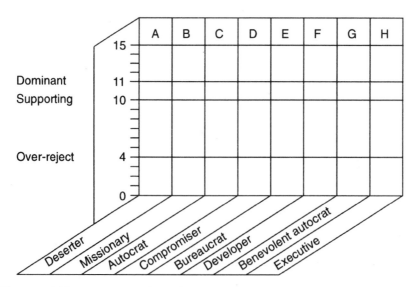

Figure 4.8 Management style profile
Source: Reddin 1987

More details concerning the interpretation of management style profiles, analysing managerial situations and their relationship to managerial effectiveness can be found in Reddin (1970, 1987).

Source: Exercise 2 is based on Reddin 1987.

Chapter 5

Situational style theories
Some general issues

INTRODUCTION

So far, we have described and evaluated situational style theories of leadership on an individual basis, identifying the contributions and limitations of each theory in turn. However, there are a number of issues which concern all situational style theories. These are problems or dilemmas which need to be resolved if situational style theories are to make a significant contribution to developing leadership effectiveness. Some of these issues have hardly been touched upon by most situational style theorists. Others have been addressed, but radically different conclusions have been reached. Five such issues will be discussed in this chapter.

THE ISSUE OF FLEXIBILITY

The issue of flexibility has two aspects. To what extent is it possible for managers to behave differently towards subordinates in different situations and to what extent is it desirable for them to do so? The question of how far managers are able to adjust their leadership style to the situation will be discussed first.

The main implication of situational style theories of leadership is that leaders will be able to influence the work behaviour and attitudes of their followers more effectively if the leadership style they employ is appropriate to the particular situation with which they are faced. In virtually all situational style theories, it is proposed that this objective should be achieved by training managers to recognize which leadership style is appropriate in different situations so that they will be able to adopt more appropriate styles when faced with those situations. Vroom and Yetton (1973), for example, state that one of the purposes of their approach is to 'encourage people to examine critically the leadership methods they use in concrete situations in order to better fit their "style" to the situational demands' (p. 208). One leadership theorist, however, apparently takes exactly the opposite view. Fiedler argues that it would be difficult for people to change their leadership styles to suit the situation, because this would entail altering their personality, as reflected by their LPC score. It would be much easier he suggests to change the situation to match their style. This leads to the concept of 'leader match' – a training programme designed to teach managers: (a) how to diagnose their own preferred style; (b) how to assess the favourableness of their leadership situation; and (c) how to change their leadership situation to match their preferred style (Fiedler and Chemers 1984).

Of course, Fiedler is right in claiming that it is difficult to change someone's personality. Nevertheless, personality does not necessarily determine behaviour in the narrow way in which Fiedler appears to believe. The same person may behave boisterously at a party and with hushed reverence at a church service. Their personality has not changed. They have merely adapted their behaviour to the very different requirements of the two situations. Similarly, there seems no reason to believe that managers cannot behave differently towards subordinates in different situations at work. Indeed, Fiedler is well aware of this. If one examines how leaders are recommended to change their leadership situation, one finds that many of the suggestions involve a change in behaviour. For example, Fiedler and Chemers (1984) suggest that leaders might improve their leader–member relations by organizing some off-work group activities which include their subordinates (e.g. picnics, bowling, softball teams, excursions, etc.), or modify their task structure by inviting subordinates to work with them on the planning and decision-making phases of group tasks, or decrease their position power by trying to be one of the gang through socializing and playing down any trappings of power and rank given to them by the organization. However, these are the very things which any other leadership theorist might suggest in order for a manager to change his or her style, say from task centred to person centred or from directive to participative. Thus Fiedler is placed in the untenable position of claiming that leaders must change their situation because they cannot change their behaviour and then suggesting that one of the ways in which they can change their situation is by changing their behaviour!

Unfortunately, Fiedler cannot afford to take the view, as other situational style theorists do, that leaders should change their style to match the situation. If they did so, their LPC score would no longer indicate their leadership behaviour with any degree of accuracy. LPC scores might still predict their preferred leadership style, but they would not tell us what managers actually do when interacting with their subordinates. Thus Fiedler's interpretation of the relationship between LPC scores, situational favourableness and leadership effectiveness would become untenable.

Research by Kennedy (1982) throws further doubt on Fiedler's views on the question of leader flexibility. Fiedler's interpretations of LPC scores have primarily been concerned with the characteristics of high and low LPC leaders. The characteristics of middle LPC leaders have largely been ignored. Kennedy compared the performance of 697 high, middle and low LPC fire officers, coastguard cadets, army company commanders, battalion staff officers and first sergeants. Middle LPC leaders were defined as those who fell in the middle 25 per cent out of the LPC scores in the sample. Kennedy found that the performance of the middle LPC leaders was more consistent than that of the high or low LPC leaders in that it varied less between different situations. He also found that it was above average in six of the eight situations covered by Fiedler's theory and superior to both high and low LPC leaders in five of them. Kennedy suggests that the superior performance of the middle LPC leaders may be due to the fact that they are more flexible, not overly constrained by one-goal orientation, and therefore better able to employ the behaviours that will maximize performance.

Kennedy's work is, however, consistent with Reddin's (1970) 3-D model of leadership. Virtually alone amongst leadership theorists, Reddin regards the ability of leaders to adopt different leadership styles as a variable. He calls this 'style flex'. Some managers, he says, have low style flex and can only use one style effectively, while others with high style flex can perform a variety of styles effectively. It may well be that those with high style flex correspond to those who have middle LPC scores and those with low style flex correspond to those who obtain either very high or very low LPC scores. Reddin's position seems much more tenable than extreme positions taken by either Fiedler or Vroom and many other leadership theorists. It also has important practical implications. Some managers may have the capability to learn how to perform different styles and thus increase their style flex. Others may be less flexible and find it extremely difficult to learn how to perform a different style, and to attempt to pressurize them into doing so may not only be a waste of time but also very distressing for the person concerned. In such cases, it might be better not to attempt to increase the number of styles they can perform, but to help them to perform their existing style more effectively.

Having discussed whether it is possible for leaders to vary the leadership styles they adopt, however, the question still remains as to whether it is desirable for them to do so. Despite the increasing popularity of situational style theories, earlier leadership style theorists such as Likert (1967) and Blake and Mouton (1978) continued to insist that there is 'one best way' to lead. Blake and Mouton, for example, state categorically that rejection of 'one best way' of conducting human relationships is equivalent to rejecting the proposition that effective behaviour is itself based on scientific principles or laws. On the other hand, for Hersey and Blanchard (1982) consistency is not a matter of using the same style all the time. Instead consistency is using the same style for all similar situations and varying the style appropriately as the situation changes. In their view, managers are consistent if they direct subordinates and sometimes discipline them when they are performing poorly, but support and reward them when they are performing well.

The evidence with respect to flexibility in use of leadership styles is mixed. When asked, subordinates typically state that they would prefer a leader who is consistent in the style he or she employs. For example, Sadler (1970) asked

1,589 people drawn from all functions and all levels of two companies in the UK to express a preference for one of four leadership styles – tells, sells, consults and joins. The consultative style was the one most consistently preferred and was also the one associated with the highest levels of satisfaction with the company and confidence in management. Conversely, the lowest satisfaction with the company and confidence in management was shown by those who felt that their managers did not correspond at all closely to any one of the four styles. Their descriptions of managerial behaviour showed that they regarded their bosses as weak, indecisive, inconsistent, incompetent and lacking in human relations skills. Other examples of studies which showed that subordinates preferred leaders who were consistent rather than flexible in the style they employed are described by Bass (1990).

On the other hand, evidence from research on situational style theories such as those of Fiedler, House and Vroom suggests that both performance and satisfaction can be higher when leaders employ a style which is appropriate to the situation. According to Bass (1990), it seems that flexible leadership will be judged more favourably if the shifts in a leader's style or behaviour are meaningful and explainable to those who are evaluating the leader as shifts to accommodate the requirements of the circumstances. If no such change in requirements is perceived, he suggests, consistency will be prized in a leader for the ease of its predictability and its fitting in with colleagues expectations. Thus, it may also be useful for managers who vary their leadership style to signal their intentions of doing so clearly, so that the style which they adopt does not come as a surprise to the subordinate. It is all very well for Hersey and Blanchard (1982) to say that consistency is adopting the same styles in the same situations, but unless the subordinate is capable of 'reading' the situation in the same way as his or her boss, the boss's behaviour could still appear arbitrary and unpredictable to the subordinate. According to Rackham and Carlisle (1978) skilled negotiators use behaviour labelling. That is, they tend to give an advance indication of the class of behaviour they are about to use. So for example, instead of just making a proposal, they begin by saying, 'If I could make a suggestion', thus giving warning that a proposal is coming. In the same way, it may be that subordinates would find it easier to respond to changes in leadership style if the leader gave clear verbal and non-verbal signals of the style to be adopted in a forthcoming interaction so that the subordinate would know what to expect.

It is worth noting, however, that subordinates may vary, not only in their ability to pick up such cues, but also in their willingness to respond to them. Early in his career, the author worked in a small operational research team, led by a project leader who varied his style according to the stage which the project had reached. In the early stages, when the problem-solving methods were being developed, he was both friendly and participative, eliciting ideas from his subordinates, tolerating disagreement and joining in good-humoured banter. When the problem-solving methods were defined, the work became more routine as data were collected and analysed. As the deadline for the final report approached, he became much more directive and intolerant of disagreement, socializing, banter and anything else which interfered with task completion. He would still listen to and act on serious points of disagreement if they could be shown to be valid, but he was obviously much less interested in hearing alternative viewpoints at this stage. Two of his subordinates, one of whom was the author, had no difficulty in coping with this change in style. We recognized the signs of what behaviour the project leader regarded as appropriate and responded accordingly. The third subordinate, however, continued to behave as he had done in the early stages of the project, disagreeing with the project leader, suggesting alternative strategies and showing resentment when his ideas were rejected. After a number of stand-up arguments, the project leader decided that he could no longer work with this subordinate and he was transferred to another team. This episode suggests that there may well be the equivalent of style flex in subordinates. In other words, subordinates may differ in the range of leadership styles which they are prepared to accept in a leader.

THE ISSUE OF GROUP VERSUS INDIVIDUAL LEADERSHIP

Leadership theories and research differ in the extent to which they are based on an individual or a group level of analysis. In early leadership style research, such as the Ohio State studies, subordinates' descriptions of their leader's behaviour were averaged, and it was this average score which was related to outcome variables such as work performance and satisfaction. In Fiedler's research on the Contingency Model, data concerning leader–member relations were obtained from superiors rather than subordinates, but here too the ratings are concerned with the leader's relations with subordinates as a group rather than as individuals. Similarly, his theory assumes that leaders will behave in the same way to all subordinates.

Other leadership theorists allow for the individual treatment of subordinates to varying degrees. Vroom distinguishes between individual and group problems (Vroom and Yetton 1973; Vroom and Jago 1988). This permits different subordinates to be allowed different degrees of participation in arriving at solutions to individual problems. However, the model suggests that the same problem-solving type should be used with all members of a group with respect to group problems. According to Schriesheim (1979), research into Path–Goal Theory (e.g. House 1971) has used individual rather than averaged group ratings of leader behaviour. Nevertheless, Schriesheim points out that many of the items on currently used leadership scales asked subordinates to describe the leader's behaviour towards the group rather than towards the individual furnishing the description, so an average or group measure was still being used. Furthermore, even if the measure asked how the leader typically treated the individual rather than the group, this would only allow for differences in the way the leader behaved towards different group members. It would not allow for the leader who behaved differently towards the same group member on different occasions.

Hersey and Blanchard (1969, 1977, 1982), on the other hand, suggest that leaders should vary their style according to their subordinates' maturity in relation to a specific task. This implies not only that the more mature members of a leader's group should be treated differently from the less mature, but also that an individual subordinate should be treated differently when performing different tasks if there are significant variations in his or her ability and motivation with respect to these tasks. Finally, Graen's Vertical Dyad Linkage (Leader–Member Exchange) theory of leadership is based on the proposition that leaders almost invariably behave differently towards different subordinates, some becoming a favoured in-group, and others an out-group with whom the leader has a more contractual relationship. This theory will be described in more detail in the next chapter.

The issue of group versus individual leadership has important practical implications. It presents managers with a dilemma. If they treat all subordinates in the same way, then some subordinates may react less favourably than others, because the particular leadership style adopted is less appropriate in their particular case. On the other hand, if managers treat subordinates differently, then this could lead to feelings of resentment if this is perceived as treating some subordinates better than others. Adams's (1963, 1965) Equity Theory can to some extent help to resolve this dilemma. According to Adams, it is not absolute differences in outcomes between people which give rise to feelings of inequity. Rather, feelings of inequity arise when the ratio between an individual's inputs and outcomes differs from the ratio between other people's inputs and outcomes. Inputs include such things as ability, effort, experience, seniority, and so on, while outcomes include factors such as pay, promotion, praise, considerate supervision, and so on. Thus a subordinate might not feel that it was inequitable for a colleague to receive superior outcomes from their mutual boss, provided that these were regarded as being commensurate with the colleague's greater ability, effort, experience or seniority. Under these circumstances, therefore, it might be considered quite acceptable that a boss should consult a senior, experienced subordinate but not the remainder of the group which happened to be composed of young, inexperienced subordinates.

However, feelings of inequality could still occur where subordinates perceive levels of inputs and outcomes differently from their managers or perceive their legitimacy for differential treatment differently. For example, the other subordinates might not regard a colleague who is consulted as being any more knowledgeable than they are. Alternatively, they might not think that a particular attribute, such as seniority, justifies a colleague being given a more interesting job to do. The example quoted at the end of the previous section provides a case in point. All three subordinates were of a similar age, experience and qualifications. All three would have preferred a friendly, participative style of leadership. The only difference was that two of the subordinates were willing to accept a more distant, directive style in the interests of completing the project on time while the third was not. Had the project leader responded to this situation by allowing the third group member greater participation in decision-making than the other two, the latter would undoubtedly have regarded this as grossly inequitable. Research into equity theory has shown that such feelings of inequity are likely to have adverse effects on work performance and satisfaction (Mowday 1987). Where differential treatment of subordinates is likely to give rise to significant feelings of inequity, therefore, the adverse consequences may more than outweigh any benefits which could result from treating subordinates differently.

THE ISSUE OF CULTURAL DIFFERENCES

There is considerable evidence that both preferences for different leadership styles and their effectiveness vary between cultures. It has already been noted that the replication of the Boys' Club experiment by Lewin et al. (1939) in Japan found the democratic groups to be less clearly superior to the autocratic groups than had the original American study (Misumi and Peterson 1985). In another replication study, Meade (1967) compared the effects of democratic and authoritarian leadership on the preferred leadership style, absenteeism, time taken to complete projects and quality of work of groups of ten-year-old Hindu boys living in North India. The authoritarian style was superior to the democratic on all criteria.

The most comprehensive data concerning the prevalence of and preference for different leadership styles come from Hofstede's (1980, 1991) massive survey of over 116,000 IBM employees in 67 different countries. He developed a Power Distance index based on employees' responses to questions concerning the extent to which they were afraid to disagree with their boss, the extent to which their bosses used an autocratic or paternalistic decision-making style and the extent to which they preferred their bosses to use such a style. Hofstede found high power distance values for Latin countries (both Latin European countries, like France and Spain and South American) and for Asian and African countries, but lower values for the USA, Great Britain and its former dominions, and the remaining non-Latin parts of Europe. In relation to the Lewin et al. study and its replications, it is interesting to note that India comes 10th out of 50 countries and three regions on Power Distance, whereas Japan comes 33rd and the USA 38th.

However, it should be noted that preferences for different leadership styles can vary within the same geographic area or ethnic group. For example, Redding and Casey (1976) concluded that although managers in Malaysia, Indonesia, South Vietnam, Thailand, the Philippines, Hong Kong and Singapore favoured an autocratic style of leadership more than Western managers, those from Hong Kong and Singapore were somewhat less favourable towards it than managers from the other five countries. Similarly, Dorfman and Howell (1988) found that in Taiwan directive leadership displayed by one's superiors correlated 0.44 with subordinates' satisfaction with work for those subordinates who had strong beliefs in the key values of Chinese culture, but only 0.19 for those who did not. Furthermore, while contingent reward behaviours were positively correlated with work satisfaction in both groups, there was a positive correlation (0.29) between contingent punishment behaviours and work satisfaction among subordinates who had strong beliefs in the key values of Chinese culture, but negative correlation (−0.22) for those who did not.

According to Bass (1990), erroneously adopting the wrong leadership style is one of the reasons why managers of one nationality managing subordinates of another may fail. However, it may not be enough simply to adopt the right leadership style. According to Smith and Peterson (1988), how a leadership style is performed may also vary from one culture to another. Thus, a supervisor who frequently checks up that work is done correctly may be seen as a kind father in one setting, as task-centred in another, and officious and untrustful in another. Smith and Peterson report a series of studies carried out in different cultures in which subordinates were asked to rate the leadership style of their superiors and then asked to complete a further series of specific questions, asking about the superiors's behaviour much more precisely. It was found that eight to ten of the 36 specific behaviours correlated consistently positively with one or other of the style measures in all the countries sampled. For example, talking sympathetically with a subordinate who has personal difficulties is seen as considerate in all cultures, and frequently talking about work progress is seen as task-centred in all cultures. However, the remaining 16 behaviours show wide and frequently significant differences between countries in correlation with the style measures. For example, a supervisor who talks about a subordinate's personal difficulties to his colleagues when the person is absent was deemed inconsiderate in Britain and the USA, but considerate in Hong Kong and Japan. Similarly, the supervisor who shows disapproval of latecomers to work is seen as task-centred in Britain and Hong Kong, unfriendly and inconsiderate in the USA, and neither of these things in Japan.

The existence of such differences further reduces the generality of conclusions concerning appropriate leadership behaviours based on research carried out in any one culture. Not only may leadership styles vary in acceptability and effectiveness between cultures, but even if the manager is aware of the appropriate style to adopt in a particular culture, he or she may still perform it in an inappropriate manner. Both leadership and interpersonal skills have been identified as major factors influencing the success of parent country managers managing subordinates from a different culture (Bass 1990). However, Smith and Peterson's analysis suggests that the skills required may vary from culture to culture, requiring a new set of skills to be learned when managing people from a different culture. The question of leadership and interpersonal skills will be taken up in Chapter 6.

Furthermore, as we have already seen with respect to Taiwan, cultural differences within the same country may also influence preferences for different leadership styles. Hofstede (1991) found that Power Distance scores were inversely related to occupational level in France, Germany and Great Britain. Occupations with the lowest status and education level (unskilled and semi-skilled workers) showed the highest Power Distance values, while those with the highest status and education level (managers of professional workers) showed the lowest Power Distance values. The range of power distance scores between these two extremes was of the same order of magnitude as the difference between the highest and lowest scoring countries. Thus it appears likely that in these countries the acceptability of different leadership styles would vary according to the social class of the followers.

Within any one country, the way in which followers respond to leaders may also be influenced by sex or ethnic origin of either the leaders or the followers. Jago and Vroom (1982) found that females who were perceived to be autocratic were negatively evaluated, whereas males who were perceived to be autocratic received positive evaluations. Rice et al. (1980) studied the reactions of male followers to male and female leaders at the West Point Military Academy. They found that followers with traditional attitudes towards women described the group atmosphere more favourably in groups with male leaders than in groups with female leaders. However, followers with more liberal attitudes towards women described the group atmosphere similarly in groups with male and female leaders.

King and Bass (1974) suggested that it is important for black supervisors of black subordinates to have upward influence in their organizations and for this influence to be visible to subordinates. Bass (1990) interprets this as meaning that such supervisors may need additional symbols of authority as well as higher level support to make their position credible. In a laboratory study, Richards and Jaffee (1972) found that white subordinates behaved differently when supervised by blacks and that some of these behaviours impeded the effectiveness of black supervisors. They also suggested that black supervisors may have to emit a different pattern of behaviours in order to be deemed as effective as their white counterparts. In another laboratory study carried out by Mayhand and Grusky (1972), a black supervisor employed a close, punitive style of supervision with black and white subordinates. The productivity of the black subordinates increased during the study, but they subsequently tended to express adverse views concerning the supervisor and the experiment. Conversely, the white subordinates subsequently expressed more favourable attitudes towards the supervisor and the experiment itself, but their productivity during the study decreased. Mayhand and Grusky explain these results as follows. They suggest that the white subjects in the experiment tended to conceal their 'real' attitudes towards the supervisor in order to appear accepting of blacks, whereas the black subjects did not feel the need to conceal their true feelings. On the other hand, the white subjects responded adversely to the actual negative behaviour of the black supervisor in the experiment and the decline in their productivity could be attributed either to greater stress or to latent hostility towards the punitive supervisor.

Such research suggests that followers may not respond in the same way to female or minority group leaders as they do to male or majority group leaders. This has both theoretical and practical implications. Most leadership theories are based on the behaviour of white male American leaders and followers. Thus it is possible that their conclusions are not necessarily valid for other groups. Support for this contention can be found in a study carried out by Rice *et al.* (1982, quoted Adams and Yoder 1985). They used data from their earlier study of male and female leaders at West Point to test the validity of Fiedler's Contingency Model. They found that correlations between male leaders' LPC scores and group performance were negative in groups with liberal followers and positive in groups with conservative or traditional followers. However, the correlations were just the opposite for female leaders. According to Adams and Yoder, these data suggest that the Contingency Model cannot be applied to female leaders without major changes.

The practical implications of the studies quoted above is that female and minority group leaders may find that they are unable to influence followers to the same extent as male or majority group members or that they have to behave differently in order to exert the same influence. Such different ways of behaving may, for example, involve being less assertive, and employing persuasion because the other group members would not accept direct orders, or it may involve being more assertive than male or majority group members would have to be to obtain the same effect. In a survey of managers and management students, Rasmussen (1991) found that female respondents were more likely than male to regard active listening as representing a passive or nurturing stance. Rasmussen states that some female respondents stated that they had consciously distanced themselves from nurturing roles – or at least from entering additional situations in which they are expected to take a nurturing stance. One female manager said, 'I have a difficult enough time holding my own. If I don't go nose-to-nose with those guys [other managers in her organization], they'll walk all over me.'

Conversely, male or majority group leaders may find that they have to behave differently towards female or minority group members from the way they would towards subordinates of male or majority group subordinates in order to have the same effect on work performance and satisfaction. Furthermore, such effects undoubtedly change over time. As attitudes towards relations between the sexes and between ethnic groups change, so will the way leaders behave towards followers and the ways in which the followers react. This was powerfully illustrated during an interpersonal skills course on which the author was a tutor. In a role play practice session, a manager in his late fifties interviewed a female 'subordinate'. He treated her in a somewhat avuncular fashion, showing a great deal of concern for her feelings and suggesting in a sympathetic manner ways of overcoming the performance problems she faced. After the interview, he received very positive feedback from the interviewee, who said that she felt that the interviewer had treated her very well. The interviewer was not surprised that the interview had been a success. He said that most of his staff were female and he knew how to manage them. In his second interview, by coincidence, the interviewee was also female. He used exactly the same technique and at the end of the interview, to his amazement, received vehemently negative feedback concerning his insultingly patronizing manner.

It follows that it is impossible to generalize about the effectiveness of different leadership styles in relation to the sex or ethnic origin of the leaders and followers. We are living in a period of transition as far as the relationships between men and women and between different ethnic groups are concerned. Thus earlier research, such as that from the 1970s quoted above, may describe situations which no longer exist. Furthermore, as we have seen, even when the general pattern of relationships between different groups changes, the attitudes and behaviour of individual group members may change at a different rate. Thus different members of the same group may respond in very different ways to the same leadership style.

THE ISSUE OF SPECIFICITY

Leadership style theories describe leadership styles at a relatively high level of abstraction (Callaghan and Wright 1992). Saying that a leader's style of behaviour is participative or autocratic or task-centred or relationship-oriented indicates only in very general terms what leaders actually do when interacting with their followers and tells us nothing about how well they do it. It is almost as if leadership theorists believe that people already know how to be participative, task-centred, and so on, and simply need to be told in which circumstances such styles are appropriate for them to employ the styles successfully. Anyone who has observed an inept democratic leader reduce a meeting to shambles or an inept autocrat being ignored by subordinates who regard him or her as a joke, knows this is not true. Each of the styles identified by behavioural leadership theorists involve certain activities and these activities can be performed more or less well. Democratic leadership inevitably involves consultation, consultation involves asking questions, and such questions can be asked skilfully or unskilfully. Similarly, task-centred leadership involves influencing subordinate behaviour towards the achievement of organizational goals, but there are many different ways of influencing behaviour and these too can be performed well or badly. In other words, to be of practical utility for the development of leadership effectiveness, it is necessary not only to identify which leadership styles are appropriate in different situations, but also to provide a detailed description of how to perform such styles and perform them well. This is an issue which will be discussed in more detail in the next chapter.

THE ISSUE OF COMPLEXITY

Introducing the situation as a variable influencing the effectiveness of different leadership styles had the effect of increasing the complexity of situational styles theories to a marked degree. Even the simplest of situational style theories is much more complex than the earlier 'one best way' style theories which simply exhorted managers to adopt the same leadership style in all situations. Nevertheless, it will be apparent that all situational style theories are only partial theories. Even the most complex of them do not encompass all the different types of leadership behaviour and situational variables which have been identified. Given that carrying out a comprehensive test of the more complex of existing situational style theories, such as House's Path–Goal Theory, is prohibitively difficult, there is little likelihood of a valid, comprehensive situational style theory being developed in the foreseeable future. The behavioural sciences are simply not sufficiently advanced to enable the development and testing of a situational style theory incorporating all the relevant variables and showing all their complex interactions in a systematic way.

Furthermore, even if such a theory were developed, it would probably be capable of being understood by no more than a few specialist leadership researchers and would therefore be of little use to practising managers. Situational style theories of leadership, in effect, seem to suffer from a conflict between being comprehensive and being comprehensible. One of the most popular theories with trainers and personnel managers, Hersey and Blanchard's Situational Theory, is also one of the simplest, identifying only two leadership dimensions and one situational variable. Conversely, one of the most comprehensive situational style theories, House's Path–Goal Theory, which incorporates four leadership dimensions and a large and growing number of situational variables, has had comparatively little use as a vehicle for leadership training.

CONCLUSIONS

In retrospect, it is apparent that situational style theorists set themselves a formidable task. It is difficult enough to develop descriptions of leadership styles which do justice to the complexity of leadership behaviour, but which are still simple enough to use for teaching and research purposes. However, this problem pales into insignificance beside that of attempting to identify, measure and establish the relationships between all the situational variables which may influence the appropriateness of a particular style. If one adds to this differences between leaders in their ability to perform different styles, the problem of deciding whether to treat followers as a group or as individuals, and all the differences in ways in which followers may respond due to differences in cultural background, class, sex, ethnic origin and so on, then it is hardly surprising that it has proved impossible to develop a valid, comprehensive situational style theory of leadership. Furthermore, even if such a theory were developed, it would not necessarily remain valid. In fifty years' time, social norms concerning the types of behaviour which are legitimate means of influence between leaders and followers may have changed, and it may be necessary to modify theories of leadership accordingly.

Nevertheless, situational style theories of leadership have made a useful contribution towards understanding the relationship between leadership behaviour and leadership success and effectiveness. From the practical point of view, situational leadership theories are in large measure diagnostic procedures. They represent attempts to help managers to identify different leadership situations and to stipulate which leadership styles would be most appropriate in these situations. As theories, they attempt to do this in a mechanistic way. That is, they suggest that in situation A, style X is most appropriate, in situation B, style Y is most appropriate, and so on. Viewed in this light, the fact that such theories have been only moderately successful is hardly surprising. Deciding what would be the most appropriate way to interact with other human beings in order to achieve some desired objective cannot be reduced simply to following a set diagnostic procedure. Inevitably human judgement is also involved.

Taylor and Wright (1988) comment that interpersonal skills involve 'reacting adaptively to the relatively unpredictable', and this applies equally to leadership. There are quite simply too many variables involved in leadership situations for a simple diagnostic procedure infallibly to identify the most appropriate style to be adopted. This is also the case in other professions, even those whose diagnostic procedures are more advanced than those of situational leadership theorists. A diagnostic procedure may help a mechanic to identify a fault in a car or a doctor to identify what is 'wrong' with a patient. Their knowledge of their respective fields will help them to know what to look for, what the symptoms are likely to signify, and what remedial action is likely to be effective. If the problem is a complex one, however, their diagnoses are likely to be a matter of reasoned judgement, rather than simply working through a set diagnostic procedure in a mechanical fashion. Furthermore, if their first attempts at remedial action are not effective, then they will learn from this experience, react adaptively, and try something else which they believe is more likely to be effective next time. It would be naive to expect that leadership would or could be any different.

This, then, is the main practical value of situational leadership theories. They do not, in themselves, provide an infallible guide to leadership behaviour. However, they do help leaders to be more aware of the factors involved in leadership situations, and the effects they may have. Thus leaders who have a knowledge of situational leadership theories, and have also had an opportunity to practise their application in training exercises, are more likely to be able to choose an appropriate leadership style than those relying on the older, somewhat naive, 'one best way' theories. Furthermore, they will be more likely to be able to react adaptively and select a more appropriate style if the first one they choose proves to be inappropriate, instead of sticking rigidly to a style which patently is not working.

Nevertheless, diagnostic skills are not the whole of leadership, any more than they are the whole of car mechanics or the practice of medicine. All involve taking certain actions in order to achieve desired ends, and taking them skilfully in order to be successful. As we have already noted, this is a major area of weakness in situational leadership theories. They tend to describe the behaviours required to perform a particular leadership style only in very general terms. It would be horrifying to consider a surgeon, for example, being trained with as little attention to the development of precise skills as the typical situational style theorists pay. Undoubtedly, there are different styles of operation, ranging from the slow and careful exploratory operation to the quick 'in and out', where speed is of the essence, because the patient may die if the operation takes too long. However, it is virtually at this level of description at which situational leadership theories stop. They do not describe in detail how to perform their different leadership styles, nor do they describe how to perform them well. These are issues which will be taken up in the next chapter.

EXERCISE 3: THE PROJECT LEADER

Bill is a project leader with ORCON, an operational research consultancy. He has just presented the final report on his latest project to the client. It is concerned with the probable effects of the opening of the Channel Tunnel on the demand for car ferries operating on long sea crossings to and from certain more distant destinations. Bill is pleased with the report and the client's response was very favourable. However, it has been a very tiring and emotionally draining project.

Work on the project began four months ago. The project team consisted of Bill as project leader and three team members, Peter, Karen and Miles. Bill is an experienced OR scientist in his early thirties. The team members are all in their mid-twenties, recent graduates and with similar length of service with ORCON. In the first two months of the project, the team developed a model of cross-Channel travel. They identified the major destinations to which people travel and estimated the total journey times, distances to be driven by those travelling by car and cost of travel to and from these destinations by different cross-Channel routes. They also arranged for a market research organization to carry out a questionnaire survey which elicited from cross-Channel passengers data concerning how important they regarded these and other aspects of cross-Channel travel. During this part of the project, Bill used a participative leadership style, encouraging the team members to make suggestions on what factors should be included in the model and how they should be measured. The model which was finally agreed was very much a team effort, incorporating ideas from all the team members. The team undoubtedly worked hard during this phase of the project, but there was also a relaxed atmosphere and a great deal of good-humoured banter in which Bill joined as much as anyone.

After about two months, the model had been developed and there now remained a great deal of routine work to be done to enter the data into the model, analyse the data to establish what changes in travel patterns might result from the opening of the Tunnel and write the final report which would make recommendations concerning actions the client should take in the light of the team's findings. The deadline was very tight and it was in fact touch and go whether the team would be able to complete the report and submit it on the agreed date.

At this point, Bill's manner changed. He no longer solicited suggestions from the team members. If suggestions were made he firmly stated that there was no time to change things now; they had to proceed with the model as it was or they would never finish the report on time. When Peter pointed out a flaw in the model which was too serious to be ignored, Bill did agree that the model would have to be changed. However, while he was glad that the flaw had been noticed before it was too late, it was obvious that he was annoyed that it had not been noticed and rectified earlier. During the whole of the second half of the project, Bill's manner was brusque and businesslike. He smiled rarely and he became quite irritable if the team members became too light-hearted in their approach to the work when he was with them.

Two of the team members, Peter and Karen adapted very quickly to this change. They did not express disagreement with or suggest changes to the project plan unless it was absolutely necessary. They also reduced the amount of banter when Bill was around and certainly did not direct any towards him. Miles, however, continued to behave in the same way he had during the first half of the project. He continued to propose changes in the model, to disagree with Bill about methods of data analysis and to make facetious comments in Bill's presence. This resulted in several serious arguments, shouting matches would be a good way of describing them, in which Bill said that Miles's behaviour was preventing the team from working effectively and Miles said that Bill was behaving in a petty-minded dictatorial manner. After two or three such rows, Bill decided that he could no longer work with Miles, who was transferred to another project team. Both Peter and Karen felt that Miles had behaved in an immature manner. While they preferred to participate in decision-making, they recognized that this was no longer possible if the project was to be completed on time.

In the end, the project was completed on time and the recommendations were accepted and implemented by the client. Bill and the remaining two team members celebrated together after work that evening and then Bill took the rest of the week off to recuperate.

What light do theories of leadership throw on the events described in this case? Although the case is intended primarily as a vehicle for examining issues relating to situational style theories of leadership, leadership theories described in other chapters may also be relevant.

Chapter 6

Alternative approaches to the study of leadership behaviour

INTRODUCTION

Situational style theories of the type described in Chapter 4 were the dominant form of leadership theories from the mid-1960s to the mid-1970s. However, from the mid-1970s a growing disillusionment with situational style theories and their associated means of measuring leadership behaviour began to become apparent (Schriesheim and Kerr 1977). While research into existing theories continued to be carried out and in some cases revised versions of these theories were produced, no major new situational style theory of leadership has been developed since that time. Instead, leadership theorists began to develop a variety of alternative approaches to the study of leadership. One renewed area of interest was the study of the personality characteristics associated with successful and effective leadership. Theories and research in this area will be examined in Chapter 8. Other theorists and researchers began to develop alternative behavioural approaches to the study of leadership. However, unlike the previous decade when there had been one dominant approach to the study of leadership behaviour, the situational style theory, leadership theory after the mid-1970s became much more fragmented. There developed a wide variety of different types of behavioural theory, many of which had little in common except the fact that they did not employ leadership style as a central feature of their models of leadership. These alternative approaches to the study of leadership behaviour will be discussed in the present chapter.

SPECIFIC LEADERSHIP BEHAVIOURS

During the latter half of the 1970s there were a number of indications that some leadership theorists were beginning to recognize the need to develop more precise descriptions of leader behaviour. For example, Campbell (1977) argued that the study of leadership had been hurt by over concentration on 'theory'. There was a need, he stated, for many more descriptive studies that attempted to develop reasonable taxonomies of what leaders and followers actually do when they interact. Describing actions in 'stylistic' or general terms was not sufficient; leadership behaviour must be described very carefully in concrete terms. In particular, leadership training courses must deal with observable behaviours which the individual should be able to exhibit when the course is completed, rather than making generalized arguments for being more employee-centred, production-centred, and so on.

A similar argument was put forward by Yukl (1981). He states that it is apparent that broadly defined categories of behaviour such as consideration and initiating structure provide too general and simplistic a picture of leadership. They fail to capture the great diversity of behaviour required by most kinds of managers and administrators. Even some of the more elaborate taxonomies that have been proposed, he states, fail to include some of the most relevant aspects of leader behaviour, such as providing praise and recognition, setting specific performance goals, providing tangible rewards for effective performance, providing necessary training and coaching, and inspiring confidence and

Table 6.1 Yukl's (1994) taxonomy of managerial practices

Planning and organizing: Determining long-term objectives and strategies, allocating resources according to priorities, determining how to use personnel and resources to accomplish a task efficiently, and determining how to improve coordination, productivity, and the effectiveness of the organizational unit.

Problem-solving: Identifying work-related problems, analysing problems in a timely but systematic manner to identify causes and find solutions, and acting decisively to implement solutions to resolve important problems or crises.

Clarifying roles and objectives: Assigning tasks, providing direction in how to do the work, and communicating a clear understanding of job responsibilities, task objectives, deadlines, and performance expectations.

Informing: Disseminating relevant information about decisions, plans and activities to people that need it to do their work, providing written materials and documents, and answering requests for technical information.

Monitoring: Gathering information about work activities and external conditions affecting the work, checking on the progress and quality of the work, evaluating the performance of individuals and the organizational unit, analysing trends, and forecasting external events.

Motivating and inspiring: Using influence techniques that appeal to emotion or logic to generate enthusiasm for the work, commitment to task objectives, and compliance with requests for co-operation, assistance, support, or resources; setting an example of appropriate behaviour.

Consulting: Checking with people before making changes that affect them, encouraging suggestions for improvement, inviting participation in decision-making, incorporating the ideas and suggestions of others in decisions.

Delegating: Allowing subordinates to have substantial responsibility and discretion in carrying out work activities, handling problems, and making important decisions.

Supporting: Acting friendly and considerate, being patient and helpful, showing sympathy and support when someone is upset or anxious, listening to complaints and problems, looking out for someone's interests.

Developing and mentoring: Providing coaching and helpful career advice, and doing things to facilitate a person's skill acquisition, professional development, and career advancement.

Managing conflict and team building: Facilitating the constructive resolution of conflict, and encouraging co-operation, teamwork, and identification with the work unit.

Networking: Socializing informally, developing contacts with people who are a source of information and support, and maintaining contacts through periodic interaction, including visits, telephone calls, correspondence and attendance at meetings and social events.

Recognizing: Providing praise and recognition for effective performance, significant achievements, and special contributions; expressing appreciation for someone's contributions and special efforts.

Rewarding: Providing or recommending tangible rewards such as a pay increase or promotion for effective performance, significant achievements, and demonstrated competence.

Source: Yukl 1994

commitment. In 1975, therefore, a research programme was instituted in order to identify meaningful categories of leadership behaviour at what Yukl calls 'an intermediate level of abstraction'. This research programme has resulted in a series of categorization systems which have been refined continually as the research progressed (Yukl and Nemeroff 1979; Yukl 1981, 1989, 1994; Yukl *et al.* 1990). The latest version (Yukl 1994) has fourteen middle-range categories of leadership behaviour (called 'managerial practices') and a much larger number of specific component behaviours. These are listed in Table 6.1. A questionnaire (the Managerial Practices Survey) has been developed in order to measure the extent to which managers use these behavioural categories in interactions with subordinates and others. However, attempts to relate the use of such practices to managerial effectiveness have so far met with only moderate success. Yukl *et al.* (1990) report six validation studies with samples of beauty salon managers, military cadets, insurance sales people, elementary schools principals, home economics programme leaders and department heads in high schools employing a variety of independent measures of managerial effectiveness. One of the managerial practices, supporting, was not associated with managerial effectiveness in any of the studies, although it was correlated with measures of subordinate satisfaction. All the others were significantly correlated with managerial effectiveness in at least one of the six studies, but none was significantly correlated with managerial effectiveness in more than three studies. Nevertheless, Yukl *et al.* claim that the correlations were higher than is typical for behaviour description questionnaires when used with a criterion of leadership effectiveness which is independent of the behavioural descriptions and is reasonably accurate.

Another example of research which examined the effectiveness of more specific leadership behaviours is Oldham's (1976) study of the motivational strategies used by supervisors. He identified six such strategies:

1 Personally rewarding (e.g. congratulations for a job well done).
2 Personally punishing (e.g. verbal criticism).
3 Setting goals.
4 Designing information feedback systems.
5 Placing personnel – to match their skills and needs.
6 Designing job systems – to match skills and needs.

The extent to which 45 middle managers in 10 stores used these categories was rated by the managers themselves, and their superiors and subordinates, and their managerial effectiveness was rated by their superiors. The managers also filled in leadership style questionnaires measuring their consideration and initiating structure. All the strategies, except personally punishing were related positively and significantly to ratings of effectiveness. The measures of consideration and initiating structure were also positively related to the measures of managerial effectiveness, but less closely than the motivational strategies. Oldham concludes that in this particular organization, motivational strategies – the actual behaviours used by supervisors to motivate subordinates – were better predictors of middle-management performance than leadership style.

Other theorists have attempted to develop a model of more specific leadership behaviours and their effects on subordinate behaviour based on the principles of operant conditioning developed by Skinner (1953). Sims (1977) suggests that organizational leaders can be regarded as managers of reinforcement contingencies for their subordinates. They let their subordinates know when and how a task is to be accomplished, through techniques such as goal setting, and then administer rewards and/or punishments contingent on the subordinate's level of performance. Luthans and Kreitner (1975) refer to the three components involved in this process as antecedents, behaviour and consequences and their application to the management of reinforcement contingencies is illustrated in Figure 6.1.

In a study of 143 young professionals, Sims examined the effects on subsequent subordinate performance of three types of contingent reinforcement, positive reward behaviour (e.g. praise, interest, help with problems), advancement reward behaviour (e.g. recommendation for promotion), and punitive behaviour (e.g. reprimand, dismissal). He found that positive reward behaviour had a significant positive effect on subsequent performance, advance-

Antecedents		Behaviour		Consequences
What comes before	$\longrightarrow$	What happens	$\longrightarrow$	What comes after
Supervisor behaviour (e.g. goal setting)		Subordinate behaviour (e.g. reaches goal)		Supervisor behaviour (e.g. praise)

Figure 6.1 The leader as manager of reinforcement contingencies

ment reward behaviour was positively related to subsequent performance, but not at a statistically significant level and punitive reward behaviour was unrelated to performance. Similarly, in a study of 128 employees in a large merchandizing organization, Szilagyi (1980) found that positive leader reward behaviour had a significant positive effect on subordinate performance and satisfaction, while punitive behaviour had a significant negative effect on subordinate satisfaction but had no significant effect on performance.

On the basis of these and other similar studies, Sims (1980) concluded that reward behaviour tends to have a much stronger effect on subordinate performance than punitive behaviour and that punishment tends to be a result rather than a cause of employee behaviour. Subsequent research has tended to support Sims' views with respect to contingent reward behaviour. For example, Podsakoff *et al.* (1982) carried out a questionnaire survey concerning the behaviour of managers and supervisors in a non-profit organization and found that those who provided contingent rewards had subordinates who performed better and were more satisfied than other subordinates. In the case of managers and supervisors who provided contingent punishment or rewards which were not contingent on performance, there was no relationship between leader behaviour and subordinates' performance. However, other studies have produced conflicting results with respect to punishment.

Arvey and Jones (1985) state that, based on the research evidence available, it does not appear possible to draw clear conclusions about the effects of punishment on general levels of work performance or job satisfaction. Different studies have suggested that there may be either positive or negative effects or no relationship at all. As Sims suggested, however, the influence of punishment seems to be less strong than that of reward. On the other hand, punishment seems to have greater effectiveness when directed at specific target behaviours. The results of studies which have investigated the use of punitive systems to control specific behaviours, such as absenteeism, have generally been positive when these tactics are used in combination with a reward system of some type.

One of the reasons for such conflicting results may be that responses to punishment are particularly sensitive to the manner in which it is administered. Baron (1990) points out that many managers find transmitting negative feedback to subordinates one of the most difficult and unpleasant tasks they must perform and avoid doing so as much as possible. As a result, they often refrain from criticizing their subordinates until the frequency or severity of performance problems – and the managers' annoyance with them – rise to extremely high levels. At this point managers do finally deliver feedback, but because of the strong emotions present, it is often biting, sarcastic and harsh. More to the point, Baron states, it frequently violates the basic principles for the effective delivery of performance feedback, in that such annoyance derived feedback is often inconsiderate in tone, contains threats, attributes poor performance to internal causes and is general rather than specific in content.

Thus the fact that operant conditioning researchers have found that punishment is often unrelated to performance and can even have a detrimental effect may result in part from the fact that it is often done badly. Some support for this view can be found in Arvey *et al.*'s (1984) study of the attitudes towards discipline of 526 hourly paid workers in a large chemical plant. They found that the workers had a negative attitude towards supervisors who administered discipline in an inappropriate manner – in a childish or petty fashion, being typically angry, and so on – but a positive attitude towards supervisors who applied discipline in a consistent manner.

Arvey and Jones (1985) suggest that a 'good' supervisor is not necessarily one who seldom or never disciplines employees, but is one who administers discipline in a constructive or 'fair' manner. Thus punishment that is applied soon after the infraction occurs, is administered consistently among and within employees, is accompanied with a clear explanation for the discipline and applies a penalty which is not unduly harsh, will be more effective than punishment that is administered haphazardly, with little explanation, and so forth. Similar conclusions are drawn by Ball *et al.* (1992) on the basis of an extensive review of the research literature on punishment. They argue that punishment can be a valuable and positive leadership tool when managed properly. Therefore, the question which should be asked is not *whether* punishment should be used in organizations, but *how* should punishment be used in organizations.

Another leadership theorist who has developed a model of leadership based on operant condition is Komaki. Komaki *et al.* (1986) suggest that three operant-based categories of behaviour are associated with supervisors' effectiveness in interpersonal attempts to influence their followers in accomplishing work-related goals. These are performance antecedents (providing instructions about performance), performance monitors (collecting performance information information) and performance consequences (indicating knowledge of performance). They infer from operant conditioning theory that an effective manager would make appropriate behaviours clear, accurately and fairly appraise performance and regularly provide consequences contingent on performance. An ineffective manager, on the other hand, would probably leave tasks ambiguously defined, appraise performance sporadically, if at all, and provide infrequent or non-contingent consequences for performance.

Komaki (1986) carried out a partial test of these hypotheses in an observational study of 24 managers in a medical insurance firm. Twelve of these managers (the effective group) had been rated and ranked by their superiors as being in the top 28 per cent of managers in terms of motivating others and the other twelve (the marginal group) had been rated as being in the bottom 28 per cent. Komaki found that the effective group were significantly more likely to monitor performance by observing employees at work or inspecting the products of their work. Other methods of monitoring performance, such as asking the employees themselves or asking others about their performance, were not related to effectiveness. Performance antecedents and performance consequences were also found to be unrelated to rated effectiveness.

Komaki suggests that performance monitoring was expected to be related to supervisory effectiveness because it is a prerequisite to the providing of contingent consequences. Managers who monitor were thought more likely to possess accurate information which they could use when providing performance consequences. She suggests that the fact that no differences in performance consequences were found between effective and marginally effective managers does not necessarily mean that consequences are unimportant when motivating others. Rather than providing more consequences, effective managers may be more likely to provide contingent consequences, and the extent to which the consequences were contingent was not measured in this research. Komaki also suggests that antecedents such as providing instructions and reminders were not expected to distinguish betwen effective and marginal managers, as managers typically err in the direction of providing far more antecedents than they do monitors or consequences. A subsequent study by Komaki *et al.* (1989), however, produced results which conflicted with her earlier study in one respect. It was found that success in a sailing regatta was significantly related to the use of *both* performance monitors and performance consequences by the skippers during the races.

In a later laboratory study, Komaki and Citera (1990) attempted to establish why performance monitoring has positive effects on performance. Sixty manager-subordinate pairs engaged in a simulated administrative task were role played by female undergraduate students. A monitor group in which managers collected information (e.g. sampled the work) was compared with an antecedent group in which managers conveyed information (e.g. provided instructions). It was found that subordinates spent significantly more time talking to the manager about their performance and the managers provided significantly more consequences to the subordinates in the monitor group than in the antecedent group. Furthermore, a sequential analysis of the comments made by managers and subordinates during their discussions revealed a pattern of reciprocal interactions. Monitoring appeared to stimulate subordinates into talking about their own performance and this in turn set the stage for managers to provide consequences and continue monitoring subordinates' performance.

It will be apparent that the operant conditioning approach to leadership theory and research has had some success in identifying more precise leadership behaviours and demonstrating their effect on subordinate behaviour and attitudes. Nevertheless, much of the work so far carried out in this area has a number of limitations. First, it typically considers a relatively narrow range of leader behaviours. Leaders do much more when interacting with their followers than simply setting goals, rewarding, punishing and giving feedback, important as these activities may be.

Second, the studies carried out by operant conditioning theorists largely ignore the question of skill. The behaviours they consider can be performed more or less well, and this too has an effect on how the subordinate responds to them. As we have seen, the way in which people respond to criticism, negative feedback and other forms of punishment depends to a considerable extent on the manner in which they are administered. Much the same considerations apply in the case of praise. Praise done well can have beneficial effects, but done badly – for example, with respect to a inappropriate aspect of performance or in front of the wrong people – it can give rise to adverse reactions such as embarrassment, resentment and loss of respect for the person giving the praise.

Third, much of the research and theory based on an operant conditioning approach to leadership does not take sufficient account of the crucial question of individual differences between subordinates. Some may resent criticism more than others, some may respond well to praise while others find it embarrassing, some might be highly motivated by the offer of a pay rise while others may prefer the opportunity to do more challenging work, and so on. Thus general solutions are likely to be less effective than those designed to suit the needs of specific subordinates. Recognizing the individual needs of subordinates and modifying the way they are treated accordingly is also something which requires considerable skill on the part of the manager.

In their more recent work, it is apparent that Sims and his colleagues have recognized these limitations and begun to address them. Some of the later studies of role played manager–subordinate interactions (e.g. Sims and Manz 1984; Gioia and Sims 1986; Gioia et al. 1989) have investigated a wider variety of leader behaviours. In particular, Gioia and Sims (1986) developed an organizational verbal behaviour categorization system comprising fifteen managerial and twelve subordinate behaviours. These studies examined such questions as the influence of differing levels of subordinate performance on managers' verbal behaviour and causal attributions. However, they did not include a measure of the managers' performance and thus do not add to our knowledge of the specific leadership behaviours associated with managerial success or effectiveness. Sims and Lorenzi (1992) note the importance of both skills and individual differences. They give advice on how to deliver a constructive reprimand. They also state that an effective manager must be concerned with individual perceptions concerning reward behaviour, because what the manager perceives as a reward may not be rewarding to the subordinate or may even be a disincentive. The manager therefore requires information concerning employee preferences for different rewards. This information, they state, can be obtained from the subordinate mainly on an informal basis, through personal conversations. However, they do not give advice on how to conduct such conversations skilfully.

AN INTERPERSONAL SKILLS MODEL OF LEADERSHIP

Wright and Taylor (1984, 1985, 1994) argue that the concept of skill has been unjustifiably neglected in behavioural theories of leadership. Such theories describe, often in very general terms, the types of behaviour which are said to be associated with successful or effective leadership, but little is said about how to perform such behaviours well. However, more detailed advice on how to interact effectively with people at work can be found in the writings of interpersonal skills trainers, particularly those concerned with the development of interviewing skills. Examples include work on counselling disturbed or frustrated employees (Maier 1952, 1955), selection interviewing (Kahn and Cannell 1957) and performance appraisal interviewing (Maier 1958; Randell *et al.* 1972; Randell *et al.* 1984).

During the mid-1970s, Wright and Taylor had worked with Randell and his colleagues on appraisal interviewing courses and later extended their approach to interviewing skills training to other types of interactions, such as counselling, grievance and disciplinary interviewing (Gill and Taylor 1976) and audit interviewing (Taylor and Wright 1977). As this work progressed, it became apparent that the skills which they were developing were not limited to any one managerial situation, that is, there was a set of 'core skills' which could be employed whenever a manager interacted with his or her subordinates or others within an organizational context.

Rather to their surprise, therefore, Wright and Taylor came to the conclusion that they were training their course participants in leadership skills. It was also apparent that the approach to interviewing skills training which they and other trainers were taking at that time tended to fragment the development of such skills. While the interpersonal skills required in different managerial situations overlapped considerably, they tended to be taught on different courses and described in separate books, or at best different chapters in the same book, each devoted to different types of interview. As Argyle (1981: xv) put it, 'Management skills came to be seen primarily as a number of discrete, set-piece performances, such as various kinds of interview, each of which could be trained'. What was lacking was a general model of the interpersonal skills required for the effective management of people at work in a wide variety of different situations. Wright and Taylor therefore decided to develop such a model.

Wright and Taylor (1994) propose that the interpersonal skills of leadership can be described in terms of three levels of analysis (set out on p. 116):

Table 6.2 Verbal components of manager–subordinate interactions

(a) Components for gathering information

Component	Appropriate use	Inappropriate use
Open questions e.g. 'Tell me about . . .' 'Could you describe what you think are . . .'	For introducing topics and encouraging subordinates to talk at length so avoiding simple 'yes' and 'no' answers.	For obtaining specific details.
Probes e.g. 'Could you tell me more about . . .' 'What do you mean by . . .'	Generally follow open questions to elicit more information about a particular topic or event.	Can miss point if more general information not collected first. Pointed and persistent probing on sensitive issues can be seen as intrusive.
Closed questions e.g. 'How long did it take?' 'Did you receive my draft report?'	Establishing precise information (dates, numbers, etc.) and receiving simple 'yes' and 'no' responses.	For gaining broad information, opinions, feelings, etc.
Comparisons e.g. 'What are the relative merits of . . .?'	Getting subordinates to explore and reveal their own needs, values and opinions.	Where the 'pairs' are unrealistic or irrelevant.
Hypotheticals e.g. 'What would you do (have done) about (if) . . .?'	Getting subordinates to think about a new topic or area.	When a subordinate lacks knowledge or experience of the situation described.
Multiples A stream of questions or statements strung together covering several points.	None. The respondent usually answers the last question or the one most convenient for him/her to answer.	Always inappropriate.
Lubricators e.g. 'Ye-es', 'Go on', 'mmm', 'Ah ha'.	Indicating to subordinates that you are listening and want them to continue.	With over-talkative subordinates. Over-used they become intrusive and inhibiting.

Table 6.2   (Contd)

Component	Appropriate use	Inappropriate use
Inhibitors e.g. 'Oh', 'I see', 'Yeah, but. . . .'	Signalling that enough has been said. Tone of voice may indicate surprise, indignation or non-acceptance of views expressed by the other.	With reticent subordinates. For frank and open discussion. Where frustration or emotion is being expressed.
Bridges e.g. 'I think that's all we need to say on that topic, now let's turn to . . .'	Providing a smooth link between one topic and another and indicating clearly what the next one is.	When the previous topic has not been adequately dealt with from the subordinate's point of view.
Restatements e.g. 'What you seem to be telling me is that . . .'	To confirm or crystallize ideas.	When used disparagingly, or reproachfully, sarcastically or cynically.
Summaries e.g. 'What we seem to have discussed and decided so far is that . . .'	Drawing together the main points of a discussion and avoiding discrepancies. It can also help in gaining commitment to action.	If used prematurely.

(b) Components for giving information

Component	Appropriate use	Inappropriate use
Factual statements e.g. 'I shall be in conference all morning.' 'The next train to London is at 4.30.'	When they help the subordinate to solve a problem, make a decision, etc.	When they are irrelevant to the problem or decision, often the result of an inaccurate evaluation of the subordinate's situation.
Self-disclosure e.g. 'I always feel anxious before giving a presentation.' 'I had a similar problem back in 19XX.'	Establishing increased rapport, decreasing subordinate's self-consciousness or feelings that he/she has a unique problem.	When disclosure deflects discussion away from subordinate's problem, particularly if leading to premature advice, or if it dumps additional problems on the subordinate.

Table 6.2 (*Contd*)

Component	Appropriate use	Inappropriate use
Evaluative statements e.g. 'Accountants are typically narrow-minded; they don't see the broad picture.' 'It is better to be honest with a customer even at the risk of losing a sale.' (n.b. Shades into praise/criticism if about subordinate.)	Where it would be helpful for the subordinate to know the manager's feelings on a particular subject	Can antagonize, alienate or lead to lip-service if subordinate has different values.
Feedback e.g. 'Your action nearly caused a strike.' 'Your manner is upsetting me.' (n.b. Shades into praise/ criticism when evaluative.)	When it provides subordinate with important information which will allow him or her to respond to a situation more adaptively in future.	When punitive (seen as criticism), smug, or unnecessary (negative information already known).

(c) Components for influencing behaviour

Component	Appropriate use	Inappropriate use
Orders e.g. 'Do it now.' 'This is the way it will be done.'	With subordinates who need or prefer clear, precise instructions. Where compliance is vital due to special circumstances (e.g. time constrains, emergencies, etc.)	Where the benefits do not justify any resentment or stifling of ideas which may result.
Requests e.g. 'I have a problem . . .' 'Could you next time then please . . .'	With subordinates who are more motivated by being asked or may contribute useful ideas to the problem.	With subordinates who need or prefer clear, precise instructions.
Advice/suggestions e.g. 'You could improve on that by . . .' 'The disadvantage of doing that is . . . but this way . . .'	With subordinates who prefer guidance and may be influenced in the desired direction by the 'logic of the situation' (e.g. those lacking experience).	Where compliance is essential and advice may be ignored.
Promises e.g. 'then I'll give you the opportunity to tackle bigger projects'.	Where the task may lack intrinsic reward and extrinsic reward must be introduced for motivational purposes.	Where the promises cannot be fulfilled. When the subordinates will perform the task effectively anyway.

Table 6.2   (Contd)

Component	Appropriate use	Inappropriate use
Threats/warnings e.g. 'I will make you regret it'. 'and I shall begin disciplinary proceedings'.	Where compliance is essential and cannot otherwise be achieved (e.g. advice ignored, no available rewards, etc.). Where foreknowledge of potential adverse consequences would be useful to the subordinate.	When more positive methods are available. Where threats cannot be fulfilled. When the subordinate would perform adequately anyway.
Explanations e.g. 'because . . .' 'The reason is that . . .'	With those subordinates who are more motivated by understanding the reasons for doing something.	When the explanation will be rejected, leading to unproductive argument.
Praise e.g. 'I think that was well done because . . .'	To provide immediate feedback about the subordinate's standard of performance in a specific area and appreciation of it.	If too general, imprecise or late. When used in a patronising way without conviction.
Criticism e.g. 'Where you went wrong was . . . but this could be overcome by . . .'	To provide feedback on substandard performance in a particular area with emphasis on how to do it better next time.	When used negatively without emphasis on how to do it better. When it is likely to impair performance further due to resentment aroused.
Leading e.g. 'Surely you must agree that . . .' 'Don't you think that . . .' 'You *do* see why . . .'	To gain compliance or acceptance by signalling the expected answer. Can be used to emphasize	For encouraging reticent subordinates to express their views, feelings, etc. For gaining commitment

(d) Components for handling emotion to enable the interaction to proceed on a rational basis

Component	Appropriate use	Inappropriate use
Apologies e.g. 'First of all I must apologise for . . .'	When used confidently and constructively to eliminate a source of grievance which might inhibit rational discussion.	If too abject, off-hand, or patronising.

Table 6.2   (Contd)

Component	Appropriate use	Inappropriate use
Reflectives e.g. 'You seem to be upset about . . .' 'You feel it would be unfair to . . .' (i.e. reflecting back the *emotional* content of what is expressed).	To indicate, without evaluation, a concerned awareness of the subordinate's emotions or frustrations and to provide an opportunity to discharge these by letting the subordinate work through the problem(s).	If used evaluatively, reproachfully or disparagingly. Where the manager cannot handle criticism or abuse. In situations of severe time constraint. For checking particular points of information or fact.

Source: Wright and Taylor 1994.

Primary components

These are the questions, statements and non-verbal cues which managers use when interacting with subordinates and others at work. They can be used for four main purposes, gathering information, giving information, influencing behaviour, and handling emotions. Such primary components are regarded as the basic building blocks which go to make up the manager's contribution to the interactions as a whole. In Table 6.2 the verbal components of manager–subordinate interactions identified by Wright and Taylor are listed, together with an indication of the situations in which their use would be appropriate or inappropriate.

Structural factors

This refers to the way in which the primary components are sequenced, or in longer interactions to the way in which the interaction as a whole or topics covered within it are introduced, sequenced, resolved, linked together, and so on. Under this heading, Wright and Taylor (1994) also identify what they call 'gambits'. These are recurring patterns of components, many of which are well known in the interpersonal skills literature, which are intended to achieve a particular purpose within an interaction. Some examples are given in Table 6.3.

The overall approach

Two aspects of the manager's overall approach to the interaction are considered. One is the extent to which the manager is willing to allow the subordinate to influence the content of the interaction. Six different approaches, allowing the subordinate differing degrees of influence on the content of interaction are identified and their potential advantages and disadvantages described (see Table 6.4). The other is the extent to which the manager wishes

Table 6.3 Gambits used in manager–subordinate interactions

Structuring method	Description	Appropriate use	Inappropriate use
Trap setting	Consists of a series of leading questions, which aim to produce compliant responses from the subordinate, until the manager is ready to spring the trap with a leading criticism such as 'so you admit you were wrong then'.	To get the subordinate to provide, without realizing it, information which will prove he/she is at fault in some way.	Rarely successful in the long term. Having fallen into the trap the subordinate is likely to be resentful and defensive. His/her self-esteem may be eroded by the tactic.
Praise before blame	The manager praises the subordinate for his/her achievements, and then criticizes him/her for areas of performance which have been poor.	If done skilfully with enough weight given to the praise in relation to the blame, the subordinate may be more willing to accept criticism because his/her good points have also been recognized.	When the praise is brief and general, while the criticism is lengthy and specific.
Blame before praise	The manager points out the subordinate's deficiencies, and then, having gained his/her agreement to an improvement plan, uses praise to restore confidence and commitment.	A high-risk strategy. May be appropriate in disciplinary situations when there is a valid need to bring home to the subordinate the importance of improving his/her performance, but do not want the subordinate to feel completely demotivated.	Usually inappropriate. The praise at the end may give the subordinate the impression that his/her poor performance is not a serious problem after all. Also the subordinate may be so demoralized that he/she does not respond positively to the praise.
The funnel technique	Begins with an open question, followed by a narrowing series of probes or other more precise questions. Ends with a closed question or summary.	To gather information, define problems, and identify solutions.	When the manager already has sufficient background information to ask a precise question.

Table 6.3 (Contd.)

Structuring method	Description	Appropriate use	Inappropriate use
The inverted funnel	Begins with a narrow question, and moves progressively to more open ones.	To establish which area is worth probing further, or whether an area is worth probing at all.	When the manager has a clear idea of which areas he/she wants to probe.
The tunnel sequence	Consists of a series of questions of the same degree of openness. For example, a series of closed questions, or a series of narrow probes.	To enable the manager to elicit a lot of specific information in a short time. To pin the subordinate down to specific factual information when he/she is attempting to evade an issue by talking generalities.	The unvarying question style may not give the subordinate the opportunity to elaborate on points, which might result in important contextual information being lost.
Hammering the point home	Consists of a series of orders, requests, explanations, pieces of advice, interspersed with leading questions.	To ensure that a clear-cut conclusion is reached and understood by the subordinate, by restating the same conclusion several times in different ways.	If the manager continues once the subordinate has understood, the subordinate is likely to become irritated and resentful.

Source: Wright and Taylor 1994

to conduct the interaction in a warm friendly manner or one which is cold and businesslike, emphasizing differences in status. It is at this third level of analysis that Wright and Taylor's model most resembles traditional leadership theory. However, an important difference is that, as shown Table 6.4, they identify the specific behaviours and structural devices associated with each approach.

In summary, Wright and Taylor (1994) regard the interpersonally skilled leader as one who:

- has a wide variety of verbal components (question and statement types) at his or her disposal and is able to select the one most appropriate for the situation and particular purpose at hand, and to perform it well, with the appropriate non-verbal cues;
- can structure interactions effectively by organizing these questions and statements into purposeful sequences which steer the interaction towards its objective(s);
- can develop an approach for the interaction, which is appropriate to the objectives in question and the probable reactions of the subordinate.

Table 6.4   Approaches to manager–subordinate interactions

Approach	Description	Potential advantages	Potential disadvantages	Typical components
Tell	The manager tells the subordinate the decision, without asking his or her opinions or giving any specific inducements to accept it.	Saves time, particularly in emergencies. May be useful as a last resort, when other methods fail.	Useful information may be ignored. Subordinates may resent the approach and be reluctant to comply.	Orders, requests, suggestions, advice.
Tell and sell	The manager tells the subordinate the decision, pointing out the advantages of compliance and/or disadvantages of non-compliance.	Can be brief and to the point, getting the message over in a clear, precise and unequivocal manner.	Inhibition of independent judgement, defensiveness, overt conflict or passive acceptance without motivation to change.	Orders, explanations, requests, praise, threats, promises, leading, evaluative statements, inhibitors, criticism, summaries.
Tell and listen	The manager tells the subordinate the decision then allows expression of his or her thoughts or feelings about it.	Decreased defensiveness, more favourable attitude towards the manager. Less resistance to change may result.	Can develop into cosy chat with no clear-cut conclusions. Overt conflict or passive acceptance may still occur.	Orders, requests, evaluative statements, praise, criticism, *then* open, comparisons, hypotheticals, lubricators.
Ask and tell	The manager asks the subordinate for his or her views on a problem before telling him or her the decision.	Solution is less likely to be irrelevant. The subordinate may be more motivated for having been consulted.	Subordinate may still feel his or her solution to be better and resent being told what to do.	Open, probes, comparisons, hypotheticals, lubricators, closed, restatements, summary, *then* orders, requests, leading, threats, promises, evaluative statements.

Table 6.4   *(Contd)*

Approach	Description	Potential advantages	Potential disadvantages	Typical components
Problem solving	The manager and subordinate analyse a problem together and attempt to find a mutually acceptable solution.	Generation of new ideas, development of clear-cut solutions, subordinate highly motivated.	ordinate may lack ideas, produce impractical or organization-ally unaccept-able solutions, or be unwilling to participate.	Open, probes, comparisons, hypotheticals, lubricators, bridges, restatements, summaries, praise, advice, explanations, reflectives, factual statements
Ask and listen	The manager asks the subordinate to talk about some problem area and listens attentively.	Subordinate may feel much better for having discussed the problem. Useful information may be gained.	The basic problem may remain unresolved.	Open, comparisons, hypotheticals, lubricators, reflectives, self-disclosure

Source: Wright and Taylor 1994

Wright and Taylor's interpersonal skills model has two main advantages. First, it provides a vehicle for the development of core interpersonal skills which can be used in a wide variety of different managerial situations. Second, it provides an integrated framework for the development of such skills which allows feedback to be given at three different levels of analysis. Descriptions of the appropriate behaviour at the approach or style level alone, which is what behavioural theories of leadership usually provide, is of limited value as it does not tell the trainee how to put the approach into practice. Conversely, descriptions of the appropriate behaviour at the component or structural level alone, as a set of unrelated factors, can be confusing. However, the analytical framework developed by Wright and Taylor allows the approaches to be used as higher level unifying concepts, within which the verbal and non-verbal components can be organized. This makes them easier to understand and remember, without losing sight of the precise behaviours which need to be changed in order to produce an improvement in leadership performance. An example of advice given to an interpersonal skills trainee, incorporating both the component and approach levels of analysis, might be: 'Next time you have to carry out an interview of this type, it would be worth trying a problem-solving approach with a looser structure and more open and probing questions, rather than a tightly structured tell and sell with a great many closed and leading questions.'

It will be apparent, however, that Wright and Taylor's interpersonal skills model of leadership is extremely complex. They argue that this is less of a drawback than might appear at first sight, because they see their model primarily as a framework for interpersonal skills development which will enable the manager, preferably with the help of a skilled tutor, to identify the specific behavioural skills which he or she most needs to practice next. Thus the manager does not need to learn and remember the whole model in detail. It is more important that he or she is able to master those aspects in which an improvement in skill would have greatest impact on his or her managerial performance.

Nevertheless, the complexity of the model makes it impossible to subject the model as a whole to a rigorous scientific test. Some support for individual elements of the model can be found in interviewing skills research. In a study of employment screening interviews, for example, Tengler and Jablin (1983) found that open questions gave rise to significantly longer responses than closed questions. In another study, Folger (1980) found that closed questions were seen as more dominant than open questions. However, as Wright (1993) points out, relatively little research has been carried out into the specific verbal behaviours associated with successful interviewing.

Other studies have attempted to test the validity of certain aspects of the interpersonal skills approach to leadership. Alban Metcalfe (1982, 1984) analysed the verbal content of successful, moderately successful and unsuccessful role played performance appraisal interviews. The appraisers' verbal behaviour was classified in terms of 22 behaviour analysis categories based on the system developed by Rackham and Morgan (1977). The success of the interviews was assessed in terms of the extent to which the appraisees stated at the end of the interviews that they really wanted to improve their behaviour and that the interview would help them to do a better job. Alban Metcalfe found that in successful interviews there was significantly more use of positive evaluation, being supportive, testing understanding, summarizing, checking out and inviting participation, but significantly less use of giving information, negative evaluation, disagreeing, attacking and shutting out.

Johnston (1990) carried out observational studies of the relationship between specific leader behaviours and the effective leadership of problem-solving groups. Two were laboratory studies using post-graduate management students as subjects and one was a study of real life problem-solving groups in a mail order organization. There were three groups in two of the studies and five in the third, but in the latter case only three groups were selected for detailed study. In each case, the solutions produced by the groups were assessed by independent judges and on the basis of their ratings the most successful, moderately successful and least successful groups were identified. Behaviour of leaders and group members were classified in terms of two levels of analysis.

Behaviours were first classified in terms of a four-fold classification system consisting of inviting participation, supportiveness, goal setting and problem solving. The leaders' problem-solving utterances were then further classified in terms of eighteen sub-categories, again based on previous work in the field of behaviour analysis.

Johnston does not quote statistical significances in relation to his data. Nevertheless, inspection of his data shows that in all three studies the leaders of the most successful groups differed from the moderately successful and least successful groups in the following respects. The most successful leaders spoke less in relation to other group members than the moderately and least successful leaders. The successful leaders' utterances were also more balanced with respect to the four main categories of behaviour. All leaders had a higher proportion of utterances in the problem-solving category than in the other three, which is not surprising in view of the fact that they were leading problem-solving groups. Nevertheless, the most successful leaders had fewer utterances in the problem-solving category than the other leaders and more than them in each of the other three categories. With respect to the sub-categories, the most successful leaders had a greater proportion of utterances in the seeking proposals, making procedural statements, summarizing, testing understanding and clarifying categories and fewer utterances in the making suggestions, making statements about content, ignoring suggestions and disagreeing without giving reasons categories than did the moderately and least successful leaders. Overall, Johnston's results leave a strong impression that successful leaders gave greater emphasis to managing the group's problem solving as opposed to making their own contribution to the solution than did less successful leaders.

Like Alban Metcalfe, Callaghan analysed the verbal content of successful, moderately successful and unsuccessful role-played appraisal interviews (Callaghan 1991; Callaghan and Wright 1994). The success of the interview was assessed by means of an eight-item questionnaire completed by the interviewees immediately after the interview. The interviewer's and interviewee's verbal behaviour was classified in terms of six functions: rewarding, deterring, guiding, enquiring, attending and informing. This relatively small number of categories was used in order to permit the data to be analysed by means of sequential analysis.

In a static analysis of the data it was found that all six leader behaviours differed significantly between successful, moderately successful and unsuccessful interviews. In the successful interviews, interviewers enquired and attended more, but rewarded, deterred, guided and informed less.

In a sequential analysis of the data it was found that the most likely response to interviewer enquiring was, as might be expected, interviewee informing. However, in the moderately successful and unsuccessful interviews, interviewee rewarding was also a probable response, suggesting that in these interviews questions were often used to elicit agreement as well as information. Similarly, the most probable response to interviewer attending was interviewee informing in the successful interviews, whereas it was interviewer informing in the moderately successful and unsuccessful interviews. This suggests that the successful interviewers may have been using attending behaviour to encourage the interviewee to continue talking, whereas the unsuccessful interviewers were using it to take control of the speaking turn. Finally, interviewer rewarding was the most probable behaviour to follow interviewer deterring in the least successful interviews. This may indicate that these were evaluative interviews in which rewards such as praise were used in conjunction with criticism or negative feedback, which could go some way towards explaining why these interviews were less successful despite the greater use of rewarding behaviour by the interviewers.

Finally, Baverstock (1993, 1994) carried out an analysis of verbal behaviour associated with the successful handling of emotional reactions in role-played interviews using Stiles's (1992) eight-fold classification system. She found that the most successful interviewers, as assessed by the interviewees, employed significantly more advisement behaviours, but only a moderate level of reflectives. As might be expected, the least successful interviewers used the lowest number of reflectives, but it was the moderately successful interviewers who made greatest use of reflectives. This is contrary to the conventional wisdom on counselling, based on the work of Rogers (1951), and suggests that the types of behaviour associated with successful handling of adverse emotional reactions in an organizational environment may differ significantly from those required in the therapist–client relationship. Further research into the social skills of organizational and political leadership has been carried out in Spain by Gil and Garcia Saiz (Garcia Sais and Gil, 1993a, 1993b; Gil and Garcia Saiz, 1993). For example, Gil, Rodriguez Mazo and Garcia Saiz (1995) recently carried out an experimental study of the effectiveness of social skills training for managers. Eight trained judges assessed the performance of nine course members in role played interviews carried out before and after an 80-hours training course. Comparison of the two interviews revealed significant improvments in a variety of verbal, paralinguistic and nonverbal communication behaviours relating to self presentation, giving instructions, appraisal, motivating the interviewee and negotiation.

It will be apparent that the research so far carried out into the interpersonal skills of leadership has largely been conducted at what Yukl (1981) calls an intermediate level of abstraction. That is, it is concerned with more specific forms of behaviour than leadership styles, but for the most part does not extend to the more detailed elements of behaviour, such as questions and statement types. Nevertheless, some common themes are beginning to emerge from this research. In particular, three of the four studies discussed demonstrate the importance of gathering information, listening to other people's responses and avoiding such behaviours as negative evaluation, disagreeing, criticizing and ignoring other people's contributions.

On the other hand, there are inconsistencies between studies. For example, Baverstock found that successful interviewers used a greater amount of advising, whereas the other studies found such behaviours as giving information, making suggestions and guiding were employed more by less successful interviewers. Similarly, Alban Metcalfe found that there was significantly more positive evaluation in successful interviewers whereas Callaghan found that rewarding behaviours were used less in more successful interviews. In some cases, such differences may arise because the interactions were set in different contexts. For example, Baverstock's subjects, unlike those in the other studies, were deliberately primed to be angry, depressed or anxious concerning some work problem. Thus they may have been more inclined to assess favourably a manager who was willing to suggest potential solutions to their difficulties. In other cases, differences between studies may arise because of differences in the skill with which particular behaviours are used. The conflicting results found by Alban Metcalfe and Callaghan led me to review my own experience of the use of praise in interpersonal skills training in an attempt to remember all the different ways in which I had seen praise fail to achieve its intended objectives. I produced the following list (Wright 1993):

1 It was expressed badly. The praise was vague and general, instead of precisely defining what the person had done well.
2 It was closely associated with blame or criticism. If a manager continually praised a subordinate then hit him or her over the head with a rolled-up newspaper, the subordinate would be very likely to begin to duck on hearing praise. If the manager continually praises a subordinate and immediately follows it with blame, much the same effect is likely to occur.
3 The manager realizes that he or she has alienated a subordinate and unsuccessfully attempts to recoup the situation by the lavish use of praise.
4 The manager employs inappropriate non-verbal cues, either using those associated with deception or overdoing those associate with sincerity, which can have the same effect.
5 Despite the lavish use of praise, the subordinate is alienated by a single unfortunate comment on the part of the manager.
6 The subordinate finds praise embarrassing and the more he or she is praised the less he or she likes it.

In other words, using praise effectively is a skill and doing it badly is likely to have quite different effects from doing it well.

However, this draws attention to another limitation of the research so far carried out into the interpersonal skills of leadership. Simply counting the amount of praise or any other specific behaviour in an interaction and relating this to the interviewee's subsequent behaviour and attitudes does not really get to the heart of what is meant by interacting skilfully with other people. Doing something skilfully involves selecting the appropriate behaviour for the circumstances and performing it well. Studies such as Callaghan's which examine sequences of manager and subordinate behaviours within an interaction are very rare and none of the studies described above attempts to assess how well as opposed to how often the managers perform different specific behaviours. This is not surprising. Developing measures of specific leadership behaviours capable of reliably reflecting the precise nuances involved in a well-phrased question or sincerely expressed praise would be an extremely daunting task. While the studies described above are beginning to build up a body of research evidence concerning interpersonal skills and, perhaps equally important at this stage, a body of research methodology for the study of interpersonal skills which can be used by future researchers (Callaghan and Wright 1992), it seems likely that much of the advice given by interpersonal skills trainers will for the foreseeable future be based more on their professional experience than rigorous research evidence.

Finally, it should be noted that all the research described in this and the preceding section has been carried out either in the USA or the UK. The extent to which it applies in other countries or other cultures is therefore unknown. There is strong evidence that many aspects of non-verbal behaviour vary between cultures (Wolfgang 1979). There is also evidence, although mainly anecdotal, which suggests that the effects of different types of verbal behaviour may vary between cultures (Wright 1994). In one of the few systematic, data-based studies carried out in this area, Wilson *et al.* (under review) found significant differences between the verbal behaviour of British and Philippine managers in appraisal interviews. British managers both rewarded and deterred more than Philippine managers, but Philippine managers asked more closed questions. The Philippine subordinates on the other hand deterred and enquired significantly less than their British counterparts. Such differences in behaviour are largely consistent with previous research into cultural differences between the two countries, such as that of Guthrie (1966), Szanton (1966) and Hofstede (1991). Ivey and Galvin (1984) state that work with different populations suggests that the microskills model of interpersonal skills training works well across cultures, but the actual skills and skill sequences may change in different cultures. The anecdotal evidence quoted by Wright (1994) and the empirical study carried out by Wilson *et al.* (under review) strongly suggest that the advice given by interpersonal and leadership skills trainers concerning the types of verbal behaviour required to interact effectively with other people may need to be different in different cultures.

THE LEADER–MEMBER EXCHANGE (VERTICAL DYAD LINKAGE) MODEL OF LEADERSHIP

The Leader–Member Exchange (LMX) Model of leadership was developed by Graen and his associates (see, for example, Graen and Cashman 1975 and Dansereau *et al.* 1975). It was initially called the Vertical Dyad Linkage Model, but in recent writings the term Leader–Member Exchange Model is more commonly used.

As we saw in Chapter 5, early behavioural theories of leadership assumed that members of a group would be sufficiently homogeneous for a leader to adopt the same leadership style with all its members. The same assumption can also be found in certain early situational style theories, such as Fiedler's. In later theories, such as Path–Goal and Vroom and Yetton's Normative Model, this assumption is often discarded in favour of the idea that leaders could and should behave differently towards different subordinates. However, the LMX Model was the first major leadership theory to give a central role to the different types of relationships which can develop between leaders and individual group members.

The central concern in the LMX Model is the quality of the relationship between leaders and subordinates. It is suggested that, on unstructured tasks, leaders may offer certain subordinates increased autonomy, influence on decision-making, open and honest communication, support for their actions, and confidence in and consideration for them. These subordinates may then reciprocate by expending more time and energy on their work and assuming greater responsibility and commitment to the success of the entire unit or organization. If this happens, such subordinates become members of an 'in-group' or 'cadre'. Over time, the in-group members become trusted assistants and the leader may become more dependent on them, not only to ensure adequate functioning of the group, but also to deal with problems which may arise within the unit. Whether such a relationship is offered to a subordinate will depend on a variety of factors, such as the leader's judgement of the subordinate's dependability, 'readiness' to take on more responsibility, compatibility with the leader in terms of technical competence and interpersonal skills and so on.

Subordinates who are not offered such a relationship or respond inappropriately when an offer is made become members of an 'out-group'. As such, they have a more contractual relationship with the leader. In effect, they are 'hired hands', who agree to fulfil the requirements of the job and accept the legitimate authority of their specified superiors in exchange for wages, continued employment and other benefits.

In some research on LMX theory, this categorization of leader–member relations has been extended to include a middle group of subordinates which falls between the in-group and the out-group. Examples include Graen and Cashman (1975), Liden and Graen (1980) and Vecchio and Godbel (1984). Graen and Scandura (1987) take this idea further and suggest that relationships between superior and subordinate can range from 'mentor–protégé' at the highest level to 'overseer–peon' at the lowest, with many gradations between these two extremes.

The research evidence with respect to the LMX model has generally been supportive. In a study of 60 managers in a housing division within a large public university after a major reorganization, Dansereau et al. (1975) obtained subordinates' perceptions of the extent to which their superiors were willing to allow them to influence their work role. On the basis of these data, the subordinates were divided into two nearly equal groups, those designated 'in' with their superior who perceived that they had the opportunity to develop their role and those designated 'out' with their superior who reported less of a chance to develop their role. It was found that only 15 per cent of units showed all members as either 'in' or 'out' with the superior, while the remaining 85 per cent of the units showed a mixture of 'in' and 'out' members. Furthermore, in-group members reported receiving greater attention, support and responsiveness to their job needs from their managers and less difficulty in dealing with them than members of the out-group. They also reported spending more time and energy in communicating and administering activities than out-group members. In subsequent research, it has been found that subordinates with a higher quality relationship with their superiors show greater involvement with the more responsible administrative activities and lower involvement in the less responsible routine activities, have higher career prospects and lower labour turnover, communicate much more frequently with their managers about administrative and technical matters, show greater agreement with their superior concerning aspects of the job situation (e.g. severity of job problems facing the subordinate) and produce greater resources for their own subordinates (see Graen and Scandura 1987; Graen 1990).

Initially, the LMX model was simply a descriptive theory. It described different types of relationship between superiors and subordinates, but did not give any explicit advice concerning how such relationships could be changed. This question has been taken up in more recent research. In a field experiment carried out by Graen *et al.* (1982), managers of information processing technicians in a large public service organization were given training based on the LMX model designed to help them to develop higher quality relationships with their subordinates. In addition to learning about the LMX model and its uses, the managers were given training in how to conduct one-to-one conversations with their unit members. The training sessions, which included role-played practice, covered such things as the general structure of the conversations, the use of specific questions and techniques in order to stimulate discussion of subordinates' gripes, concerns and job expectations, active listening skills, and sharing the managers' own job expectations with subordinates.

Measures taken before and after the training showed significant improvements for the leadership trained group as compared with the control group in a variety of areas, including productivity, leader–member relations, leader support, the motivating potential of the job, and members' loyalty and job satisfaction. The trained group and their subordinates improved their productivity (measured by number of completed cases per hour) by an average of over 16 per cent, with no significant effects on quality of output, resulting in a projected annual costs savings of over $5 million systemwide.

An important additional finding was that employee growth need strength (GNS), measured by Hackman and Oldham's (1975) questionnaire, moderated the effect of leadership training on productivity. High GNS subordinates showed a 52 per cent improvement in productivity, while medium and low GNS subordinates showed no gains. Similar results were obtained in a field experiment on a comparable sample carried out by Graen *et al.* (1986). In this study, the high GNS group showed an increase of 55 per cent in productivity (measured by weekly output records) over the control group, with a significant decrease in errors, while the medium and low GNS groups demonstrated no significant improvements.

Graen *et al.* (1986) suggest that these findings can be explained by the fact that the aim of the training was to encourage and enable leaders to offer greater vertical collaboration with each employee. This offer of collaboration can be seen as a form of challenge to the subordinate, which he or she may or may not choose to accept. High GNS subordinates, they argue, are more likely to accept such an opportunity, and experience high internal work motivation resulting in gains in productivity.

Another moderator variable which has been found to affect the effectiveness of training using the LMX model is the initial quality of the working relationship between superior and subordinate. Scandura and Graen (1984) found that following leadership training, productivity and job satisfaction rose more among those subordinates who initially had low quality leader–member relations than among those who had a high quality working relationship. This can be explained by the fact that subordinates with poor leader–member relations can be expected to benefit more from an improvement in the situation than those who already have good relations with their superior.

These more recent studies introduce a strong situational element into the LMX model. There had, in fact, been an implicit situational factor in the original Vertical Dyad Linkage model, in that it was said to apply only to unstructured tasks. However, this was merely stated to be the case rather than based on research as in the case of GNS. In effect, what the LMX model now states is that on unstructured tasks high GNS subordinates will respond more positively to attempts on the part of the manager to develop high quality leader–member relations, and the effects will be greater the worse the current working relationship with the subordinate. Furthermore, the training programme described by Graen *et al.* (1982) shows how a start can be made towards developing such a better quality working relationship. As they point out, such relationships develop over time, and only the first stage of this development was included in their experiment. Nevertheless, unlike most other leadership theorists, Graen and his associates have stipulated the precise behaviours which leaders need to perform in order to improve their leadership effectiveness and have shown how managers can be trained to perform such behaviours skilfully. Thus their work provides a useful link between traditional leadership theory and the operant conditioning and interpersonal skills approaches to leadership described earlier in this chapter.

Another recent development has been the extension of the VDL/LMX model to include horizontal relationships within teams as well as vertical dyadic relationships between leaders and followers. In their study of 31 professional work teams in a public sector organization, Uhl-Bien and Graen (1992) found that team member perceptions of the quality of working relationship within a team was significantly related to their own assessments of team effectiveness. However, such perceptions were not related to the project leaders' assessments of team effectiveness or to those of outside raters who were familiar with the work of the team members. Although in its early stages, this research provides another useful link with an important area of current interest, the study of team leadership and self-managing teams, to be discussed in the next chapter.

On the other hand, the LMX model says little about how to manage people who either work on structured tasks or have low growth need strength. In this case, the manager may have the more contractual relationship with the subordinate described earlier, but this is not explicitly stated, nor does the model say anything about how to manage such contractual relationships more effectively. It may also be the case that there are still other situational variables yet to be discovered which moderate the effectiveness of leadership training based on the LMX model. However, Graen and his associates seem to be attempting to build up the LMX model gradually over time, rather than produce a complete leadership theory at first attempt. Thus such questions may be taken up in future research.

ATTRIBUTION PROCESSES AND LEADERSHIP BEHAVIOUR

Green and Mitchell (1979) propose that an important influence on managers' behaviour towards their subordinates is the attributions which they make concerning the causes of subordinates' performance. Based on previous research, they argue that such attributions are central to the following leader behaviours:

Rewarding and punishing subordinates' performance

Regardless of ability, performance is evaluated most positively and consequently most rewarded when success is seen as being accompanied by effort. Similarly, when failure is seen as being due to lack of effort, poor performance is most severely punished. However, when there is an external cause for the performance, such as task difficulty or luck, good performance is not likely to result in rewards, while poor performance is likely to produce sympathy or support on the part of the leader.

Closeness of supervision

Supervising subordinates closely is likely to be self-perpetuating because the supervisors attribute satisfactory performance to their own presence rather than the subordinates' efforts.

Expectancies about subordinates' future performance

If the subordinates' performance is attributed to stable factors (such as ability or task difficulty), the leader is likely to expect a similar level of performance in future. If expectations are based on unstable causes, such as effort, expectations about future performance are less predictable.

Aspirations the manager might hold for the subordinate

If a subordinate's successes are seen as being caused by high ability and effort and his or her failures by external factors, such as a difficult task or bad luck, then there is a greater likelihood that the leader will provide the subordinate with more achievement-related activities. On the other hand, if successes are seen as being the result of external factors (e.g. easy task, office politics or luck), and failures as being due to lack of ability, then the leader is less likely to provide achievement opportunities or to assign difficult tasks to the subordinate concerned.

Green and Mitchell (1979) suggest that there are a variety of other factors which may influence attribution processes in manager–subordinate interactions. Among them are the following:

Distinctiveness, consistency and consensus

Poor performance on a particular task is likely to be attributed to external factors (such as the assignment being too difficult) under the following circumstances:

- High distinctiveness: the subordinate performs well on other types of task.
- Low consistency: the subordinate has done well on this type of assignment in the past.
- High consensus: everyone seems to perform this task poorly.

Conversely, if the subordinate performs poorly at other tasks, has performed poorly at this task before, and no one else seems to have trouble with the task, the poor performance is more likely to be attributed to internal causes (Mitchell and Wood 1980). According to Green and Mitchell (1979), leaders are more likely to depend upon consistency and distinctive information about a subordinate than on consensus information when assessing the subordinate's performance.

The leader as observer (actor/observer effect)

In general, people explain the behaviour of others in terms of internal causes, such as effort or ability, while attributing their own behaviour to situational causes. Thus, leaders are likely to blame subordinates for their failures, attributing poor performance to such factors as irresponsibility, whereas subordinates are likely to blame external factors, and resent what they feel to be the leader's unfair treatment of them.

Self-serving bias

In the case of successful outcomes, causal attributions concerning one's own behaviour tend to take a somewhat different form from that described above. While people tend to blame their failures on external factors (such as an impossible task, not enough help, or bad communication), they tend to attribute their successes to internal factors (such as hard work, perseverance, insight or creativity). Thus, leaders may be tempted to attribute their unit's successful ventures to their own efforts and its failures to external causes, perhaps their subordinates. They may also be reluctant to attribute subordinates' poor performance to external factors because this could reflect badly upon themselves, and prefer to attribute them to internal causes.

Consequences of the subordinate's behaviour

Leaders are more likely to attribute poor performance to internal factors, and to respond in a punitive manner, when a subordinate's action has major adverse repercussions as opposed to incurring minor difficulties.

According to Green and Mitchell (1979), such causal attributions may influence the leadership style which a manager adopts towards a subordinate. For example, if the performance of a subordinate is attributed to lack of understanding of the task, it seems likely that the manager will respond with structuring behaviour. Mitchell and Wood (1980) suggest that attributions made concerning the causes of poor performance may affect specific leadership behaviours. When an internal attribution is made, for example, the leader may be expected to attempt to change the subordinate's behaviour by such means as feedback, punishment or training. Conversely, when an external attribution is made, the leader might be expected to pay more attention to changing the situation or task, by such means as providing more help or better information. Mitchell and Wood (1980) carried out two studies of the effects of causal attributions on supervisors' responses to incidents of poor performance among nurses in a hospital setting. As predicted, they found that:

1 consensus, consistency and distinctiveness helped in determining attributions;
2 internal attributions led to punitive responses on the part of supervisors;
3 supervisors used more internal attributions and punitive responses when the consequences of poor performance were serious.

However, Green and Mitchell (1979) note that personal or organizational policies may limit the effects of attribution processes on leader behaviour. The leader may decide that it is too difficult to identify the true causes of a particular type of subordinate behaviour and therefore adopt a policy of applying the same punishment in all cases. For example, the leader may insist that all instances of lateness shall receive the same punishment, irrespective of claimed mitigating circumstances. Alternatively, organizational policy may dictate how instances of poor performance are handled and the leader may have little discretion in the way he or she responds (see section on substitutes for leadership, pp. 134–7).

Even when causal attributions have limited immediate effect, however, they may still have long-term effects on the leader's behaviour towards and relationships with subordinates. Unless false attributions are corrected, there is a strong possibility that self-fulfilling prophesies and vicious circles may develop. A subordinate who works hard and is falsely accused of slacking may decide that it is not worth trying in future and thus apparently confirms the false attribution. Similarly, a subordinate who unjustly gains a reputation for being a mediocre performer may be given routine tasks to do and as a result becomes bored and turns into a mediocre performer. In other words, false beliefs concerning the causes of behaviour could result in a subordinate becoming the type of out-group member described in VDL/LMX theory. Of course, the reverse may also happen. A subordinate who is praised when successful through luck may subsequently work harder in order to maintain his or her reputation as a good performer. Similarly, a subordinate who gains a reputation for being a good performer may be given more challenging work, which he or she finds motivating and performs well as a consequence. Equally, however, such inaccurate positive attributions could have adverse effects. The subordinate may become unjustifiably complacent or be allocated job assignments beyond his or her capabilities. It is important, therefore, that managers are aware of the biases which may distort their judgements concerning the causes of other people's behaviour and attempt as far as possible to compensate for their effect when assessing subordinates' performance.

While we have concentrated on manager–subordinate interactions in this section, it is worth nothing that false attributions concerning the causes of behaviour could also have detrimental effects on other relationships within organizations. For example, the late arrival of important supplies or information from a fellow manager could be attributed to internal factors (lack of co-operation) rather than external (pressure of work). Thus, it is important to bear in mind potential sources of bias whenever judgements about the reasons for people's behaviour are made.

SMITH AND PETERSON'S EVENT MANAGEMENT MODEL

According to Smith and Peterson (1988), organizational life does not present organization members with discrete problems, but with an unending flow of 'events', as the studies of Mintzberg, Stewart, Kotter and others show (see Chapter 2). They argue that every leader must struggle with the need to adapt his or her behaviour to forms which will be experienced by others in the manner intended. Smith and Peterson criticize situational style theories of leadership on the grounds that they pay insufficient attention to cognitive variables. They argue that the way leaders and followers respond to each other depends not solely on the objective characteristics of the situation, but also upon the way they interpret the situation. However, situational style theories envisage the relationship between variables as being static. That is, certain types of situational variables are seen as determining which leadership style will be the most effective. Smith and Peterson, on the other hand, see the contingencies which regulate relationships between leaders and followers as being mediated by perceptual processes. Thus the leader's environment is by no means a fixed and static entity. Leaders may construe it in a variety of ways, depending upon such things as the degree to which their attention is drawn to it, the reasons they invoke for what is happening, and their own particular motives at the time.

Similarly, the way in which followers respond to the leader's behaviour will depend on the way they construe the situation. Peterson (1979, 1985) showed that subordinate reactions to a particular leadership style varied sharply, depending upon whether they felt the style was required by the situation. For instance, school teachers reacted positively to being told what needed to be done, except when they judged that they already knew what was required.

Thus all events have multiple meanings and leaders must constantly choose from which of a series of possible sources they will derive their event meaning. Initially, these choices may be made consciously. Over time, however, they become substantially routinized to the point where some leaders expect that certain sources are the most potent and active in defining meaning, whereas others for the most part may be disregarded. The potent or active sources of event meaning direct the leader's attention towards or away from various aspects of the work situation, thereby affecting what is seen and the conscious construction of events.

Based on Hosking and Morley's (1988) model of leadership skills, Smith and Peterson (1988) take the view that leaders frequently have the requisite social skills to carry through the process of influence and negotiation. What they lack is the ability to 'find their way around', or develop the network of contacts which gives them the necessary know-how. Only when this is developed can they exercise their existing skills and knowledge. Smith and Peterson therefore see effective leadership training not as a matter of inculcating appropriate styles, but of training for choice. Leaders often need to learn, they state, how to choose which sources of information or demands upon them to attend to, and how to choose which specific behaviours stand the best chance of implementing their intentions. A first priority in leadership training might therefore be to increase trainees' awareness that even the decision to operate on the basis of choices which are largely programmed ones is itself an implicit act of choice. In many circumstances it may also be the right choice, but the purpose of training should be to subject this to systematic review.

Smith and Peterson (1988) do not, however, make specific suggestions concerning the way such training could be carried out. Effective training, they state, always arises out of some diagnosed need and the training methods adopted would need adaptation to the specific circumstances identified. Once such a focus is determined, a wide variety of established training procedures can then be useful in diagnosing culture, identifying choices and rehearsing alternative solutions. Among those mentioned are Stewart's (1982) exercises designed to help managers to identify who are the people they most need to influence and what choices are open to them in doing so, and Schein's (1987) process consultation.

In summary, Smith and Peterson's event management model serves the useful function of drawing attention to the importance of perception and judgement in leadership. In particular, it convincingly argues that objective descriptions of leadership situations are not sufficient to enable us to predict how people will respond to them, because such situations are subject to many different interpretations by those involved. However, the model does not itself give practising managers any specific advice on ways in which they can improve the effectiveness of the choices they make with respect to sources of information on which they rely or on the behaviours they should adopt in order to achieve their goals. Furthermore, my own experience of interpersonal skills training leads me to question whether all managers already have all the skills they need to interact effectively with other people within organizations. It is not really a question of making a choice between training in leadership behaviours or perception. Both have a useful role to play.

SUBSTITUTES FOR LEADERSHIP

Kerr and Jermier (1978) developed a leadership theory which, paradoxically, identifies factors which reduce the need for leadership within organizations or render it ineffective. They argue that for organization members to maximize organizational and personal outcomes, they must be able to obtain both (a) guidance on how to perform their tasks or roles and (b) good feelings stemming from recognition from other people or intrinsic job satisfaction. However, such guidance and good feelings need not necessarily be provided by the hierarchical leader; it is only necessary that somehow they be provided. Where other sources of guidance and good feelings are deficient, the opportunity for a formal leader to exert influence is great and formal leadership ought to be important. On the other hand, if other sources provide guidance and good feelings in abundance, the hierarchical leader will have little chance to exert downward influence and formal leadership will have little effect.

Kerr and Jermier (1978) distinguish between two sets of factors which may reduce the possibility and/or necessity of leadership within organizations, 'neutralizers' and 'substitutes'. Neutralizers are characteristics of the subordinate, the task or the organization which make it effectively impossible for relationship and/or task leadership to make a difference. Substitutes for leadership are characteristics of the subordinate, task or organization which render relationship and/or task leadership not only impossible but also unnecessary. Kerr and Jermier argue that this distinction is important because the substitutes for leadership provide a person or thing acting or used in place of the formal leader's negated influence, while the neutralizers do not, creating an 'influence vacuum' from which a variety of dysfunctions may emerge.

A list of potential neutralizers and substitutes for leadership is given in Table 6.5. Kerr and Jermier (1978) state that all fourteen characteristics have the capacity to counteract leader influence and can therefore be termed neutralizers. However, only some can act as substitutes for leadership. For example, subordinates' perceived 'ability, experience, training and knowledge' will tend to reduce the leader's influence, but whether they also act as substitutes for leadership may depend on how accurate these perceptions are. Subordinates with high ability and self-esteem may perform well without the need for supervisor influence. On the other hand, false perceptions of competence and unfounded self-esteem on the part of subordinates may simply have a neutralizing effect. 'Subordinate indifference towards organizational rewards' and 'organizational rewards which are not under the leader's control' are examples of characteristics which do not render formal leadership unnecessary, but merely create conditions in which effective leadership may be impossible. Kerr and Jermier (1978: 396) state: 'When no one knows where control over rewards lies, ... or when rewards are linked rigidly to seniority or to other factors beyond anyone's control, or when rewards are perceived to be unattractive altogether, the resulting influence vacuum would almost inevitably be dysfunctional.'

In summary, the authors state that few organizations would be expected to have leadership substitutes and neutralizers so strong as to overwhelm the leader totally or so weak as to require subordinates to rely entirely on the leader. In most organizations, it is likely that substitutes exist for some leader activities but not for others. Effective leadership, they conclude, might therefore be described as the ability to supply subordinates with needed guidance and good feelings which are not being supplied by other sources.

Research on substitutes for leadership has produced mixed results. In a field study of police officers, Kerr and Jermier (1978) showed that when powerful leader substitutes, such as 'intrinsically satisfying work' and 'task-provided performance feedback' exist, the leader's supportive behaviours fail to contribute significantly in predicting organizational commitment. In a second study of police officers conducted by Jermier and Berkes (1979), the results suggested that 'social organization' could act as a substitute for supportive leadership, 'work group established norms and role structures' could neutralize the need for coordination by the formal leader, and 'ability, experience and job knowledge' tended to substitute for instrumental leadership.

In a study of hospital workers, Howell and Dorfman (1981) studied the effects of seven potential substitutes for leadership on the relationship between supportive and instrumental leadership and organizational commitment and job satisfaction. Only one strong substitute was found, 'organizational formalization' substituting for the instrumental leadership of work assignment in relation to organizational commitment. In a follow-up study, Howell and Dorfman (1986) differentiated between professional and non-professional hospital

Table 6.5 Neutralizers and substitutes for leadership

Characteristic	Relationship-oriented, supportive, people-centred leadership: consideration, support, and interaction facilitation	Task-oriented, instrumental, job-centred leadership: initiating structure, goal emphasis, and work facilitation
of the subordinate		
Ability, experience, training, knowledge.		Neutralizer or substitute
Need for independence.	Neutralizer	Neutralizer
Professional orientation.	Neutralizer or substitute	Neutralizer or substitute
Indifference towards organizational rewards.	Neutralizer	Neutralizer
of the task		
Unambiguous and routine.		Neutralizer or substitute
Methodologically invariant.		Neutralizer
Provides its own feedback concerning accomplishment.		Neutralizer or substitute
Intrinsically satisfying.	Neutralizer or substitute	
of the organization		
Formalization (explicit plans, goals, and areas of responsibility).		Neutralizer
Inflexibility (rigid, unbending rules and procedures).		Neutralizer
Highly specified and active advisory and staff functions.		Neutralizer
Closely knit, cohesive work groups.	Neutralizer or substitute	Neutralizer or substitute
Organizational rewards not within the leader's control.	Neutralizer	Neutralizer
Spatial distance between superior and subordinates.	Neutralizer	Neutralizer

Based on: Kerr and Jermier 1978

workers. They found that 'intrinsically satisfying tasks' and 'importance placed on organizational rewards' were strong substitutes for leader's support among professional employees. However, contrary to predictions, 'task feedback' was not a strong substitute for supportive leadership among professionals and no strong substitutes for instrumental leadership were found for either the professional or the non-professional groups.

While the research described above has not produced the expected results in many cases, it does show that certain individual, task or organizational characteristics can sometimes neutralize or substitute for the effects of formal leadership. This has a number of implications for leadership theory and practice. As Kerr and Jermier (1978) point out, all leadership style theories have in common the assumption that, either generally or in any one situation, there exists a leadership style which will be effective. Substitutes for leadership theory, on the other hand, suggests that there are circumstances where effective leadership is impossible or irrelevant. This, Kerr and Jermier suggest, may help to explain why leadership theories are often only weakly supported or do not receive any support in research studies. The theories may be valid, but only when effective leadership is possible.

From the practical point of view, substitutes for leadership theory serve the useful function of drawing attention to the fact that leader behaviour is not the only influence on leader effectiveness. No matter how able they are, leaders' effectiveness can be undermined by organizational practices and conditions which prevent them from exerting influence over their subordinates. Thus improving leadership effectiveness may not merely be a matter of training leaders in order to increase their ability, which is the solution usually suggested by leadership theorists. It may also be a question of redesigning organizational practices to eliminate or at least reduce the effects of factors which neutralize the leaders's effectiveness. Conversely, substitutes for leadership theory suggests that it may be possible to reduce the amount of formal leadership which is required within organizations, without impairing organizational effectiveness, by enhancing the effects of characteristics which act as substitutes for leadership, providing this can be done in such a way that such characteristics do not instead act as neutralizers.

CONCLUSIONS

The six approaches to the study of leadership described in this chapter illustrate the wide variety of different factors which needs to be taken into account when attempting to explain leadership success and effectiveness. The style adopted by the leader in different situations may be important, but there are also the specific behaviours the leader employs, how skilfully these are performed, the nature of the relationship between the leader and his or her followers, the attributions which managers make concerning the causes of their subordinates' performance, how the leader perceives and construes events within the organizational environment, and whether this environment facilitates or hinders the leader's attempts to influence the behaviour of his or her followers. It would, of course, be unrealistic to expect leaders consciously to bear in mind all these factors while an interaction with followers is actually taking place. However, a common theme running through many of the approaches outlined in this chapter is skill – skill in performing specific behaviours and skill in accurately interpreting events. Such skills, once developed, become part of the leader's natural behavioural repertoire. Thus, like many other skills, they can be performed 'without thinking'. Sometimes, because the outcomes we are attempting to achieve are important, we may consciously attempt to act skilfully, but even then performing the skill does not call for the intense concentration required during the early stages of skill acquisition. This is not to say that, once developed, skills can safely be ignored. Skills may become 'rusty' through disuse or we may become complacent and fail to use them when they are required. There is also the challenge of continual improvement – making skills which are already at a high level even better. Nevertheless, the development of the types of skills associated with the leadership theories described in this chapter does offer the possibility of making use of the insights of leadership theories without the necessity of continually referring back to the theories themselves.

Two further approaches to the study of leadership behaviour remain to be considered. One is the study of the behavioural aspects of charismatic leadership. As the study of charismatic leadership has also been concerned with the personality of such leaders, examination of this topic will be delayed until Chapter 9. The other is the concept of self-management. In part, this represents a development of Kerr and Jermier's ideas on substitutes for leadership. If employees manage themselves, then, in theory at least, there should be less need for leadership. The issue of self-management is taken up in the next chapter.

EXERCISE 4: CRITICAL INCIDENT

Case

William Bean is Administration Manager at the Head Office of Solent Oil and Cake, a leading manufacturer of compound animal feeding stuffs and vegetable oils. He has just returned from two weeks' holiday. Before he went on holiday, he authorized the payment of a special bonus to six process workers who had carried out vital maintenance work the previous weekend. As soon as he returned from holiday, he received an irate phone call from the Personnel Manager complaining that one of his subordinates, Victor Ridsdale (the Office Manager), had irresponsibly and inexcusably exceeded his authority and stopped the bonus. As soon as she discovered what had happened the Personnel Manager had authorized the payment herself, but a threatened strike which would have closed down the whole factory was only narrowly avoided. Bill has sent for Victor, and he has just entered Bill's office.

VR *Hello Bill, You wanted to see me. How was the...*

WB (interrupting) Yes, what on earth were you doing stopping the special bonus last week? I've hardly been back an hour and my phone hasn't stop ringing. The Personnel Manager's complaining, the Production Manager's complaining, the Maintenance Manager's complaining. I simply cannot understand what you thought you were doing.

VR (with some heat) *Look, I'm fed up with this. It wasn't my fault. I was only trying to protect you and maybe save the company some money, and everyone seems to think I have committed a major crime. If other people had done their jobs properly, the problem would never have arisen in the first place, but I'm the only one who is being blamed.*

WB Wait a minute, why did you say that that you were trying to protect me?

VR *Well, there was an anomaly in the note you left authorizing the special bonus and I thought that if the wrong bonus was paid we would get the blame.*

WB I didn't see anything wrong with the note. What was the problem?

VR *What it said in words didn't match the computer code. The words said the workers were to be paid double time for the extra work, but the computer code only said time and a half. There was obviously a typographical error somewhere, but I wasn't sure where. So I decided that the best thing to do was to delay payment until you got back and could sort it out.*

WB But how did you get involved in the first place? Wages aren't your responsibility.

VR *The Wages Supervisor brought the note to me. She had noticed the anomaly and didn't know what to do about it, so she asked my advice. People seem to think I'm something like your deputy so they often come to me when you are away. I can't always help them but I do my best.*

WB So what did you do?

VR *I advised her not to pay it. The way I saw it, if we paid them double time when they were only due time and a half, we would never get the money back. However, the Wages Supervisor wasn't willing to take responsibility for stopping the payment, so I decided that the best thing to do was to delay payment until the whole matter could be sorted out. I didn't stop the payment. I simply wrote across the note 'Delay payment until Mr Bean returns', and signed it.*

WB Then what happened?

VR *As you have no doubt heard, the process workers were upset and there was nearly a walk-out.*

WB That could have been pretty serious for the company.

VR *Yes, but fortunately it didn't happen.*

WB Yes, but what would have been worse for the company, losing a small amount of money to the process workers or having a strike?

VR *The strike, obviously, but I didn't see what else I could do at the time.*

WB Didn't you think of checking with anyone?

VR *The Wages Supervisor said that she had tried to contact the Personnel Manager, but she was out for the day.*

WB Was there anyone else you could have consulted apart from the Personnel Manager?

VR *The Maintenance Manager, I suppose, or the head of the production department.*

WB OK, and if you had done that, you would have been seen as a smart young manager with his eye on the ball instead of someone who nearly caused a strike.

VR *OK, I take your point. I'll check out my facts before jumping in with both feet next time.*

WB Excellent. If you take that message on board, at least something good will have come out of this whole business. Is there anything else we need to talk about whilst we are on this subject?

VR *Well, if you could keep me informed of any special payments or anything unusual which is likely to come up when you are going away, that would be useful.*

WB Good point. If people are going to come to you with problems affecting the department when I am not here, you need to be better briefed. Perhaps it would be a good idea to have regular briefing meetings irrespective of whether I am planning on being away. After all, I could be ill or simply out of the office for any number of reasons. What do you think of that?

VR *That would be very useful. Yes, I'd welcome that.*

WB Good. I'll set that up. Now, about all these people who have been complaining. I think we need to let them know your side of things. I'm not saying they won't still be aggrieved, but I think we should be able to smooth things over a bit. How do you think we should . . .?

Exercise

Analyse the above manager–subordinate interaction in terms of the leadership concepts, theory and research discussed in this chapter. Material from other chapters may also be introduced where relevant.

A longer version of this exercise can be found in Wright and Taylor (1994).

Chapter 7

Self-management

INTRODUCTION

In recent years there has been a considerable growth of interest in and enthusiasm for the concept of enabling people to manage their own behaviour at work, thus reducing the need for formal leadership. This concept has been derived from a number of different theoretical sources and has been given a variety of different names, including self-management, self-managing teams and empowerment.

A major source for the development of ideas concerning self-management was work in the area of job design. The concept of increasing the amount of control which people have over their working lives, either individually or in groups, has been a common theme in job design theory, research and practice for many years (Bucklow 1966; Davis 1966). For example, Walker (1950) described a job enlargement programme which introduced greater interest, variety and responsibility into the workers' jobs. One of the tenets of Herzberg's (1968) theory of job enrichment was that workers should be given greater responsibility by such methods as removing controls, increasing accountability of individuals concerning their work, granting additional authority to an employee and so on. Similarly, in Hackman and Oldham's (1976) Job Characteristics Model, autonomy is one of five core job dimensions which are predicted to increase internal work motivation, job satisfaction and quality of work performance. In the Job Characteristics Model, autonomy is defined as the degree to which the job provides substantial freedom, independence, and discretion to the individual in scheduling the work and determining the procedures to be used in carrying it out.

In Britain and elsewhere in Europe, much of the early work on job design was carried out within the context of socio-technical systems theory. Put briefly, socio-technical systems theory is concerned with identifying the conditions which secure the best match between the social and technical systems within an organization (Trist 1977). It grew out of Trist and Bamforth's (1951) research on autonomous work groups in the British coalmining industry. They proposed allocating 'responsible autonomy' to primary work groups and ensuring that each of these groups has a satisfying sub-whole as its work task and scope for flexibility in work pace. It was also proposed that group members should be trained for more than one role so that interchangeability of tasks would be possible within work teams. Emery (1959) argued that a work group which has a degree of autonomy and a wide sharing of the skills needed for its task will be able to provide a degree of continuity in performance which is unlikely to be achieved under the control of a supervisor. Under these circumstances, he suggests, the first-level supervisor would be less concerned with wielding sanctions. Effective supervision would entail integrating the activities of different work groups and planning further ahead so that groups receive sufficient support and servicing to keep them functioning. Since Trist and Bamforth's development of the concept, autonomous work groups have been introduced into a large number of widely differing organizations, including an Indian textile mill (Rice 1958), an American coalmine (Trist *et al.* 1977), the Volvo car assembly plant at Kalmar (Gyllenhammer 1977) and a British confectionery factory (Wall *et al.* 1986).

Based in part on socio-technical systems theory, Hackman and Oldham (1980) extended their work on job design to encompass not only the design of jobs for individuals, but also the design of work for groups and of groups for work. In particular, they suggested that, under certain circumstances, self-managing teams could provide an alternative to individual job enrichment. They define self-managing work groups as 'intact (if small) social systems whose members have the authority to handle internal processes as they see fit in order to generate a specific group product, service, or decision' (Hackman and Oldham 1980: 164). They argue that designing enriched work for groups rather than individuals is feasible when employees have strong needs for both personal growth and significant social relationships, when the overall climate and organizational style is likely to be supportive of self-managing groups and when existing technological, personnel and control systems are hospitable to the formation of such groups.

It will be apparent even from this brief description of job design theory and practice that allowing employees greater autonomy has significant implications for the way people are managed and manage their own behaviour at work. A number of writers have explored these implications in more detail within the context of leadership theory.

INDIVIDUAL SELF-MANAGEMENT

Luthans and Davis (1979) proposed the concept of behavioural self-management, based on Bandura's (1977) social learning theory. They suggest that instead of simply responding to environmental events, managers can achieve greater self-control by becoming more aware of the behavioural contingencies which regulate their behaviour and exerting greater control over these contingencies. The methods most frequently used to increase individual self-control involve changing either the stimulus situation or the consequences of actions. Thus a manager who is continually interrupted by long telephone calls may change the stimulus situation by asking the switchboard to take all calls during a certain period of the day or simply placing a two-minute time limit on all calls. The manager then monitors his or her behaviour and provides reinforcing consequences if the amount of long telephone calls is significantly reduced. The reinforcement may be a covert reward, such as feeling pleased, or an overt reward, such as taking a ten-minute 'time out' to read a trade journal or taking a coffee break.

An expanded list of self-management procedures was developed by Manz and Sims (1980). They also based their approach on Bandura's social learning theory, but further suggested that such procedures could be regarded as substitutes for leadership. Manz and Sims' list of self-management procedures include the following:

Self-observation   Systematically gathering information about aspects of one's own behaviour which one wishes to change, thus establishing the basis for self-evaluation, which in turn provides information on which to base self-reinforcement.

Specifying goals   Setting oneself specific goals for one's work effort. According to Manz and Sims, setting specific goals not only results in improved performance and goal attainment, but their achievement also seems to possess strong reinforcing properties, subsequently leading to further goals in the pursuit of organizational objectives.

Cueing strategies   The gradual limiting of discriminative stimuli that precede maladaptive behaviour while simultaneously increasing exposure to stimuli evoking more desirable behaviour.

Incentive modification   Self-administered rewards and self-administered punishment. Manz and Sims (1989) later suggested that although self-administered punishment can be used as a self-management strategy, it is generally not very effective. For example, a mild degree of guilt can sometimes be useful, but when it becomes excessive or habitual it can undermine motivation and effort.

Rehearsal   The systematic practice of the desired performance, either overtly or in imagination.

The self-management procedures described so far are exclusively behavioural strategies. Manz and Sims (1989) later extended their work on self-management, or self-leadership as they came to call it, to include cognitive strategies. These are concerned with the ways in which people perceive and process information about work and how they can constructively manage patterns of thinking, which in turn influence behaviour. They argue that, while behavioural strategies are useful and important, thinking is the core of self-leadership.

Manz and Sims (1989) identify two closely connected cognitive-based self-leadership strategies. The first involves the use of natural rewards which derive from the task itself to generate constructive thinking and feeling about one's effort. One way of doing this is by actually building natural rewards into tasks. Enjoyable tasks, according to Manz and Sims (1989), engender feelings of competence, self-control and purpose. These in turn promote constructive and positive thoughts and feelings about work which motivate employees to higher performance. Actions which managers can take to increase the likelihood of their subordinates experiencing such thoughts and feelings include helping them to discover what gives them a feeling of purpose, providing them with the opportunity to take on worthwhile challenges and experience a sense of meaning in their jobs, and giving them the autonomy and guidance necessary to develop the confidence and master the skills necessary to perform the job well. The authors also suggest that the power of natural rewards can be tapped by managing the focus of one's thoughts. That is, one can focus on the naturally rewarding aspects of tasks while performing them, rather than focusing on the disliked aspects, which inevitably leads to negative feelings about the work.

The second cognitive-based self-leadership strategy identified by Manz and Sims (1989) is to establish constructive thought patterns. In order to succeed in this difficult process, they suggest, each person needs to analyse, challenge and manage his or her beliefs, imagined experiences and self-talk. Beliefs are particularly important in that they can become self-fulfilling prophesies. Positive expectations increase the probability of achieving something, whereas negative expectations often lead to failure. Mental images, such as visions of the likely outcomes to problems, can also influence subsequent actions and orientation towards work and life. For example, imagining what it would be like to fail could either deter someone from performing a particular activity at all, or so undermine self-confidence as to bring about the very failure which is being imagined. Conversely, however, positive mental imagery can be used to rehearse an activity or to develop self-confidence. Finally, people can change their internal dialogues. For example, instead of indulging in destructive self-criticism if a work assignment goes badly, one can take a more constructive, analytical approach, saying to oneself: 'What went wrong? I know I can do better than that. What can I do to improve my performance next time?'

Manz and Sims (1980, 1989) suggest a number of ways in which managers can encourage subordinates to engage in self-leadership. They can act as models for others to learn from, both by the way they behave and by exhibiting effective thought patterns. They can evoke self-leadership through the use of directed questions on such topics as how well subordinates think they are performing, what targets they feel they should aim for, how pleased they are with their performance, whether they have thought about trying different work methods which they might enjoy more, and so on. Such questions can be combined with constructive suggestions, instruction and guidance on the effective implementation of self-leadership behaviours. When subordinates exhibit desirable self-leadership behaviours, the manager should then provide social reinforcement in the form of verbal encouragement and other forms of support. Initially, the manager reinforces performance-related behaviours, but as time goes by the reinforcement shifts to the process of self-leadership itself. That is, the manager's primary function becomes one of encouraging, guiding and reinforcing processes such as self-imposed goal setting, self-reinforcement, employees' building natural rewards into tasks, and developing constructive thought patterns rather than that of directly providing instructions and reinforcing subordinate performance.

Finally, Manz and Sims (1980, 1989) identify a range of situational factors which are likely to influence the appropriateness of attempts to develop self-management techniques in subordinates. These include:

The nature of the task   For example, the amount of discretion it allows, the extent to which it is largely creative, analytical or intellectual in nature.

The availability of time   For example, in a crisis situation, the time may simply not be available for the development of self-leadership capabilities.

The importance of subordinate development   The extent to which the organization emphasizes short-term efficiency or the long-term development of subordinates.

The characteristics of the subordinates   For example, individual employees' eagerness, desire and capacity for self-leadership and the extent to which they share organizational goals.

SELF-MANAGING TEAMS

Manz and Sims (1984) further developed their ideas on self-management to include the concept of self-managing teams. They regard the self-managing team as a natural extension of their work on self-leadership and see it as a type of collective or group self-leadership (Manz and Sims 1993). According to Manz and Newstrom (1990), the central defining characteristic of a self-managing team is an organization's serious effort to place a high degree of both decision-making power and opportunities for self-control within a work group. This strategy is typically based on three beliefs:

1 That employees are capable of such autonomy and creative effort.
2 That they desire to assume such responsibilities.
3 That the organization will benefit from results such as improved productivity and reduced levels of conflict.

Based on job design and job enrichment research, Manz and Newstrom predict that self-managing teams will produce increased levels of motivation, job satisfaction and performance with accompanying decreases in employee absenteeism and intentions to resign.

Inevitably, the nature of self-managing teams varies considerably between organizations. Nevertheless, certain typical characteristics can be identified (Manz and Newstrom 1990; Manz and Sims 1993). They usually complete a whole or distinct part of a product or service, and thus possess a relatively whole task function with which they can identify. They are typically provided with a substantial degree of decision-making autonomy and control over their work behaviour on a day-to-day basis. Examples include assigning jobs to team members, training team members, deciding on work methods, setting team goals, selecting team members, recording quality, adjusting production schedules, and so on. Inevitably, introducing self-managing teams changes the authority structure within the larger organization. Teams commonly select their own internal team leaders, replacing the former supervisor role. The next highest level of management, what used to be foremen, then become what are typically referred to as team co-ordinators or team facilitators. In one plant, described by Manz and Sims (1984), such team co-ordinators were jointly selected by management and the existing co-ordinator team and often the people chosen were existing internal team leaders. Each team was assigned a co-ordinator and a co-ordinator might have responsibility for one to three teams.

The introduction of self-managing teams brings about marked changes in the role of the external leader of such teams. Rather than giving instructions, commands and reprimands and assigning tasks and goals, as did the traditional foreman or supervisor, the role of the team co-ordinator or team facilitor, as the name suggests, is to help the team to make its own decisions and control its own behaviour. In other words, according to Manz and Sims (1993: 210): 'Leading teams requires an approach that centers on helping teams to lead themselves.' They suggest that the following types of behaviour are necessary for leaders of self-managing teams:

- Encouraging self-goal setting.
- Encouraging self-evaluation.
- Encouraging high self-expectation.
- Facilitating self-problem solving.
- Developing self-intiative and responsibility.
- Encouraging within-group conflict resolution.
- Providing training.
- Encouraging opportunity thinking.

The time taken to introduce a fully functioning self-managing team system can vary considerably. A large financial service organization studied by Sims et al. (1993) converted to a team organization over a single week-end, albeit after extensive analysis and planning. Many people expected a short-term decrease in quality and productivity immediately after the change. According to Sims *et al.* (112), 'the opposite happened. Many of the quality indicators immediately shot up. Backlogs seemed to disappear. It was almost as if the teams were determined to show that this new organization was better from the very beginning.'

On the other hand, Lawler (1992) suggests that teams may not reach full maturity until they are two to four years old, and even at maturity still need a management person to help them solve their internal problems and monitor their decision-making processes. Manz and Newstrom (1990, 1993) argue that when starting up a new operation, it is important to focus on getting the technical systems right before attempting to introduce radically new forms of social organization. When self-managing teams were introduced into a new paper mill, it was envisaged that the development of mature self-managed teams would take from five to eight years, with a gradual transition across the four stages portrayed in Figure 7.1 (Manz and Sims 1993: 68). This illustrates an evolution from start-up teams under the direct leadership of the team manager with no rotation of member skills and responsibilities to (ultimately) self-managing teams which would have the requisite skills and abilities within the team to perform assigned responsibilities. At that stage, team members would exercise control over their own problems and rotate among various co-ordinating and scheduling roles. Figure 7.1 portrays the way in which the role of team manager was expected to change as they moved from direct supervision (stage one) to positions of shared authority (stage two) to boundary managers and leaders (stages three and four).

EMPOWERMENT

Another strand in the increasing interest in self-management is the work of those organizational theorists and practitioners advocating the empowerment of employees. Empowerment is a concept which has been employed in a much wider context than those we have discussed so far, in that it has been widely used by social scientists concerned with the issue of powerlessness among disadvantaged members of society, such as ethnic minorities, women and the handicapped (Conger and Kanungo 1988a).

When employed in the context of self-management, the term empowerment tends to be used to signify the sharing of power through the delegation of authority. A recent OB text, for example, defines empowerment as 'the process by which managers help others to acquire and use the power needed to make decisions affecting themselves and their work' (Schermerhorn *et al.* 1994: 473). Conger and Kanungo, on the other hand, prefer to regard empowerment as a process of enhancing feelings of self-determination and self-efficacy (convictions of their own effectiveness) among organizational members. They argue that delegation or resource sharing is only one set of conditions that may, but not necessarily will, enable or empower subordinates. There are various

Stage 1 : Start-up team

Authority
Expert
Teacher
Problem solver
Coordinator
Team supervisor
Mentor

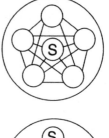

Stage 2: Transitional team

Shared authority
Monitor
Helper
Example setter
Teacher
Evaluator
Information provider
Link to other teams

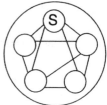

Stage 3: Well-trained, experienced team

Manager of boundary
Auditor
Expert
Resource provider
Goal-setting guider
Information provider
Protector/buffer

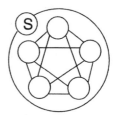

State 4: Well-trained, mature team

Boundary leader
Shared valued
Coach
Champion
Counselor
Resource provider
Supporter
Shared responsibilities

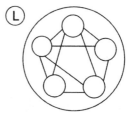

Figure 7.1 Proposed evolution of self-managing teams in a paper mill
Note: S = supervisor or manager; L = leader.
Source: Manz and Newstrom 1993

other conditions of empowering and the process of delegation is therefore too restrictive in scope to accommodate the complex nature of empowerment.

Conger and Kanungo identify a number of management practices that heighten a sense of self-efficacy and thus result in subordinates experiencing a sense of empowerment. These include:

1 Leadership practices such as:
● expressing confidence in subordinates accompanied by high performance expectations;

- fostering opportunities for subordinates to participate in decision-making;
- providing autonomy from bureaucratic constraints. For example, clerks in the Marriott hotel chain are empowered to eliminate minor charges on hotel bills if they are questioned by guests, and customer service clerks at Wal-Mart are empowered to refund the money for returned items, even without a sales slip (Luthans 1992);
- setting inspirational and/or meaningful goals;
- providing feedback on performance. Words of encouragement may be used to provide a feeling of empowerment even if the individual fails to achieve the desired outcome (e.g. 'We may have lost to the competition, but I'm proud of your performance. We will do better next time.');
- acting as a model. According to Conger and Kanungo, a supervisor's exemplary behaviours can empower subordinates to believe that they can behave in a like manner or that they can at least achieve some improvement in performance.

2 Contingent/competence-based reward systems that emphasize innovative/unusual performance and high incentive values.

3 Jobs that provide task variety, personal relevance, appropriate autonomy, low levels of established routines and rules, and high advancement prospects.

It will be apparent that, despite their disparate origins, many of the concepts discussed in this chapter are beginning to be integrated into a common approach to self-management. Conger and Kanungo (1988a) include such concepts as participation, autonomy and job enrichment as factors giving rise to feelings of empowerment. Lawler (1986) advocates what he calls 'high-involvement management'. Using this approach, individuals at the lowest levels in organizations are given more information, knowledge, power and rewards by means of such practices as job enrichment and self-managing teams. This is combined with a leadership style which builds trust and openness, provides and communicates a vision, moves decisions to the proper location and empowers others. Manz and Newstrom (1990) state that the underlying theory for self-managing teams stems from both basic job design theory and socio-technical systems theory. Similarly, Lawler (1992) notes that much of the early work on self-managing teams was done in Europe, based on the socio-technical approach to work design. Wall et al. (1986) point out that the properties prescribed for autonomous work groups parallel the hallmarks of Hackman and Oldham's Job Characteristics Model and note that several writers (e.g. Rousseau 1977) have argued for a synthesis of the two approaches. Finally, although they did not use the term in their earlier writings, Manz and Sims (1993) have recently stated that empowerment, especially team empowerment, is central to creating effective self-leadership. Rather than examining the implications of these various concepts separately, therefore, we will evaluate the approach as a whole.

THEORETICAL UNDERPINNING OF SELF-MANAGEMENT CONCEPTS

Although self-management is an area of great current interest and enthusiasm among organizational theorists and practitioners, in many respects it represents a re-emergence in a new form of ideas which were popular in the 1950s and subsequently discarded. An obvious example is the assumption that participation is the one best way to lead (see Chapter 3). Another is the assumption that all people have a need for autonomy and self-direction. For example, both Lawler (1992) and Manz and Sims (1993) cite as a source of their approach McGregor's (1957) Theory Y, which states that the motivation, the potential for development, the capacity for assuming responsibility, and the readiness to direct behaviour towards organizational goals are present in all people.

However, this view of motivation was widely criticized in the 1960s. In particular, Schein (1965) argued that early motivation theorists had greatly underestimated the importance of individual differences in motivation. Human needs and motives, he stated, assume varying degrees of importance to each person, creating some form of hierarchy, but this hierarchy itself is variable from person to person, from situation to situation and from one time to another. Early theories of job enrichment, such as that of Herzberg, were also criticized for giving insufficient consideration to individual differences. Hulin (1971), for example, argued that all workers do not have the same needs, aspirations or desires and thus it cannot be assumed that all workers would be satisfied and motivated by an enriched job.

More recent theories of job design have therefore incorporated individual differences as a moderator variable influencing the extent to which employees would react favourably to an enriched job. Hackman and Oldham, for example, suggest that the influence of job characteristics on such outcome variables as motivation, satisfaction and performance will be influenced by the employee's 'growth need strength' (the extent to which the individual has a high need for personal growth and development). A meta-analysis of five studies which examined the moderating effect of growth need strength on the relationship between job characteristics and performance carried out by Fried and Ferris (1987) confirmed this contention. The association between 'enriched' job characteristics and performance was negligible (0.10) in the case of low growth need strength people, but much higher (0.45) in the case of high growth need strength people.

However, the extent to which individual differences are taken into account by writers on self-management varies. Writers on empowerment tend to assume, either implicitly or explicitly that everyone has a need for autonomy and self-determination. For example, Conger and Kanungo (1988a) state that everyone has a need for self-determination and a need to control and cope with external demands. This may well be true, but the extent to which people have such a need and also the extent to which they feel capable of controlling and coping with particular environmental demands may vary. Thus an increase in responsibility may be one person's empowerment and another's source of stress.

As we have seen, Manz and Sims (1980, 1989) identify a number of situational factors which are likely to influence the appropriateness of attempts to develop self-management techniques in subordinates on an individual basis, including the individual employee's eagerness, desire and capacity for self-management. In their writings on self-managing teams, however, they largely ignore the issue of individual differences. Indeed Manz and Newstrom (1990) specifically state that the concept of self-managing teams is based on the belief that employees desire autonomy, decision-making power and opportunities for self-control. It is also noticeable that although they quote the Job Characteristics Model as support for the concept of self-managing teams, they do not mention the key concept of growth need strength and Hackman and Oldham's contention that this both varies between employees and moderates the effect of job characteristics on their motivation, job satisfaction and performance.

On the other hand, Lawler (1992) does note that individual differences can influence the effectiveness of self-managing teams. He states that, like job enrichment, work teams are most effective with individuals who desire complex, challenging work. For those individuals who prefer repetitive tasks, work teams are highly undesirable. Lawler also suggests that work teams differ from individual job enrichment in that they require individuals who enjoy social interaction and value social rewards. As meetings are important and frequent, he suggests that people who dislike meetings are unlikely to thrive in a team environment. Furthermore, operating in a team environment, Lawler argues, often requires an individual to have higher skill levels than does operating alone in an enriched job. Individual job enrichment does not demand that individuals have interpersonal skills or group decision-making skills since many decisions are made by individuals and not groups.

Lawler's comments clearly have important implications for the selection of people to work in self-managing teams and decisions concerning whether attempts should be made to enrich people's jobs and empower them on an individual basis. However, he does not pursue these matters further.

ORGANIZATIONAL COSTS AND BENEFITS OF SELF-MANAGEMENT

The data concerning the organizational benefits of self-management in its varying forms are almost uniformly favourable. Impressive improvements in productivity and quality are reported in individual organizations. Some examples are as follows:

- An automobile battery plant organized around teams reported productivity savings of 30 to 40 per cent compared with traditionally organized plants (Manz and Sims 1993).

- A distribution organization achieved productivity improvements of 10 per cent per year, cost savings of 10 to 20 per cent of earnings and customer service quality levels of over 99 per cent in the four years since the introduction of self-managing teams (Manz and Sims 1993).
- An engineering company found that products which formerly took 16 weeks to build were being completed in 10 days following the introduction of self-managing teams (Yeatts et al. 1994).
- A manufacturer of quality rings reduced the time taken from receiving an order to shipping the product from 30 calendar days to 10 (Yeatts et al. 1994).

Favourable results have also been reported in wider ranging reviews of research studies. For example, Pasmore et al. (1982) analysed the results of 71 studies of autonomous work groups and found that positive effects on quality, employee attitudes and safety were reported in all cases, on productivity in 89 per cent of cases, on absenteeism in 86 per cent, on costs in 85 per cent and on labour turnover in 81 per cent. For a number of reasons, however, such results must be treated with caution. First, researchers and practitioners are naturally more reluctant to report their failures than their successes. The high proportion of studies with successful outcomes, therefore, may to some extent reflect the fact that unsuccessful studies are not available to review because they have not been published. Second, the studies which are reported vary considerably in quality. For example, Pasmore et al. gave the percentage of cases reporting an improvement on each dimension rather than the amount of improvement because statements such as 'productivity increased' or 'costs were dramatically reduced' were all that was available in some cases. Third, in many studies several variables are changed at the same time, making it difficult to establish to what extent any one particular variable contributed to any beneficial effects. For example, changes in pay rates often occur when autonomous working groups are introduced. Kelly (1978) argues that the significance of pay incentives has been seriously underestimated as a causal factor in the increases in output and product quality associated with the introduction of autonomous work groups. A meta-analysis of 17 socio-technical studies carried out by Beekun (1989) provides some support for this view. Interventions with a change in pay were found to result in 67 per cent more productivity than those which did not change pay.

On the basis of both individual studies and meta-analyses of research into self-managing teams, Goodman et al. (1988) conclude that self-managing groups positively affect productivity, and overall the effects of self-management on productivity are stronger than those of alternative interventions. However, they also note that the magnitude of the effect is not well known. Their best judgement, looking across all studies, is that self-managing groups have a modest impact on productivity. Similarly, on the basis of a more recent review of the research on self-managing teams, Cohen and Ledford (1994) come to the conclusion that they have a modest positive impact on performance, product quality, productivity and attitudes of team members. Nevertheless, Cohen and Ledford also state that overall there has been a paucity of high-quality studies on self-managing teams and echo the earlier observation by Goodman *et al.* that, in general, the more rigorous the design, the more modest the results of the study. For example, a longitudinal quasi-experimental study of autonomous work groups in a confectionery factory carried out by Wall *et al.* (1986) revealed that they had substantially enhanced intrinsic job satisfaction and produced a more short-term increase in extrinsic job satisfaction, but had not demonstrably affected job motivation, organization commitment, mental health, work performance or voluntary labour turnover.

It is much more difficult to find hard evidence concerning the effectiveness of empowerment on an individual basis. Ripley and Ripley (1993), for example, claim that empowerment programmes can have numerous beneficial effects within organizations, including increased motivation to reduce mistakes, increased opportunities for creativity and innovation, improving customer satisfaction, increased productivity, increased competitiveness and so on, but do not quote any supporting evidence. It could, of course, be argued that the evidence from job enrichment research provides some support for the concept of individual empowerment. Locke *et al.* (1980), for example, carried out a review of 13 job enrichment studies which revealed an improvement in performance ranging from −1 per cent to 63 per cent with a median performance improvement of 17 per cent. Nevertheless, such global data could hide extensive individual differences. Thus whether empowering someone on an individual basis has beneficial effects could depend on the motivation and ability of the person concerned.

It is also difficult to find detailed comparative data on the costs involved in introducing and operating the various self-management systems discussed in this chapter. Such costs could arise in a number of areas. First, new plant or equipment may be necessary to operate the new work systems. Where introducing self-management involves relatively simple increases in autonomy, such as empowering clerks to make refunds without reference to their superiors, such costs may not arise. Where self-management interventions are complex and require complete changes in production systems, however, they could be extremely expensive. For example, a report on the Volvo car assembly plant at Kalmar stated that investment costs were estimated to be 10 per cent higher than in a conventional factory, and in the first two years of operation these did not seem to have been offset by significant improvements in efficiency and economic performance or by any marked reduction in levels of absenteeism or labour turnover (Anonymous 1976).

Second, as Lawler (1992) points out, team members need higher skills than those working on their own, and there are numerous reports of the extensive training which team members and team co-ordinators or facilitators receive in order to enable them to work effectively in a team environment. According to Rehder (1994), General Motors has invested millions of dollars in ongoing team member training at the factory where they introduced a teamwork production system for their new line of Saturn cars. Team members spend 250 to 750 hours in intensive training, with a large portion of this time devoted to such topics as team and consensus building, leadership, problem identification and solving, and total quality management.

Third, there may be costs in operating a self-management system if workers who are empowered to make decisions do not make the right ones. Conger and Kanungo (1988a) note that although they focused on the positive effects of empowerment, it is conceivable that such practices could have negative effects. Specifically empowerment might lead to overconfidence and, in turn, misjudgements on the part of subordinates. Because of a sense of false confidence in positive outcomes, organizations might persist in efforts that are, in actuality, tactical or strategic errors. When evaluating the effectiveness of self-management systems, therefore, it is important to bear in mind that there may be costs involved which need to be offset against any gains which are reported.

EMPLOYEE COSTS AND BENEFITS OF SELF-MANAGEMENT

As we saw in the Pasmore *et al.* (1982) survey, autonomous work groups were reported to have had a positive effect on employee attitudes in all 71 cases reviewed. Other reviews of research and reports of individual cases are also virtually unanimous in showing that self-management in its various forms is associated with an increase in levels of job satisfaction.

Nevertheless, there are also indications that there may sometimes also be costs involved as far as employees are concerned. Among them are the following.

Job losses and insecurity

There are numerous reports of job losses associated with the introduction of self-management. According to Schermerhorn *et al.* (1994), there is a trend in the hotel industry to eliminate managers and empower subordinates to provide a better service to customers. For example, the Hyatt Hotel Corporation gave hourly workers more say in their jobs and more responsibilities after laying off 20 per cent of their management staff. Similarly, although the introduction of autonomous work groups in the confectionery factory studied by Wall *et al.* (1986) did not demonstrably affect work performance, it did have productivity benefits at the organizational level because the reduced need for supervision led to reduced indirect labour costs. Not surprisingly, the fact that the introduction of self-managing teams can reduce the need for supervisory staff can produce feelings of insecurity. For example, Manz and Newstrom (1990: 53–4) state that in the mill which they studied there was 'a haunting, if not always stated, fear among some of the team managers that they risk(ed) managing themselves out of a job'. This fear is by no means unfounded. According to Manz and Sims

(1993), the number of managers is typically reduced with a team system. In fact, they state, one of the major sources of saving that derives from a team system is a delayering of management and supervisors. They also state that when an organization changes to teams, managers must be guaranteed that they will not lose their jobs because of the new system. However, they add that this does not mean that they will necessarily be doing the same job or performing the same duties as before. They claim that managers and supervisors who are displaced are typically reassigned to more technical specialized positions or will be covered over a longer period through normal attrition. On the other hand, they also state that some supervisors may retire or quit rather than accommodate themselves to a team system and in 'a few cases' top management has asked a supervisor or manager who cannot adjust to leave the organization.

Similarly, Lawler (1992) states that high-involvement organizations need to do everything possible to guarantee a stable workforce. Employees will be reluctant to suggest ideas and work in ways which will reduce the number of employees needed to do the work if they are concerned that they or fellow workers will lose their jobs. However, Lawler also notes on several occasions that work teams can lead to considerable cost savings by reducing the number of employees needed at all levels within organizations. For example, he states (p. 115) that managerial teams often 'allow for leaner staffing at the management level just as teams do at the production level'. Similarly, he states that:

> Work teams can also have a significant impact on the need for supervisory personnel and staff groups. Work teams can usually take inventory and do scheduling, quality assurance and even some of the tasks typically done by middle- and upper-level management. Significant cost savings can then be realized by leaner staffing. The higher level work that is typically done by middle managers at a higher pay rate is transferred to production teams and done by individuals who are paid at a lower wage.
>
> (Lawler 1992: 99)

In any other context, eliminating the need for higher paid workers by handing on their work to lower paid workers would sound suspiciously like exploitation. Furthermore, unless the production teams are also paid a significantly higher rate of pay commensurate with their new responsibilities, the new system may not achieve the desired effects. Lawler (1977) previously noted that he had come across a number of cases in which problems had arisen in the introduction of job enrichment or autonomous work groups because workers felt that they deserved higher pay because they now had more responsibilities.

Winners and losers

It is commonly observed that while the majority of employees gain from the introduction of self-management, there are almost invariably losers as well.

Manz and Sims (1993) state that middle managers and supervisors, with some justification, frequently regard themselves as the biggest losers in a transition to a team system. Partly, as we have seen, this is because they may lose their jobs. In addition, however, those who remain have to learn a completely new role as team facilitator or co-ordinator which in many respects is a much more complex and stressful one than their previous role. In a study of twelve manufacturing plants which had introduced work restructuring programmes providing for greater employee participation, Walton and Schlesinger (1979) found that in most cases there was relatively less satisfaction or more dissatisfaction at the first-line supervisory level than in positions above or below in the same plant hierarchy.

Other employees who feel they are losers include those with specialist skills who find that their position is being eroded by the introduction of teams. For example, employees with considerable technical experience who were hired to facilitate the start-up of the mill studied by Manz and Newstrom (1990, 1993) experienced a sense of inequality. This stemmed from two sources: performance of tasks which they viewed as beneath their status and the rapid acquisition of status (and income) by other, inexperienced workers. Similarly, in the financial services company studied by Sims *et al.* (1993), senior clerks saw themselves as losers. Under the old system, they were hourly paid employees who had special knowledge and authority and a higher rate of pay, but under the new system the position of senior clerk would cease to exist.

Stress

Paradoxically, although empowerment is seen as a method of reducing stress (Schermerhorn *et al.* 1994), there is also evidence that self-management systems can also be a source of stress. Lawler (1992) notes that in some of the organizations he has worked with, employees have pointed out that it is more stressful to work in a high-involvement organization. The responsibilities, the pressures of learning and some of the interpersonal processes involved are new to many employees. However, Lawler claims that as a general rule, employees work through these issues and ultimately prefer a high-involvement approach.

Kanter (1989) suggests that the promise of freedom has a dark side: insecurity and loss of control. The new ways of managing, she states, can create an illusion of freedom combined with security. In theory, there should be a perfect marriage of risks and support – freedom when people want to take risks and support when the risks do not work out. In reality, the people at the top in organizations still wield the power, and sometimes do so in ways which people below them experience as arbitrary. Furthermore, increased autonomy within organizations also applies to top managers, freeing them to take actions which would previously have been unimaginable and which can affect the lives of those below them in the organization in an unpredictable and capricious manner. A manager whose company was undergoing drastic restructuring told her: 'For all of my ownership share and strategic centrality and voice in decisions, I can still be faced with a shift in direction not of my own making. I can still be reorganized into a corner. I can still be relocated into obscurity. I can still be reviewed out of my special project budget.' The realities of power change, and job security are important, Kanter argues, because they affect the way people view their leaders. When the illusion of simultaneous freedom and protection fades, the result can be loss of motivation.

Loss of autonomy in self-managing teams

A major cornerstone of the concept of self-management is that it enables employees to experience greater autonomy. Another of the paradoxes of self-managing teams, however, is that they may increase the autonomy of the team while at the same time decrease the autonomy of the individual team member. As Lawler (1992) points out, team membership is not optional. Individuals cannot take ownership of one part of the process and refuse to do other tasks. He also notes that when groups are cohesive, social pressure can play an important role in motivating individual performance, as valued social rewards, such as praise from other group members and acceptance by the group, depend on satisfactory individual performance. Similarly, punishments are sometimes administered by the group when individuals do not perform well. Furthermore, Lawler suggests, groups may be more effective at giving rewards and punishments than the supervisors. Often reaction from peers is more critical to employees than reaction from bosses, but perhaps more importantly, peers are often constantly present and able to give continuous reinforcement while bosses are not always present.

Some support for Lawler's views can be found in studies of self-managing teams. In the distribution warehouse studied by Manz et al. (1993), managers came to the conclusion that peer pressure was often more effective than managerial threats and that a worker would be less likely to report sick if he or she had to face team members next morning. In the paper mill studied by Manz and Newstrom (1990), one of the tasks of team leaders was ensuring that team members were not too tough in managing themselves. One team manager commented that if someone failed to pull their weight in the team (e.g. was chronically absent), the team manager might have to 'take the (figurative) lynching rope out of their hands' and try to fashion a peaceful settlement rather than mete out the more traditional punishment. Such examples suggest that in some cases at least workers may have exchanged the tyranny of the bosses for an even greater tyranny of the team.

It is worth noting, however, that the opposite problem may also occur. In the confectionery factory studied by Wall et al. (1986), the work groups were loath to discipline members who consistently broke group norms and explicitly referred these problems to the support managers. This unfortunately led to a high number of disciplinary dismissals. Line managers were aware that they had dismissed employees who, under conventional circumstances, they would not have required to leave. The absence of supervisors meant that the few employees who stepped out of line were not immediately detected. Under conventional job design systems, supervisors would take early action and perhaps protect employees from managers. In autonomous work groups, misdemeanours were typically more advanced when they came to light and warranted use of formal warning procedures.

In summary, it must be reiterated that the currently available research evidence on employee reactions to self-management in its various forms shows that the majority of workers find their jobs more satisfying as the result of the introduction of such systems and would be reluctant to return to the conventional systems of hierarchical control. Nevertheless, the evidence reviewed in this section suggests that there can be losers as well as winners as a result of the introduction of self-management and there could also be costs for all employees under some circumstances. Much will depend on the good will of the managers introducing and controlling the system. As we have seen, systems of self-management undoubtedly can have benefits for both the organization and its employees. However, both Lawler (1992) and Manz and Sims (1993) make it clear that, while organizations should try to protect employees from any adverse consequences of such systems, the primary reason for the introduction of self-management is the potential beneficial effects on organizational effectiveness. Whether all employers and all individual managers who empower their subordinates will be equally concerned with protecting people from adverse consequences resulting from the introduction of self-management is open to question. This raises the possibility of what may be termed 'exploitative empowerment'; in other words, empowering people by giving them greater responsibility, which greatly increases their workload, causing considerable stress and loss of job satisfaction without a commensurate increase in organizational rewards, while at the same time claiming that this is being done for their benefit. If this happens, disillusionment with self-management is likely to set in and any gains which the organization might have made from its introduction are likely to decline dramatically.

One of the few reports of a self-management system which failed provides an illustration of this point. Manz and Angle (1993) describe the effects of introducing self-managing teams into an insurance company in which employees already enjoyed a high degree of individual autonomy. The CEO introduced the team system, not to increase autonomy, but to provide peer pressure, thus disempowering employees and increasing his own control. Interviews with the CEO led Manz and Angle to conclude that the CEO was sincerely committed philosophically to employee participation, but his espoused theory was inconsistent with his theory in use. In this organization, the introduction of work teams led to a loss of individual self-management for employees, senior staff ignored the system, junior staff became frustrated, team meetings eventually became infrequent and unproductive, employee scepticism and apathy rose, and efficiency and co-ordination plummeted.

THE QUESTION OF AUTHORITY

While the delegation of authority and provision for greater autonomy are key elements of self-management systems, there remains the question of what authority should be retained by the managerial hierarchy and how the organization should respond when autonomy is abused or misused. According to Hackman (1990), 'falling off the authority balance beam' is one of the major pitfalls in team management. He suggests that for teams to be effective it is necessary to achieve a good balance between managerial and team authority. If the managers retain virtually all authority, dictating work procedures in detail to team members, many of the advantages that can accrue from teamwork will be lost. Conversely, if virtually all authority is assigned to the team, then this can result in anarchy or a team which heads off in an inappropriate direction. However, Hackman argues that merely deciding how much authority will be retained by management and how much will be assigned to the team is not enough. Equally important are the domains of authority that are retained and assigned. Hackman argues that managers should be unapologetic and insistent about exercising their authority about direction – the end states the team is to pursue – and about the outer limit constraints on team behaviour – the things that the team should never do. At the same time, managers should assign the team full authority for the means by which it accomplishes its work – and then do whatever they can to ensure that team members understand and accept their responsibility for deciding how they will execute the work.

Hackman argues that authoritatively setting a clear, engaging direction for a team is to empower, not to depower, it. Indeed, effective team functioning may be impossible unless someone exercises authority about direction. Having a clear direction helps to align team efforts with the objectives of the parent organization, provides members with a criterion to use in selecting its performance strategies and sustains energy within the team. When direction is absent or unclear, Hackman states, members may wallow in uncertainty about just what they should be doing and may even have difficulty generating the motivation to do anything.

Similarly, Manz and Sims (1993) state that external managerial control will always play an important role in any organization and is not incompatible with self-management. Even when self-management is deliberately encouraged, some external control by management, primarily focused on output measures or at the task boundary is commonly found and typically wanted by employees. For Van Oudtshoorn and Thomas (1993), the key managerial function in an empowering organization is to set broad outlines which establish the limits of the subordinate's empowerment, and then provide coaching and counselling to the employee in the achievement of personal and organizational goals within the limits already defined.

Lawler (1992) states that although a high-involvement organization must create a climate of fairness and openness, it should not be soft on discipline. High-involvement organizations require people who are trustworthy and capable of responsibility and employees should have the freedom which goes with that trust. However, if individuals fail to behave in the way the organization expects, Lawler argues, it is critical that the organization takes immediate strong action. Indeed, Lawler suggests that, in many respects, a high-involvement organization is less able to afford to be lenient when dealing with discipline problems than a traditional one, simply because it places less emphasis on catching and punishing troublesome employees. Thus, when they are discovered, dishonesty, theft and clear breaking of organizational policies on ethics should be dealt with in the strongest possible manner.

However, this does not tell us what the response should be if an individual or group performs badly, not because they break rules, but because they either do not devote enough effort to the task or make mistakes. There seems to be an assumption that empowerment will inevitably motivate people, but it seems unlikely that this will invariably be the case. This poses a dilemma. If management does not impose the goals which the individual or team should achieve and motivate the achievement of these goals by the use of rewards and sanctions, the individual or team could decide not to aim for high performance to the detriment of the organization. Conversely, if the organization imposes the goals, but allows individuals or teams to choose the means by which these goals are achieved then this is not true autonomy (Manz 1986). Indeed, if the organization sets performance goals which are difficult to achieve and then leaves the individual or team to decide how to achieve them, this could make the job extremely stressful. In addition to the normal pressures involved in achieving high levels of performance, there would also be the psychological pressure of being responsible for finding a solution to what may be an impossible problem. In a sense then, self-managing teams and autonomous work groups are an illusion and some writers have therefore suggested that terms such as semi-autonomous work groups would be more accurate.

The issue of what response should be made to mistakes is also important and deserves more attention than it receives in the self-management literature. Giving people more autonomy provides greater opportunity for making the wrong decision. Again, there is a dilemma. If people are blamed for making the wrong decision, then this will discourage people from making use of their authority. On the other hand, if there are no penalties for making mistakes, this could encourage recklessness. Hollander and Offerman (1990) suggest that it is unrealistic to expect leaders to distribute powers to others when negative consequences of actions will fall on the leader. On the other hand, if the leader has empowered the subordinate to make a decision which is beyond his or her capabilities, it seems unfair to blame the subordinate either, resulting in a situation where no one is responsible for actions which have adverse organizational consequences. Of course, some mistakes can be put down to the costs of developing people and set against the gains to be obtained from empowerment. However, this still leaves the question of the kind of mistakes which can be regarded as legitimate and how many. This suggests that a great deal of judgement is required to decide how much someone should be empowered, whether anyone is responsible for any mistakes made and if so who, and what should be done to rectify the situation. This is an issue which will be taken up in the next section.

IMPLICATIONS FOR LEADERSHIP

It was stated at the beginning of this chapter that the introduction of self-management was intended to reduce the amount of formal leadership required in an organization. It will be apparent from the foregoing discussion of the various approaches to self-management that, while they may reduce the amount of formal leadership required, they also have the effect of increasing both the quality of formal leadership required and the amount and quality of informal leadership.

Hackman (1986) notes that it is common for those writing about self-management to take the view that there is relatively little need for leadership in such self-managing units. However, he takes the contrary view and argues that leadership is both more important and a more demanding undertaking in self-managing units than it is in traditional organizations. Hackman has developed a model of the critical leadership functions for self-managing units. He identifies five enabling conditions that foster self-management (see Figure 7.2). These are:

1 Clear engaging direction and a well-designed performance situation.
2 An enabling unit structure.
3 A supportive organizational context.
4 Available expert coaching.
5 Adequate material resources.

Reminiscent of the Job Characteristics Model, these enabling conditions influence certain processes which are indicative of the unit's effectiveness, such as energized and aligned performance, ample effort, smooth and unconstrained task execution, which in turn produce certain performance outcomes, including clients who are pleased with the product, improved unit capability and enhanced individual growth and well-being.

The critical leadership functions for a self-managing unit, Hackman argues, are those that contribute to the establishment and maintenance of favourable performance conditions. This involves two types of behaviour: (a) monitoring – obtaining and interpreting data about performance conditions and events that might affect them; (b) taking action to create or maintain favourable performance conditions. More specifically, Hackman suggests that the leader should first assess the outcome states at the right of Figure 7.2, and then work backwards to identify (and ultimately do something about) performance conditions that may be contributing to performance problems or missed opportunities.

Hackman's (1986) model provides a useful method of analysing what the manager needs to do when leading a self-managing team. Furthermore, many of the model's precepts would apply equally to the management of individuals who are being allocated a greater degree of self-management. Nevertheless, like much of leadership theory, while the model describes what needs to be done, it says little about how this should be done. In particular, he says little about the ways in which self-management will change the nature of the interactions between leaders and followers. Other writers, however, have noted that significant changes are likely to take place.

Lawler (1992) points out that group members need training in interpersonal and team skills and the more responsibility they are given for making supervisory type decisions, the more they need group process training. Some idea of

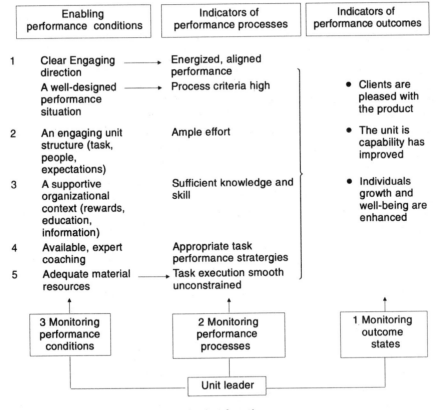

Figure 7.2 The unit leader's monitoring function: a summary
Source: Hackman 1986. Copyright ©1995 the American Psychological Association

the informal leadership behaviours that may be required by members of self-managing work teams can be gained from the study by Manz and Sims (1984, 1993) of an automobile battery plant. The types of verbal behaviour they observed during team meetings included the following:

1 Verbal rewards.
2 Verbal reprimands.
3 Allocation of task requirements.
4 Issues of work scheduling.
5 Production goal setting and performance feedback.
6 Routine announcements.
7 Special problems (e.g. quality problems).
8 Discussion of communication problems.
9 Performance evaluations for pay advancements.
10 Member entry to and exit from the team.

Similarly, the external leader of the group needs much more sophisticated leadership skills than the previous foreman or supervisor. It would appear that the external team leader (co-ordinator) is just as much a 'person in the middle', with differing expectations from those above and below in the hierarchy, as the foreman or supervisor was. According to Manz and Sims (1984, 1993), different supervisor levels in the automobile battery plant saw the team co-ordinator role quite differently. The support group (upper plant management) saw the co-ordinator's role as that of a facilitator who could help work teams to manage themselves. Co-ordinators saw their role as focusing more on the completion of achievable concrete tasks, with the facilitator's role as more of a backup responsibility. Team leaders, the immediate subordinates of the coordinators, saw the co-ordinator's job as a balance between a facilitator who does not interfere with group functioning and a resource that provides some direction.

As a result, according to Manz and Sims, team co-ordinators had to tread a fine line between overdirection and underdirection. If the co-ordinator took charge and dictated a course of action to the team, the team members could lose interest and the co-ordinators would not be acting as expected by senior management. On the other hand, teams left totally on their own to solve problems became frustrated and dissatisfied with difficult situations in which a co-ordinator provided what they believed to be inadequate direction. Manz and Sims therefore suggest that while it is useful and appropriate for the co-ordinator to have technical expertise, social skills seem to be much more important. In many ways, they state, the co-ordinator acts as a counsellor and communication facilitator. The most frequent type of co-ordinator verbal behaviour that they heard was the reflective question, throwing the burden of judgement back on the team leader or team member. The use of questions such as 'What would you do if nobody else was available?' in order to encourage team members to become more independent was also noted in the financial services organization studied by Sims et al. (1993).

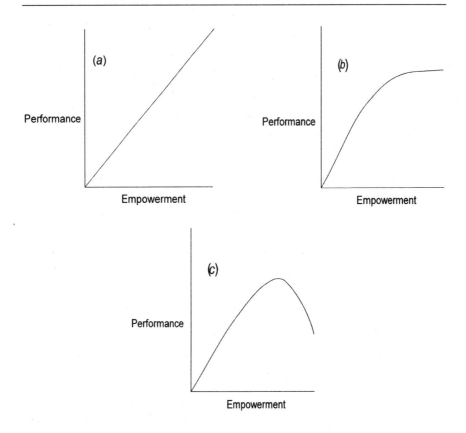

Figure 7.3 Hypothetical relationships between empowerment and performance
Based on: Hulin 1971

Verbal skills will also be needed to make judgements about how much responsibility an individual subordinate should be given when empowering subordinates on an individual basis. It has previously been noted by writers such as Vroom (1964) and Hulin (1971) that there is a variety of different possible relationships between motivational variables and organizational outcomes. In the case of empowerment, it is most unlikely that the relationship with performance is a straight line one, as shown in Figure 7.3 (a). This would imply that total empowerment would result in infinite performance and this is patently absurd. It may be that increasing amounts of empowerment result in increasing levels of performance up to a certain point but make no difference thereafter, as shown in Figure 7.3 (b). However, it seems more likely that, as shown in Figure 7.3 (c), increasing amounts of empowerment will improve performance up to a certain point and thereafter result in a decline in performance, because the job holder lacks the ability to take on further responsibility, or finds the additional responsibility stressful or finds the temptation to take advantage of the increased autonomy too great. Furthermore, the point at which this is likely to occur is also likely to differ from one person to another, depending on their abilities, desire for responsibility and autonomy, stress tolerance, trustworthiness and so on. Thus, the manager who empowers subordinates on an individual basis will need to have the ability to elicit information on all these questions in order to make sound decisions on how much responsibility the subordinate should be given and how much autonomy he or she should be allowed.

CONCLUSIONS

It is too early to come to any definitive conclusions concerning the various forms of individual and team self-management. The currently available research evidence suggests that they can have major benefits for organizations and their employees. Nevertheless, previous techniques such as participative leadership, management by objectives, job enrichment and so on have been welcomed with equal enthusiasm and have been equally well supported by initial research evidence, only for disillusionment to set in as later experience and research proved less supportive. In many respects, the disillusionment is often an overreaction as the techniques do have value and are effective; they simply did not live up to the exaggerated expectations which had been generated. I would be very surprised if this did not happen in the case of self-management. Indeed, articles suggesting that empowerment may not be as effective as it is claimed are already beginning to appear. For example, Kennedy (1994) states that empowerment has lost its appeal for many middle managers and workers. Middle managers are disenchanted because they are left to flounder by their own superiors. Workers feel that they are being put upon because they are doing more than they have ever done but are not being compensated for it. As a result, according to Kennedy (p. 11), 'Disillusionment is creeping like a fog over a process which inspired wild enthusiasm and commitment just a few years ago – and still has great strengths.' There is also opposition to the self-managing teams and other team-based systems in some parts of the American union movement. For example, Parker and Slaughter (1988), both former workers in auto plants, regard the team concept as a form of 'management by stress', which enables management to put greater pressure on workers to increase production. For them, a good example of a team with interchangeable members is a team of horses – beasts of burden of equal capabilities, yoked together to pull for a common end (determined by the person holding the whip). They state bluntly (p. 40) that 'By far the best way to deal with the team concept is to keep it out of your shop altogether.'

Therefore, it is important to be aware of the potential pitfalls which may be associated with the introduction of self-management in its various forms. I would suggest that a major potential problem is the balance between organizational and employee benefits. We have seen that there are a number of areas where these may not be entirely compatible. The proponents of self-managing teams say that jobs should not be at risk, but claim great organizational benefits from lean staffing. They state that individuals will benefit from greater autonomy, but claim that an advantage of self-managing teams is that they control the team members' behaviour more effectively than supervisors. Empowerment is regarded as a way of reducing stress, but it can also increase it. It is argued that workers should be given greater autonomy, but it is also said that management should retain authority over the most important decisions affecting employees' lives, the goals which they are expected to achieve. None of these potential conflicts need necessarily lead to the failure of a self-management system. Nevertheless, if self-management is seen by employees as a means of achieving organizational benefits at their expense, then they could fail. More than any other method of motivating employee performance, self-management relies upon the willing co-operation of employees. With disillusioned and alienated employees it simply will not work.

EXERCISE 5: THE TEAMS THAT FAILED

Case

This case examines the way in which self-managing teams were introduced into an independent property and casualty insurance firm. The firm employed 32 people. It was founded in 1941 and, until the recent appointment of a new acting chief executive officer (CEO), had operated along traditional lines. Account executives operated as relatively independent agents, each with their own network of highly personal relationships with clients. However, one of the new CEO's initial acts was to restructure the firm into self-managing work teams. This was done without the participation or the consent of the employees. The team philosophy was explained to the employees when the teams were introduced, and teams were encouraged to make decisions and solve their problems jointly. Within established company guidelines, work teams were expected to be self-managing units which carried out the activities needed for acquiring and servicing accounts cooperatively. The intention was to pass on what were formerly management responsibilities to the teams, leading to more efficient work performance. It was also apparent that the CEO felt that the company needed to increase its organization and co-ordination of work efforts. He hoped that the teams would help him to achieve efficiencies which would boost the firm's profitability.

Under the new system, three teams were created. The senior team consisted of the senior, more experienced sales producers (an industry term for agents who bring in premium money), along with administrative assistants (referred to as production assistants) and other support personnel. The junior team was similar in design except that its members were the more junior producers of the firm. Finally, the small accounts team was made up entirely of administrative personnel and handled all small accounts (those that brought in annual premiums of less than $500).

Each team was expected to meet approximately once per week. The team leaders were selected by the teams, but the acting CEO significantly influenced this process. Initial meetings often focused on company rules and procedures. The new system produced some distinct coordination and efficiency advantages. Junior team members, in particular, felt that these first meetings had been badly needed and were quite productive. Also, given the diversity of job functions on each team (sales producers, production assistants, marketing personnel and others), meetings provided a forum to discuss and co-ordinate work flow issues. Advantages identified by the junior team included clarifying individual responsibility for work, developing a more uniform approach to account handling, facilitating system development and definition and understanding of responsibilities, and designing specific responsibilities for special problems. The senior team identified similar issues, including providing more consistent customer service and developing greater knowledge of a smaller number of accounts. The team approach made it clear who was responsible for what.

Over time, however, several disadvantages of the team approach began to appear. First, tension emerged concerning the emphasis on efficiency and organization. This emphasis was fostered by the leaders of both the senior and junior teams, whose own jobs were made easier when procedures were followed closely. There were complaints about excessive paperwork. Senior team members in particular felt that rigidly following set procedures reduced their autonomy and discretion. Under the previous system, they had been able to set their own individual priorities, work schedules and so on, without first having to reach consensus with the others.

Second, the institution of separate teams resulted in a loss of agency identity and unity. For example, outside their team, other sales producers would not possess the knowledge to follow up on a sales producer's accounts if he or she were absent. Third, there was reduced customer service on small accounts because they were all dealt with by a third team which had no sales producers. Fourth, the institution of separate senior and junior teams deprived the less experienced sales producers of an opportunity to work with and learn from the senior team members. Finally, there was conflict between producers who wanted freedom from the red tape of procedures and production assistants who wanted procedures to be carefully followed to reduce their own hassles.

As a result of such problems there was a growing disillusionment with the team system. Senior producers, who did not need significant moral support from their peers to develop confidence and skills, were not motivated to support the new system, while junior sales producers, who did need this moral support, were frustrated by their non-representative, procedure focused team leadership. Eventually, team meetings became shorter, infrequent and non-productive, employee scepticism and apathy regarding the team approach rose, and efficiency and co-ordination plummeted.

In theory, self-managing teams should lead to greater autonomy. In this company, however, far from increasing autonomy, they operated as vehicles for limiting autonomy. At the end of the study, the CEO (who had become the president of the organization) was asked if perhaps he had really intended to use the 'self-managing' teams to extend and amplify his personal influence and control. He agreed, saying that 'every reason for doing the team system was control'.

Exercise

What lessons can be learned from the above case concerning the operation of self-managing teams? In particular, you may wish to consider such issues as the way in which such teams are introduced, the degree and type of autonomy they promote, whether there are differences between the needs of service and production organizations, how teams should be led, whether self-management can be facilitated more readily on an individual basis in some cases, what are the implications for staff development, the relationship between the team system and organizational rewards, and the way in which such factors influence the relationship between team systems and organizational effectiveness.

Source: Based on Manz and Angle (1993).

Chapter 8

Modern trait theories of leadership

INTRODUCTION

As we saw in Chapter 3, early research into leadership traits produced disappointing results. It appeared that few, if any, personality characteristics differentiated leaders from followers or more effective leaders from less effective leaders with any degree of consistency. As a result, interest in leadership traits declined as leadership theorists turned their attention to the study of the behavioural styles associated with successful and effective leadership.

During the 1970s, however, there were a number of indications that a rekindling of interest in the study of the relationship between personality traits and leadership was taking place. One was that certain researchers and theorists claimed that the original rejection of the trait approach to leadership had been premature in that it had been based on a misinterpretation of the research evidence. Another was the emergence of newer theories concerning the personality traits associated with successful and effective leadership which attempted to overcome some of the limitations of earlier approaches. Thirdly, there was the development of a new area of research and theory concerned with followers' perceptions of leaders' personality characteristics and their effects on followers' responses to them. Finally, after many years of neglect, there was a resurgence of interest in charismatic and related forms of inspirational leadership. However, writers on charismatic leadership have tended to incorporate hypotheses concerning both the personality traits and forms of behaviour associated with this type of leadership in their theories. It is also a major current area of research and theorizing in its own right. Discussion of charismatic leadership will therefore be delayed until the next chapter. In this chapter, the other three recent developments in the study of the relationship between personality and leadership will be discussed in turn.

REASSESSMENT OF EARLIER TRAIT RESEARCH

We have already noted that Stogdill (1974) argued that the implications of his earlier (1948) review had been misrepresented by some later writers. He claimed that, despite suggestions to the contrary, it had not demonstrated that leadership was entirely situational and that no personal characteristics were predictive of leadership. In his view, this represented an overemphasis on situational factors and an underemphasis on the personal nature of leadership. There was strong evidence that different leadership skills and traits were required in different situations, but equally there were instances in which the same qualities were required despite the differing circumstances.

Lord *et al.* (1986) went further in their reassessment of Mann's (1959) review of the relationship between personality characteristics and leadership. They suggested that not only had Mann's (1959) review been misinterpreted, but the results themselves were misleading. They reanalysed the data from the studies reviewed by Mann using meta-analysis and found average correlations between personality traits and leadership status higher than the median values originally quoted by Mann. For example, the correlation between intelligence and leadership status was 0.52 compared with the median of 0.25 reported by Mann. A further analysis, including data from subsequent studies in addition to those originally reviewed by Mann, showed that the traits of intelligence, dominance and masculinity were significantly associated with leadership status. While the correlations for adjustment, extraversion and conservatism did not reach significance, they were all positive and in the case of adjustment very close to significance.

Kenny and Zaccaro (1983) also argue that leadership traits are more stable than was previously thought. They analysed data concerning the emergence of leaders in small groups in which both group membership and tasks were varied. They estimated the extent to which a person was seen by others as a leader in different group situations and found that 49 to 82 per cent of leadership variance could be attributed to some stable characteristic or characteristics of the emergent leader. In a later study, carried out by Zaccaro *et al.* (1991), subjects worked on four different group tasks, each requiring as a primary behavioural style either initiating structure, consideration, persuasion or production emphasis. Group composition was varied for each task. They found that there was a significant tendency for the same person to be seen as a leader across group situations. On two of the four tasks, individuals ranked as leaders were more likely than non-leaders to display the required behaviours for the task. Furthermore, leader rankings were significantly related with scores on a self-monitoring test, which measures the ability to monitor and control one's own expressive behaviours. According to Zaccaro *et al.*, these results suggest that people who emerge as leaders behave in accordance with a group's functional requirements, but some group members may be more likely to emerge as leaders because they are better than others at perceiving these requirements and responding accordingly.

Note, however, that these studies refer to the personality traits associated with the emergence of leaders in small groups. They do not necessarily tell us about the personality traits associated with leadership success or effectiveness. Here the results tend to be less impressive. For example, Barrick and Mount (1991) carried out a meta-analysis of studies relating the so-called 'big five' personality dimensions to job performance. Average correlations between the personality dimensions and managerial job performance were found to be 0.22 for conscientiousness, 0.18 for extraversion, 0.08 for emotional stability and openness to experience, and 0.05 for agreeableness. The correlations for conscientiousness and extraversion were significant, but they are also very low. Thus it appears that these personality traits account for a very small proportion of the variance in managerial performance.

Although these results are concerned with managerial performance in general rather than with performance of the leadership role in particular, they do throw doubt on the idea that there is a simple, close relationship between personality and leadership performance. However, this still leaves the possibility that there exist relationships between personality and leadership performance of a more complex nature. Like the reviews quoted in Chapter 3, more recent surveys of leadership research (e.g. Bass 1990; Yukl 1994) suggest that there may be relationships between personality traits and leadership effectiveness and success, but they are not necessarily simple, positive ones. For example, Bass (1990) suggests that there is an optimum level for leader intelligence and competence. The leader should be more intelligent than the group and more able to solve the group's problems, but not too much more. Similarly, according to Yukl (1994), traits such as self-confidence and need for affiliation appear to be beneficial if they are at a moderate, rather than at a high or low level. Yet other traits, such as need for power, seem to be beneficial in some forms, but not in others. Thus, it appears that if stronger relationships between personality traits and leadership success or effectiveness are to be identified, more complex theories are required. In the next section, we will examine three such theories.

SITUATIONAL TRAIT THEORIES OF LEADERSHIP

As noted in Chapter 3, Stogdill suggested that, in order to understand the relationship between leadership and personality traits, it was necessary to take into account both combinations of traits rather than individual traits (Stogdill 1974) and the demands of the situation in which the person is to function as a leader (Stogdill 1948). In recent years, a number of theorists have been developing trait theories of leadership which go some way towards fulfilling both these requirements. The work of three such theorists, McClelland, Miner and Fiedler, will be discussed in this section.

McClelland's research on motivational traits and leadership

It does not appear that McClelland originally intended to produce a situational trait theory of leadership. Nevertheless, his research is quite clearly leading in this direction. It has been concerned with the effects on behaviour of a number of specific motives. His original work was concerned with the origins and motivational effects of the need for achievement (usually abbreviated to n Achievement or n Ach). McClelland and his associates found that people who are high in n Achievement are typically interested in excellence for its own sake rather than for rewards such as money, prestige or power; are more resistant to social pressure; choose experts rather than friends as work partners; like risky occupations; are more concerned with achieving success than avoiding failure; perform better under longer odds; pay more attention to realistic probabilities of success; choose moderate risks over either safe or speculative ones; have greater future time perspective; and come from families in which there has been a stress on early self-reliance and mastery (McClelland 1958; McClelland and Winter 1969).

According to McClelland (1975), people with high n Achievement become active entrepreneurs and create growing business firms which are the foundation stones of a growing economy. He argues that n Achievement leads to success in small business or in sales, where the key people do most of the work for themselves (see McClelland and Boyatzis 1982), and it has been found that motivation training can develop higher levels of n Achievement, leading in turn to higher levels of entrepreneurial activity and success (McClelland and Winter 1969).

However, McClelland (1975) argues that n Achievement should not be expected to be associated with managerial effectiveness and success in larger businesses. N Achievement, he suggests, is a one-person game which never needs to involve other people. As the one-person firm grows larger, however, it obviously requires some division of function and some organizational structure. Organizational structure involves relationships among people – getting people to work together, or dividing up the tasks to be performed, or supervising the work of others – and in McClelland's view high n Achievement does not equip people to deal effectively with such tasks. He argues that since managers are primarily concerned with influencing others, it seems obvious that they should be characterized not by high n Achievement but by a high need for power.

McClelland (1975) recognizes that this view is not a popular one, either with behavioural scientists, who have often favoured a participative, person-centred approach to leadership, or with the general public who feel that it is reprehensible to be concerned about influence over others. McClelland argues, however, that the need for power can be a positive as well as a negative attribute. He distinguishes between two types of power, personalized and socialized. People who desire personalized power want most of all to dominate or win out over someone else. Those who are motivated by socialized power, on the other hand, are characterized by a concern for group goals, for finding those goals that will move people, for helping the group to formulate them, for taking initiative in providing means of achieving them, and for giving group members the feeling of competence they need to work hard for them. In other words, people with a socialized power orientation not only desire power for themselves but also help their followers to feel powerful.

In large organizations, McClelland argues, the leadership motive pattern (LMP) which is associated with managerial effectiveness and success is one which combines being at least moderately high in the need for power, lower in the need for affiliation and high in self control. High n Power is important because it means that the person is interested in the 'influence game', in having an effect on others; lower n Affiliation is important because it enables the manager to make difficult decisions without unduly worrying about being disliked; and high self-control is important because it means that the person is likely to be more concerned with maintaining organizational systems and following orderly procedures (McClelland and Burnham 1976; McClelland and Boyatzis 1982). High self-control is also seen by McClelland (1975) as the key factor distinguishing a socialized from a personalized power orientation.

Research carried out by McClelland and his associates has provided empirical support for his views. In a study of over 50 managers of both high and low morale units in all sections of a large company, it was found that 80 per cent of the sales managers in charge of units with high morale had higher n Power than n Affiliation, while this was the case in only 10 per cent of the low morale units. Similarly, 73 per cent of the managers of high morale units in the research, product development and operations divisions had stronger n Power than n Affiliation compared with only 22 per cent of those managing poor morale units (McClelland and Burnham 1976). In a later study, McClelland and Boyatzis (1982) analysed the relationship between LMP and rate of promotion of 92 technical managers and 145 non-technical managers at the American Telephone and Telegraph Company. They found that among non-technical managers (e.g. those responsible for customer services, accounting, marketing, administration and administration-related functions), LMP was significantly related to subsequent promotion at eight and sixteen years after testing. N Achievement was associated with rate of promotion only at lower levels of non-technical management jobs. McClelland and Boyatzis (1982) suggest that this is because these are jobs in which individual contributions are more important than the ability to influence people. By contrast, at higher levels, in which promotion depends on demonstrated ability to manage others, n Achievement was not associated with success, but n Power was. In the case of the technical managers (e.g. engineers, plant managers, construction foremen and garage foremen), neither LMP nor n Achievement was associated with rate of promotion. McClelland and Boyatzis (1982) suggest that the lack of association between LMP and managerial success on the part of technical managers probably occurred because promotion on the technical side depended more on technical than leadership qualities.

Similar findings have emerged from other studies of technical managers. In a study of US naval officers, Winter (1979, quoted McClelland and Boyatzis 1982) found that although the leadership motive pattern was associated with success at the executive and commanding officer level, this only held true for officers in non-technical leadership positions. Success for people who held high rank because of their technical or engineering qualifications was not associated with the leadership motive pattern. The low predictive power of LMP with respect to technical managers leads House and Singh (1987) to question whether some combination of traits other than the leadership motive pattern might have higher predictive utility. They suggest that since technical supervisors constitute a substantial proportion of managers, research concerning the motivational determinants of success among technical managers is called for.

McClelland himself has suggested that it would be a mistake to assume that all leadership positions require high power motivation. Litwin and Siebrecht (1967, quoted McClelland 1975) have shown that ideally an integrative manager in a large organization is not excessively high in power motivation. Otherwise, too much time would be spent on influencing and not enough time integrating conflicting viewpoints. McClelland therefore suggests that the successful manager in this position has a more balanced profile, with moderately high power, affiliation and achievement motivation scores. By contrast, in other research, the combination of high need for power and high need for achievement has been found to be associated with managerial success (Cummin 1967), with company performance for research and development entrepreneurs (Wainer and Rubin 1969), with effectiveness of scientists, engineers and executives (Varga 1975) and with managerial performance, promotion rate and occupational choice (Stahl 1983).

A different pattern of motives associated with managerial success and effectiveness emerged from Cornelius and Lane's (1984) study of 21 centre managers and 18 curriculum directors in a company providing second language instruction. In the case of the centre managers, they found that neither LMP nor n Achievement predicted the size (and therefore importance) of the centre which they managed, the centre's administrative efficiency or the overall satisfaction of employees. The only significant relationship between motives and performance was between the manager's n Achievement and the organizational climate variable of subordinates' standards of excellence. In the case of the curriculum directors, who were in effect front-line supervisors of professional employees, n Achievement was unrelated to any of the performance measures, but LMP was positively related to centre size and negatively related to the administrative efficiency of the unit and overall satisfaction of employees. This means that although high LMP curriculum directors were appointed to larger, and therefore more prestigious work centres, it was those with high scores on the need for affiliation who performed better on the objective measures of administrative efficiency and tended to have work groups with better attitudes.

Thus, it appears that there may well be several different leadership motive patterns which are associated with managerial effectiveness or success, depending on the situation, as well as the one on which McClelland's research has concentrated. A more systematic analysis of the different motivational patterns required within different types of organization will be examined next.

Miner's role motivation theories

Miner's (1960, 1965) original role motivation theory was concerned with the motivation to manage and was limited to the domain of bureaucratic (hierarchical) organizations. During the 1980s, however, he expanded his typology of organizations to include, in addition to hierarchical organizations, professional, task (entrepreneurial) and group organizations. As the name suggests, hierarchical organizations are those in which management plays the key role. They establish work rules and regulations, evaluate job results, carry out organizational changes, judge individual competence and so on. Management induces contributions down through the hierarchy by manipulating positive and negative sanctions, and role prescriptions are specified in such documents as organization charts and written job descriptions. The large industrial corporation is an example of this type of organization. In professional or knowledge-based organizations, role requirements derive from the values norms, ethical precepts and codes of the profession rather than the management hierarchy. Members of the core profession assume the key roles and perform many of the activities which managers perform in hierarchic organizations. A law firm is an example of this type of organization. In task systems, sanctions which influence work performance are built into the task itself, rather than being mediated by higher managers or professional norms. A prime example is the entrepreneur, but others include profit centre managers, corporate venture managers, straight commission sales representatives and so on. Finally, in group systems, decisions are made by consensus or majority vote and leadership is emergent, occurs at the will of the majority, and is often rotating.

This typology, Miner (1993) argues, covers most organizational systems in modern society. However, he recognizes that other types may exist, such as patrimonial and charismatically led organizations. He also recognizes that the same organization may encompass more than one of his organizational types. For example, an organization may have within it several different systems in different parts. Thus, a large manufacturing organization with hierarchy at the top may also include research and legal systems which are largely professional, new venture teams that are largely task systems, and autonomous work groups on the shop floor that are largely group systems. Alternatively, the same organization or unit might simultaneously exhibit the characteristics of different organizational types. Thus, it is possible to have organizational systems that are mixed or composite, where no one type prevails. An example would be an organization in which some features of the work context are largely hierarchic, but an almost equal number are professional. Miner suggests that many business schools are of this type.

Miner's (1993) role motivation theories are concerned with the relationships between organizational types, role requirements for the key performers (managers, professionals, entrepreneurs or group members) and the motive patterns that fit these roles. Each type of organization, he argues, is characterized by a set of informal role requirements and a corresponding set of motive patterns (six in the case of hierarchical organizations and five each for the other types) which match these role requirements.

This leads Miner to the concept of 'motivation-organizational fit'. He argues that:

1. If the role-motivation match is good, the likelihood increases that the role requirements will be carried out and that effective performance will occur. On the other hand if the motivation pattern of the individual does not fit the role, there is an increasing likelihood that the individual will be unsuccessful.
2. When a particular organizational system is staffed appropriately (to achieve a motivational fit), it runs smoothly and produces output. Should the staffing be motivationally inappropriate, however, the system may not run at all, or if it does run it will do so at markedly reduced levels of efficiency.
3. If one studies leadership in each type of system, a particular motivational constellation should be elevated among the 'leaders', and that constellation should be more prevalent among the good (valued, high-performing) leaders than among the poor leaders. Furthermore, the managerial, professional, task and group motive patterns should predict success in the appropriate organizational system, but not the other three.

Later, however, Miner (1993) equates 'true' leadership with the role of the hierarchic manager and suggests that professional, task and group influences act as substitutes for this hierarchic influence.

Professional motives, commitments, norms, knowledge and training make hierarchic supervision largely unnecessary. Similarly commission sales people, such as real estate agents, can operate with little or no supervision because the level of their earnings tells them whether or not they are performing adequately; the substitute for leadership is built directly into the task. In group systems, co-workers take over much of the leadership function by training one another, exerting pressure to perform, even allocating compensation. There is little left for a leader to do.

(Miner 1993: 43)

The role requirements and corresponding motive patterns for managerial, professional, task/entrepreneurial and group organizations respectively are presented in Figures 8.1 to 8.4. Certain similarities to the work of McClelland will be noted. For example, the managerial motive patterns include the desire

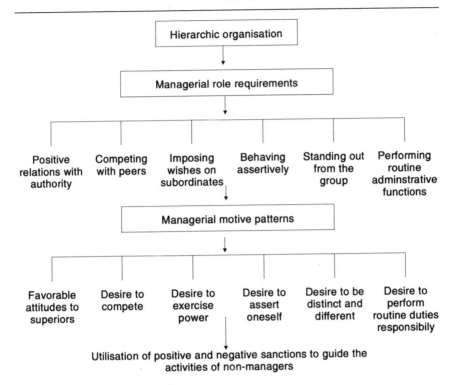

Figure 8.1 Outline of the hierarchic role motivation theory
Source: Miner 1965

to exercise power and to perform routine duties responsibly. Similarly, many of the task motive patterns match McClelland's need for achievement. One exception is the desire to avoid risk. Whereas McClelland takes the view that people who are high in n Achievement prefer a moderate level of risk, Miner argues that entrepreneurs attempt to minimize risk because risk-taking may result in business failure.

A detailed review of the research evidence concerning role motivation theories is presented in Miner (1993). Impressive results have been obtained in studies of the relationship between managerial role motive patterns and a variety of criteria such as grade level, performance ratings, advancement potential ratings, promotion rate and so on within hierarchical organizations. The results of 52 analyses of the relationship between total managerial motivation scores and criterion variables from 36 different studies are reported. In 94 per cent of cases, a significant positive relationship was found. Significant relationships between the individual managerial motive patterns and criterion variables ranged from 31 per cent of cases for Standing out from the Group to 56 per cent of cases for Competitive Situations. Equally importantly, managerial motive patterns show little relationship to criterion variables in non-hierarchical organiza-

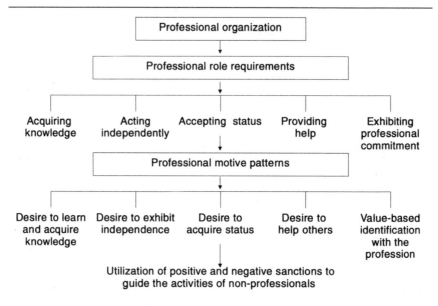

Figure 8.2 Outline of the professional role motivation theory
Source: Miner 1993

tions. In the case of total managerial motivation scores, only 12 per cent of 49 relationships from 22 different studies were significant. Furthermore, these were all negative (e.g. high-scoring research scientists and engineers being promoted *less* within their professional context).

Research into the validity of Miner's professional and task role motivation theories has produced positive results (see Miner 1993), although it is less extensive than for the managerial motive patterns, as the scales designed to measure them have been developed much more recently. No measure of group motive patterns has yet been developed and therefore the validity of this concept has not been tested.

In the case of the motivation to manage, research on managerial role motivation training provides a further source of validation studies relating to the theory. This training was originally developed by Miner (1960, 1965) with the specific objective of raising levels of motivation to manage in a research and development population, where professional activities often seem to be preferred to managerial. Miner (1993) reports on 15 studies of managerial role motivation training, involving 24 experimental groups and 11 control groups. In 96 per cent of the experimental group analyses there was an overall improvement in managerial role motivation subsequent to training while none of the controls showed a significant improvement. Only one of these studies examined the effect of managerial role motivation training on subsequent managerial success. Miner (1965) found that five years after training, those managers who had received training were significantly more likely than a

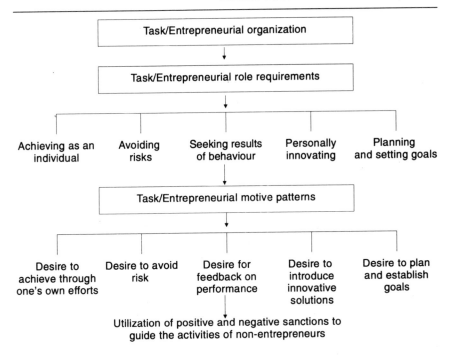

Figure 8.3 Outline of the task/entrepreneurial role motivation theory
Source: Miner 1993

matched, untrained control group to be promoted if they stayed with the organization or recommended for rehire if they left. However, there were differences in the amount to which the motivation to manage increased depending on the personality of the trainees. There was a consistent tendency for those who were more active and more independent to increase their motivation to manage, while those who were more passive and dependent were found to be largely unresponsive. Comparable training programmes have not been developed in relation to the professional, task and group role motivation theories.

Of the three theoretical approaches described in this section Miner's role motivation theories come closest to fulfilling Stogdill's suggestion that trait theories of leadership should incorporate both the demands of the situation and combinations of personality characteristics rather than single traits. Studies carried out both by Miner and his associates and by independent researchers provide evidence of the validity of his role motivation theories within the domains (types of organization) for which they are intended, but not for other types of organization. Furthermore, the results obtained in relation to the total scores for each cluster of motive patterns are more significant than those for the individual motive patterns within each cluster.

Nevertheless, Miner's treatment of leadership requires some clarification and further elaboration in certain areas. In particular, he does not adequately

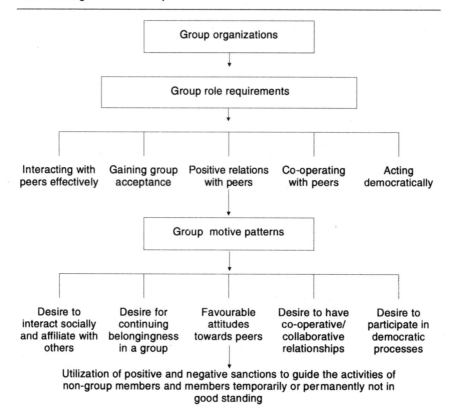

Figure 8.4 Outline of the group role motivation theory
Source: Miner 1993

reconcile his claim that a good role motivation match will be associated with more effective leadership in each type of organization with his later suggestion that professional, task and group organizations may be considered as providing substitutes for leadership. Part of the problem may be that he does not distinguish between 'neutralizers' which make it effectively impossible for leadership to make a difference and 'substitutes', which render relationship leadership not only impossible but also unnecessary. As noted in Chapter 6, Kerr and Jermier (1978) argue that this distinction is important because the substitutes for leadership provide a person or thing acting or used in place of the formal leader's negated influence, while the neutralizers do not, creating an 'influence vacuum' from which a variety of dysfunctions may emerge. Thus, it may well be that in certain respects professional, task and group organizations make it more difficult to exert leadership, but this does not necessarily mean that they render it unnecessary.

As we saw in Chapter 7, the introduction of self-managing teams does not eliminate the need for either internal or external leadership of such teams, but it does require the development of a more complex and sophisticated form of leadership. Similarly, having worked in an operational research consultancy and an industrial research laboratory as well as a business school, I have had numerous opportunities to observe subordinates attempting, sometimes successfully, to circumvent the wishes of their superiors by appealing to professional norms. However, anyone who has observed the organizationally damaging behaviour of a group of professionals engaged in a bitter struggle over status or scarce resources could be forgiven for wondering whether hierarchic leadership is quite as redundant in professional organizations as Miner seems to suggest.

Admittedly, Miner does note that it is possible to have organizational systems which are mixed or composite; where, for example, some features of the work context are hierarchic and others professional. This is undoubtedly true, but it follows that there could be both hierarchic and professional leaders within the same larger organization, who fulfil their leadership roles in quite different ways and thus actually behave quite differently as leaders. Alternatively, the same person may be expected to fulfil both roles. For example, a research laboratory section leader may be expected to provide both hierarchic and scientific leadership with respect to his or her subordinates and need to behave quite differently when performing the two roles. Both situations are potential sources of conflict. This raises the possibility that in mixed organizations, which after all are quite common, both organizational and leadership effectiveness may be associated with key personnel having an appropriate balance between different clusters of motive patterns, rather than scoring highly on one set or the other, or indeed both.

Furthermore, it is worth noting that, despite Miner's comment that research groups within a hierarchic organization may be largely professional, he includes several studies of research groups among those which are stated to be consistent with his managerial role motive theory. Thus, it would be possible to reduce the number of studies which are consistent with his managerial role motivation theory and increase the number which are inconsistent simply by redefining these groups as professional rather than hierarchical. Indeed, Miner himself is inconsistent in the way in which he classifies the study by Gantz *et al.* (1977) of scientists and engineers in a government R&D laboratory. Their finding of a positive correlation between managerial motivation and peer rating of managerial potential is regarded as supporting the validity of the hierarchic role motive theory within its domain, but their finding of a negative correlation between managerial motivation and actual promotion rate is said to indicate lack of validity outside its domain.

This suggests that the weakest part of Miner's theorizing is his typology of work and leadership situations. A somewhat more fine-grained system for categorizing work and leadership situations is required to take into account the complexities of organizational life. Another weakness of Miner's hierarchic role motive theory, pointed out by Bass (1990), is the absence of measures of subordinates' satisfaction, productivity, cohesiveness and growth. In fact, most of the measures of managerial success employed in validation studies, such as grade level and performance and potential ratings, represent superiors' perceptions of performance. As the research of Luthans *et al.* (1988) showed, however, rate of promotion may not be closely related to measures of effectiveness based on subordinate ratings. Thus, it would be useful to have more objective measures of managerial performance to establish whether managers with a high motivation to manage are genuinely more effective in the way they perform their roles or simply perceived to be more promotable by their superiors.

Fiedler's Cognitive Resource Theory

In his contingency theory of leadership, Fiedler argued that leadership effectiveness depended upon the leader's style being appropriate to the requirements of the situation (see Chapter 4). However, in his later Cognitive Resource Theory (Fiedler 1982; Fiedler and Garcia 1987), he suggests that leadership effectiveness will also depend on the leader's traits, in particular his or her intelligence and experience. He argues that intelligence will be more important in the case of directive rather than non-directive leaders, because directive leaders make the decisions themselves and tell the group what to do. They therefore need to be intelligent in order to come to the right decision. However, Fiedler proposes that three situational variables influence how much the directive leader's intelligence will affect his or her effectiveness. These are:

- the intellectual demands of the task;
- the support of the group;
- the stress in the job and in particular stress with the leader's own boss.

The influence of intelligence on the effectiveness of the leader will be greater, Fiedler argues, if the task is intellectually demanding (intelligence is not required if it is not), if the leader has the support of the group (who are therefore willing to put the leader's decisions into practice) and if the leader has a relatively stress-free job (because the calm conditions will allow the leader to think clearly and arrive at rational solutions to problems). Under these circumstances, Fiedler says, experience will not be related to leadership effectiveness. However, if the leader is under stress, this will prevent him or her from using intelligence to the best advantage, and intelligence will not correlate or even correlate negatively with leadership effectiveness, whereas experience will correlate highly. Under stress, Fiedler argues, people tend to revert to previously learned behaviour, and experience enables the leader to fall back on previous methods which have been effective in coping with task and interpersonal problems.

With respect to non-directive leaders, Fiedler says that if the leader has the support of the group on an intellectually demanding task, then it is not the leader's intelligence which will correlate with task performance, but the intellectual abilities of the group. He hints (Fiedler and Garcia 1987: 111) that certain characteristics may be important for effectiveness in non-directive leaders, such

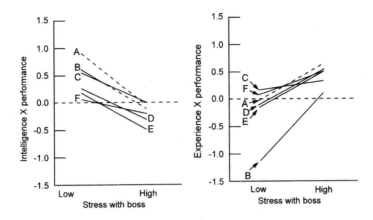

Figure 8.5 Summaries of correlations between intelligence and performance and organizational experience and performance

Subjects: First sergeants (A); company commanders (B); squad leaders (C); coastguards – high on intellectual tasks (D); staff officers (E); coast guards – low on intellectual tasks (F).

Note: All graphs show correlations as z'.

Source: Fiedler and Garcia 1987

as providing emotional support and interpersonal skills, but does not develop these ideas fully.

Fiedler and Garcia (1987) provide a detailed review of the research evidence concerning the Cognitive Resource Theory. As in the case of other complex theories, it is impossible to test the theory as a whole in any one study, because there are too many variables involved. Fiedler and his colleagues have therefore conducted a series of studies testing different aspects of the theory. In some cases, mixed results have been found. For example, there is only limited support for the hypothesis that abilities of group members will correlate with performance in groups in which a non-directive leader has the support of the group. Nevertheless, the main tenets of the theory are well supported. Figure 8.5 presents summaries of the correlations between (a) leader intelligence and performance and (b) organizational experience and performance under conditions of high and low stress with boss in studies of US Army squad leaders, first sergeants, company commanders and staff officers and US coastguards. It will be seen that all correlations are in the expected direction. Rated performance was consistently higher when intelligent leaders worked under unstressful conditions rather than stressful conditions and when experienced leaders worked under stressful conditions rather than unstressful ones. The coastguard study (Potter and Fiedler 1981) provides evidence of the interaction between intelligence and experience. As can be seen in Table 8.1, the results for all

Table 8.1 Correlations between intelligence and performance under low and high stress with boss for coastguard staff

Time in service	Low boss stress	High boss stress
All subjects	0.16 (60)	−0.27 (51)
Less than 10 years	0.73 (13)	−0.43 (16)[a]
10–20 years	−0.23 (21)	−0.28 (14)
More than 20 years	0.24 (16)	0.24 (14)

Note:
[a] Differences between correlations in the high and low boss stress columns are significant ($p < 0.001$)

Source: Fiedler and Garcia 1987

subjects are in the expected direction – intelligence correlates more highly with rated performance under conditions of low stress with boss – but the difference between the high and low stress conditions is not significant. However, there is significant difference for coastguards with less than ten years' experience, which is not present in more experienced subjects. This indicates that the effects of stress were much greater for those with relatively less time in service than for those who had been in the Coast Guard for an extended period of time. Fiedler and Garcia suggest that the more experienced subjects had presumably become less vulnerable to stress with their immediate superiors as they acquired friends in high places, gained indispensable knowledge about their jobs, or reached a more secure position in service.

Subsequent research into the Cognitive Resource Theory has produced somewhat mixed results. Murphy *et al.* (1992) carried out two studies of problem-solving in artificially created three- and four-person groups. They found that group members tended to be more satisfied with and more supportive of non-directive than directive leaders, but this did not affect performance. Consistent with Cognitive Resource Theory, the leader's technical knowledge or expertise contributed to group performance only if the leader was both trained and directive, while group members' task-relevant knowledge contributed to group performance only if the leader was non-directive. Gibson *et al.* (1993) studied the behaviour of leaders in three-person teams working on creative group tasks. They found that, under conditions of stress, more intelligent and more creative leaders tended to 'babble', that is, they tended to talk too much but say little of substance, and inhibited their group members from contributing meaningfully to the group process. On the other hand, the results of Vecchio's (1990) study of problem-solving in artificially created four-person groups were less conclusive. There was moderate support for the hypothesis that the correlation between leader intelligence and group performance would be greater for directive (low LPC) leaders than for non-directive (high LPC) leaders. However, three other hypotheses derived from Cognitive Resource Theory were not supported and the results relating to a further three hypotheses were inconclusive due to limitations of the research design.

Furthermore, while much of the research evidence supports Cognitive Resource Theory, a number of limitations can be identified. Some of these are methodological. We have already noted in Chapter 4 that it is not clear precisely what the LPC scale measures. Thus, we cannot be certain that Fiedler's results actually relate to directive and non-directive leaders, as he claims. Furthermore, there are indications that the relationship between leadership performance and experience may vary depending on the measure of experience used (Bettin and Kennedy 1990) and the relationship between leader intelligence and group performance under conditions of high and low stress may vary depending on the measure of intelligence used (Gibson 1992).

As a trait theory of leadership, Cognitive Resource Theory is very limited in scope. It takes into account only two individual difference variables and it is possible that other personality traits will influence leadership effectiveness in addition to intelligence and experience. Furthermore, the argument that non-directive leaders do not need to be intelligent seems intuitively questionable. They may make more use of the abilities of the group than directive leaders, but they will often need intelligence to evaluate the contributions of different group members and to control group discussions. Similarly, directive leaders may also need interpersonal skills to influence their subordinates, although different ones from non-directive leaders. A directive leader who gives orders in an unconvincing manner and does not know how to use the reward (and punishment) system effectively may simply become a laughing stock. Finally, the supporting evidence largely comes from work by Fiedler himself or his associates and is largely based on military and quasi-military establishments. To test the generality of the theory, it would be useful to see further studies carried out: (a) by independent researchers, (b) in different types of organization and (c) which incorporate additional personality variables and more refined measures of intelligence and experience. Nevertheless, the theory does appear to be an important breakthrough. Like Fiedler's earlier situational behavioural model, it may yet run into difficulties, but even so, if, like its predecessor, it opens up a new area of leadership research and theorizing it will have performed a very useful function.

IMPLICIT LEADERSHIP THEORIES AND THE INFORMATION-PROCESSING APPROACH TO THE STUDY OF LEADERSHIP

Implicit leadership theories have been studied extensively by Lord and his colleagues (see, for example, Lord et al. 1982; Lord et al. 1984; Lord and Maher 1993). In particular, they have been concerned with the methods that are used to process information about people and events, and how these influence the perception of leadership. Implicit leadership theories are not academic theories of leadership, but rather leaders' and followers' conceptions of the traits which characterize leaders or leaders of a certain type. Such theories help people to make sense of complex events and behaviours within the working environment by allowing such events and behaviours to be classified in terms of simpler categorization systems. They also enable predictions to be made concerning the ways in which people will behave in future, based on assumptions concerning the way in which people in a particular category usually behave. Finally, and most importantly from our point of view, implicit leadership theories influence whether a person is perceived as a leader and whether he or she is perceived as an effective leader or not. According to Lord *et al.* (1982), implicit leadership theories reflect the structure and content of cognitive categories which people use to distinguish leaders from non-leaders.

Lord and Maher (1993) argue that the ability to perform the leadership role depends on how the person is perceived by others. If a person is perceived as a leader, he or she can exert more influence than if not labelled as a leader by others. They therefore define leadership as: 'the process of being perceived by others as a leader'. The locus of leadership, they state, is not solely in the leader or solely in the followers. It involves behaviours, traits, characteristics and outcomes produced by leaders as these elements are interpreted by followers.

Lord and Maher (1993) suggest that we categorize objects and people based on their similarity or dissimilarity to prototypes of the members of that category. A prototype is an 'abstract conception of the most representative member or most widely shared features of a given cognitive category' (Phillips 1984: 126). In the case of people, these prototypes are derived from traits. To take a simple example, a prototype of a leader might be of someone who is intelligent, goal directed and responsible. Thus, someone who has these traits is likely to be perceived as a leader, but equally someone who is perceived as being a leader is also likely to be perceived as having these traits. In other words, once we attach a label to an object, person or event, this process of categorization guides how we interpret much of the subsequent information we encounter concerning that object, person or event. Over time, this additional information tends to strengthen the original categorization. If someone is categorized as an effective leader, then subsequent information is likely to be interpreted as confirming that he or she fits this category. Conversely, if a supervisor initially classifies a subordinate as a poor performer, subsequent performance information will be classified in terms of the poor performer label, even though the subordinate's performance may have improved in the meantime.

Lord and Maher (1993) suggest that the method of processing information whereby people are categorized as leaders can take a number of different forms. Leadership can either be *recognized* from the qualities and behaviours revealed through normal day-to-day interactions with others, or it can be *inferred* from the outcomes of salient events. That is, someone may be labelled as a leader either because he or she has certain attributes, such as intelligence and honesty, or because he or she is seen as being directly responsible for some favourable outcome, such as increased profits.

Table 8.2 Alternative types of processes used to form leadership perceptions

Models of perceptual processes	Data	Mode of cognitive process	
		Automatic	Controlled
Recogition	Traits and behaviours	Prototype matching based on face-to-face contact	Prototype matching based on socially communicated information
Inferential	Events and outcomes	Perceptually guided, simplified causal analysis	Logically based comprehensive causal analysis

Source: Lord and Maher 1993

Such processes may also be either *controlled* or *automatic*. Controlled processes require awareness, intent and effort, and interfere with other cognitive tasks, whereas automatic processes do not. These distinctions yield the two-by-two classification of leadership perception processes summarized in Table 8.2. Lord and Maher (1993) suggest that, because social interactions often place high information-processing demands on those involved, recognition-based processes will typically be more automatic. However, more controlled processes may be involved where leaders are not observed directly, but information relevant to leadership is socially communicated (for example through the media or co-workers). The same prototype-matching process is used to form leadership perceptions in both cases.

Lord *et al.* (1984) identified 35 attributes, such as being goal directed, informed, charismatic, decisive, responsible, intelligent, and so on, which American college students most frequently used to characterize leaders. They also identified 11 different leadership contexts, such as military, educational, business, religious, and so on. They found that there are some fairly general aspects of leadership. For example, intelligence was thought to characterize leadership in ten of the eleven contexts, the sole exception being national political leader. On the other hand, they also found that many traits only characterized leaders in specific contexts. Thus, leaders in different contexts do not share exactly the same set of traits, even though they are all recognized as being leaders. This means that leaders may have difficulty moving from some leadership contexts to others. If there is a high degree of overlap among the traits characterizing leaders in the two contexts (for example, business and finance), leaders may move from one context to the other without much difficulty. On the other hand, if there is minimal overlap (for example, sports and finance), leaders who attempt to move from one field to another may face substantial difficulties.

Lord *et al.* (1984) also asked college students to rate the extent to which they perceived a district manager described in three short vignettes as a leader. The vignettes were identical except for four or five phrases which were very prototypical of leaders (provides information, emphasizes goals, talks frequently, and specifies problems), neutral with respect to leadership (seeks information, seeks suggestions, explains actions, clarifies attitudes, and prevents conflicts), or antiprototypical of leaders (admits mistakes, withholds rewards, criticizes harshly, and neglects details). As expected, ratings of the person as a leader were highest when he was described as using prototypical leadership behaviours, intermediate for the neutral descriptions and lowest for the antiprototypical leadership behaviour descriptions. This prototype matching explained 53 per cent of the variance in leadership perceptions. Furthermore, expectations about other behaviours not described in the vignettes were influenced by the initial descriptions. That is, if the person was described as using prototypical leadership behaviours, he was expected to exhibit greater use of other prototypical leadership behaviours and a lower use of antiprototypical leadership behaviours. Conversely, if the person was described as using antiprototypical leadership behaviours, he was expected to exhibit greater use of other antiprototypical leadership behaviours and a lower use of prototypical leadership behaviours. According to Lord and Maher (1993), these results suggest that a person's initial classification in terms of leadership is based on his or her behaviour and then further inferences about the person are based on raters' implicit leadership theories (general knowledge associated with leadership categories), rather than the person's actual behaviour.

The effects of inferential processes in leadership perceptions were demonstrated in a study carried out by Rush *et al.* (1981). Undergraduate students were shown 15-minute videotapes of group problem-solving sessions. After viewing the videotapes, they were given bogus performance feedback indicating that the group they had watched was either second best or second worst out of 24 groups performing the experimental tasks. The students were then asked to make leadership ratings of the people in the videotape. The feedback manipulation was significantly correlated with leadership ratings made immediately after viewing the videotape ($r = 0.31$) and after a 48-hour delay ($r = 0.40$), even though subjects in both the 'good' and 'poor' feedback conditions viewed the same leadership behaviours. In other words, according to Lord and Maher (1993), success enhances the perception of leadership, while failure limits the perception of leadership. As we shall see, however, the strength of this effect is influenced by the extent to which the person is seen as causing the positive or negative outcomes. The more he or she is seen as causing the outcomes, the more this will beneficially or adversely affect leadership ratings.

As noted earlier, inferential processes may involve either controlled or automatic processing of information. People may think very carefully about causality, trying to assess the relative impact of the leader and other potential facilitative and inhibitive factors on what was achieved. Alternatively, they may unknowingly be influenced by factors in the situation which makes some causal sources more salient than others. A study carried out by Phillips and Lord (1981) illustrates both these processes. As in the previous study, leadership ratings were made after subjects had watched a group problem-solving task and received bogus feedback on the performance of the videotaped group. As expected, even though all subjects had viewed the same videotaped interaction, subjects gave the target person higher leadership ratings when they were told that the group had performed well rather than poorly. However, this effect was diminished if other, plausible explanations of the group's performance were given. When subjects were told that groups which had performed well were high in ability and motivation or were told that groups which had performed poorly were low in ability and motivation, then the role of the leader was discounted. On the other hand, if subjects were told that the high performing group was low in ability and motivation, then the leader was rated more highly. Conversely, if they were told that the low performing group was high in ability and motivation, then the leader received lower ratings. According to Lord and Maher (1993), this logical integration of information suggests controlled, rational processing of information.

Another, less rational factor also influenced causal attributions in Phillips and Lord's study. The videotapes shown to the subjects were filmed from two alternative camera angles which made the target subject more or less salient. Although the same behaviours were clearly visible in both videotapes, the leader was rated as a significantly more important determinant of the group's performance when he was high in perceptual salience than when he was low in perceptual salience. Lord and Maher (1993) suggest that this effect probably involves more automatic processes rather than deliberate, reflective ones.

Lord and Maher (1993) argue that the models of leadership perceptions which they put forward have different practical implications depending on the level within the corporate hierarchy being considered. They suggest that lower level leadership emphasizes automatic, recognition based processes, because lower level supervisors generally interact on a face-to-face basis with workers. As a by-product of such interaction, leadership perceptions are formed by subordinates. If the category of an effective leader is widely held by these subordinates, therefore, it would benefit the manager to learn what traits and behaviours are prototypical of effective leadership and make an effort to behave in congruence with this prototype when feasible. Lord and Maher suggest that leadership training programmes should aim towards identifying subordinates' perceptions of effective leadership in particular contexts. They comment that although behaviours and traits associated with effective leadership are thought to be consistent across situations by popular writers, there may be important differences across organizations, among different levels of the same organization, across different task domains, or even among different subordinates in a given work unit. Thus, managers new to an organization, or those with heterogeneous work groups should be sensitive to different prototypes that affect subordinates' perceptions of effective leadership in these domains.

Lord and Maher (1993) note that automatic, recognition-based processes of leadership perception are also important in the case of senior executives when they are interacting on a face-to-face basis with their team of managers. In general, however, executive-level leadership perceptions emphasize the remaining three processes in Table 8.2, because top leaders must also convey leadership to a much broader group that their immediate team of managers. In so doing, they employ less direct means of influence, such as symbolism, images, and policies that affect the organization as a whole. Thus, top executives are dependent on more controlled recognition-based processes, as well as on inferences about leadership that are drawn from key organization events.

Lord and Maher (1993) argue that to be effective, executive-level leaders must make use of perceptually derived power to influence factors that affect organizational performance, either directly or indirectly. Such power can be increased through automatic recognition-based processes if an executive fits an effective leadership prototype held by members of powerful constituencies within the organization. Senior executives can also enhance their perceptually derived power in more indirect ways by ensuring that socially communicated information about their behaviours fits a leadership prototype held by those within the organization with whom they do not interact directly, and by associating themselves in a salient manner with organizational achievements, while distancing themselves as far as possible from poor outcomes (for example, by blaming others or adverse circumstances).

However, Lord and Maher (1993) note that the methods of information processing involved in forming leadership perceptions can be particularly troublesome for atypical leaders, such as minorities and females. Because they are rarely seen in leadership roles, women and members of minority groups do not fit existing conceptualizations of typical leaders and therefore will not automatically receive credit for success, even though their unique status makes them salient. Instead, they will tend to receive closer scrutiny as their perceivers consciously, but perhaps inappropriately, consider alternative causes for their success. Thus, according to Lord and Maher, minorities and women may have a particularly difficult time managing their impressions as leaders.

The work of Lord and his associates also has implications for cross-cultural leadership. O'Connell et al. (1990) found that the cognitive categories used by Japanese students to classify leaders were quite different from those used by the American students in the study by Lord et al. (1984). According to Lord and Maher (1993), these results suggest that an understanding of cultural differences in leadership prototypes may be necessary in order for managers in foreign countries to manage effectively. For example, individuals who fit the leadership prototypes of Japanese workers may not be evaluated favourably in an American organization and vice versa. Such problems, they argue, could cause misperceptions and underutilization of managerial talent. Being perceived as a leader is crucial to effective top-level leadership, and this process could be limited by culturally bound definitions of leadership.

Lord and Maher (1993) note that the research so far carried out into the processes underlying leadership perceptions has a number of limitations. First, there may be other factors, not covered in this research, such as the subordinate's attempts at image management and the manager's non-verbal behaviour, which also influence leadership perceptions. Second, the studies did not investigate repeated perceptions of leadership and therefore do not throw light on the important question of how perceivers change categories over time. Third, the research has not explained how inferential and recognition-based processes of leadership perception are combined. Finally, they suggest that an interesting area for future research would be the study of individual differences in leadership perception processes. In the Phillips and Lord (1981) study, for example, it was impossible to identify which methods of information processing were used by individual subjects. Nevertheless, it appeared likely that some subjects emphasized rational processing, while others based their perceptions on salience, rather than each using both processes.

Furthermore, putting into practice the findings of research based on an information-processing approach to the study of leadership may be less straightforward than Lord and Maher (1993) suggest. They are undoubtedly correct in their assertion that being seen as a leader by followers helps a leader to influence them and may ultimately help the leader to be more organizationally effective. However, they do not examine the potential conflict between being seen as a leader and behaving in an effective way as a leader. Such a conflict could very well arise if followers hold a prototype of an effective leader which is an inappropriate one. Talking frequently was said to be prototypical of leaders in the study by Lord *et al.* (1984), but was not a characteristic of successful leaders in the observational studies of manager–subordinate interactions carried out by Alban Metcalfe (1984), Johnston (1990) and Callaghan and Wright (1994). Conversely, behaviours which were found to be associated with successful leadership in these studies, such as seeking information and suggestions, were classified as neutral with respect to leadership in the study by Lord *et al.* It is impossible to reach firm conclusions based on these studies, because we do not know what leadership prototypes were held by the subjects in the observational studies. Nevertheless, they do raise the possibility that at times leaders may have to perform a difficult balancing act between, on the one hand, behaving in ways that facilitate making the right decision and, on the other, behaving in ways which make them appear as effective leaders to their followers.

It is also questionable whether leadership perceptions derived from face-to-face interactions are necessarily processed solely in terms of automatic processes. There may not be time for a more controlled analysis of impressions during the interaction itself, but this by no means precludes the use of more controlled recognition-based processes at a later stage when the subordinate thinks over earlier events. First impressions can have lasting effects, but equally people may revise their opinions when they have time to think more carefully about the way in which they have been treated. Therefore, unless the manager is told about these second thoughts by the subordinate, he or she could be left with completely erroneous beliefs concerning the impression which has been made.

Even greater problems in impression management are likely to arise at the senior executive level. Subordinates often gossip about their superiors within organizations, discussing how effective they are and comparing notes about such things as how they behave in meetings, whether they contradict themselves, whether they keep their word, and so on. If Lord and Maher (1993) are correct in their statement that prototypes of effective leadership may vary widely within the same organization, then matching one's behaviour to those held by different groups may be impossible. It may be possible to match one's behaviour to the group with whom one is interacting directly, but when the impression given to this group is transmitted socially, there can be no guarantee that it will fit the leadership prototypes held by other groups or individuals within the organization. Furthermore, the more the leader tries to match his or her behaviour to prototypes held by different groups, the more he or she runs the risk of being perceived as someone who is inconsistent, which could have damaging consequences for perceptions of leadership. I am aware of two cases, one in industry and one in academic life, in which the reputation for honesty and trustworthiness of a senior member of an organization was seriously undermined because it became widely believed that assurances given in one meeting had been repudiated in another. These examples confirm Lord and Maher's view that impression management is extremely important as far as senior executives are concerned. However, they also show that it is a very complex matter, requiring careful thought about the way all aspects of behaviour will be perceived throughout the organization.

CONCLUSIONS

In this chapter, we have examined evidence that the rejection of personality traits as predictors of leadership emergence, success and performance was premature. Reanalysis of early trait research and the results of some more recent studies do suggest that influential reviews of trait research published during the 1940s and 1950s underestimated the role of personality in determining who emerged as leaders in informal groups. However, evidence that particular personality traits invariably influenced leadership performance in the same direction remained both scarce and inconclusive. Nevertheless, more recent research carried out by McClelland, Miner and Fiedler does give hope that it will be possible to make more accurate predictions of leadership performance if these are based on clusters of traits rather than individual traits and on performance in specific types of situation rather than in general. This has implications both for the selection and training of leaders. Leaders can be selected on the basis of clusters of traits required in different situations. The work of McClelland and Miner also suggests that certain personality characteristics, such as need for achievement and motivation to manage which may be beneficial in certain types of work role can be developed through training. While general intelligence is relatively stable in adulthood and therefore difficult to influence through training, it may be possible to train job-holders in problem-solving techniques which would enable them to make better use of their natural level of intelligence. In addition, training could help leaders to develop more quickly the types of experience they need in particular jobs and also to develop greater stress tolerance.

The work of Lord and his associates on implicit leadership theories has practical implications in a number of areas. It suggests that judgements of leadership performance and potential can be biased by irrational factors. Given that decisions concerning the selection, promotion and continued employment of leaders are made much more often on the basis of interviews and observation than on the basis of objective data, then it is perceived rather than actual personality traits which are more likely to influence those decisions. Thus, the findings concerning implicit personality theories remind us of the need to be aware of and to beware such biases as far as possible when drawing conclusions about potential or actual leaders on the basis of our perceptions. Conversely, Lord's work also provides potential and actual leaders with information which could be useful in attempts to manipulate other people's perceptions, thus reinforcing the need to take great care in the way we respond to such perceptions. This point has considerable relevance in relation to the response to charismatic leadership. This issue will be taken up in the next chapter.

Chapter 9

Charismatic and related forms of leadership

INTRODUCTION

The concept of charismatic leadership has a long history. Charisma was originally a theological concept, meaning a gift of God's grace which enables a human being to perform exceptional tasks (Lepsius 1986). It was introduced into the social sciences in the early years of this century by Weber. He suggested that claims to legitimate authority could be made on three grounds – rational-legal, traditional and charismatic. For Weber, a claim to authority based on charismatic grounds rested on devotion to the specific and exceptional sanctity, heroism or exemplary character of an individual person, and on the normative patterns or order revealed or ordained by him. According to Weber, the charismatically qualified leader is obeyed 'by virtue of personal trust in him and his revelation, his heroism or his exemplary qualities' (Weber 1947).

Weber's way of defining charisma contained within it the seeds of confusion and controversy. It suggests that a charismatic leader is one who both has certain extraordinary qualities and produces certain responses – trust and devotion – in followers. However, if both these factors are said to be involved in charismatic leadership, then the cause and effects of charisma are included in the same definition. A charismatic leader cannot fail to inspire devotion and trust in followers, because someone who does not inspire devotion and trust simply is not charismatic.

Charismatic leadership became a popular area of study among political scientists and sociologists, but there was little agreement concerning precisely where the origins of this mysterious quality could be located. Some identified specific attributes which were said to characterize the charismatic leader, others argued that social and historical contexts were critical in the emergence of charismatic leaders, and yet others argued that charismatic leadership involved a particular type of relationship between leaders and their followers (Conger and Kanungo 1987).

THE STUDY OF CHARISMATIC LEADERSHIP WITHIN ORGANIZATIONS

Perhaps because of its inherent ambiguity, organization theorists, and particularly leadership theorists, paid relatively little attention to the concept of charisma. However, an influential paper by House (1977) demonstrated how charismatic leadership could be studied in a more objective manner, and it has since become one of the major current areas of interest among leadership theorists. In general, organization theorists have taken an interactive approach to the study of charismatic leadership. House took the view that the starting-point for the study of charismatic leadership was the effects which the leader has on the followers. Furthermore, he suggested that such effects were more emotional than calculative, in that the follower is inspired enthusiastically to give unquestioning acceptance, willing obedience, trust, affection, loyalty, commitment and devotion to the leader, and to the cause the leader represents. Leaders who produced such effects would then be classified as charismatic and the characteristic which distinguished such leaders from other leaders and the situational factors associated with their emergence could then be determined empirically.

The role of the follower in the emergence of charismatic leadership has also been an important aspect of subsequent theories of charismatic leadership, but in general these emphasize the way a leader is perceived by followers. For example, Conger and Kanungo (1987) state that charisma must be viewed as an attribution made by followers who observe certain behaviours on the part of the leader within organizational contexts. Similarly, Bryman (1992) argues that charismatic leadership involved a particular type of social relationship between leaders and followers, in which the leader is viewed as extraordinary and special by followers and regarded with a mixture of reverence, unflinching dedication and awe. While giving a central role to follower attributions, this approach also allows for the possible influence of a variety of factors on such attributions and thus the perception of charisma. Among them are the actual characteristics of the leader, his or her behaviour, the characteristics of followers, the way they respond to the leader and the circumstances in which the leader emerges or is seen to be charismatic.

Characteristics of charismatic leaders

According to House (1977), personality traits which have been found or hypothesized to characterize charismatic leaders include extremely high levels of self-confidence, dominance, a strong conviction in the moral righteousness of their beliefs and a high need to have influence over others. Attributes noted by other writers include an ability to inspire and/or create inspirational activities (Conger and Kanungo 1987), great oratorical skill (Bryman 1992), a high degree of linguistic ability and non-verbal expressiveness (House *et al.* 1988) and emotional expressiveness (Conger and Kanungo 1988c).

A wide range of behaviours have been suggested as possible sources of charismatic leaders' influence over followers. House (1977) proposed the following: acting as a role model for the types of behaviours, values and beliefs they wished their followers to adopt; engaging in behaviours designed to create an impression of competence and success; articulating a transcendental goal; communicating high expectations for subordinates and exhibiting confidence in their ability to meet them; and the communication of messages that are especially relevant to mission accomplishment.

Conger and Kanungo (1987) suggest that charismatic leaders within organizations:

- have an idealized goal or vision of what they want the organization to achieve, which is highly discrepant from the status quo yet remains within the latitude of acceptance of their followers.
- may take on high personal risks, incur high costs, and engage in self-sacrifice to achieve a shared vision, thus enhancing subordinates' perception of their trustworthiness.
- demonstrate expertise in transcending the existing order through the use of unconventional or extraordinary means.
- engage in behaviours which are novel, unconventional, and counternormative and, as such, involve high personal risk or high probability of harming their own self-interest.
- engage in realistic assessments of the environmental resources and constraints effecting the realization of their visions, implementing innovative strategies when the environmental resource–constraint ratio is favourable to them.
- portray the status quo as negative or intolerable and the future vision as the most attractive and attainable alternative.
- articulate their motivation to lead through assertive behaviour and expression of self-confidence, expertise, unconventionality, and concern for followers' needs.
- use their personal idiosyncratic power (expert and referent) rather than their position power (legal, coercive and reward).
- exert such idiosyncratic power over followers through elitist, entrepreneurial, and exemplary behaviour rather than through consensus-seeking or directive behaviour.
- act as reformers or agents of radical changes and their charisma fades when they act as administrators or managers.

For Bryman (1992), a pivotal component of charismatic leadership is the leader's sense of mission, since a charismatic leader who is bereft of a mission or vision is almost inconceivable. He suggests that common themes to be found running through writings on charismatic and related inspirational forms of leadership are that the leader:

- has a vision;
- communicates the vision in such a way that it is fully understood and can be a focus of people's commitment;

- empowers members of the organization to fulfil the vision;
- creates an organizational culture which is consistent with the vision;
- changes organizational structures in line with the vision;
- inspires the trust of those with whom they work.

Characteristics of followers of charismatic leaders

Less research has been carried out on the characteristics of followers which lead them to respond to charismatic leaders or to regard leaders as having charismatic attributes. However, it seems likely that there are significant individual differences in this respect. As Bass (1990) observes, what different prospective followers feel about charismatic leaders is more important than what such leaders do or say. The same words or actions by a would-be leader can seem charismatic and extremely influential to ardent disciples but humbug to others.

The source of such differences could be two-fold. Either the particular leader or vision may appeal to some people more than others, or some people may be more susceptible than others to charismatic leaders or visions in general. As noted earlier, House (1977) suggested that one explanation of the emotional appeal of charismatic leaders may be that they arouse motives which are particularly relevant to mission accomplishment. Among those specifically mentioned are the arousal of need for affiliation through exhortation of love and affection for fellow human beings, arousing the power motive by military leaders through symbols of authoritarianism and an image of the enemy, and arousing need for achievement in work organizations by frequently stressing excellence as a measure of one's worth. Given that people vary in the strength of such needs, it would seem to follow that responses to leaders articulating a vision based on such motives would also vary. In a similar vein, House (1977) suggests that for a leader to have charismatic effects, it is necessary for the role of followers to be defined in ideological terms that appeal to followers. Again, given that potential followers are likely to have ideologies which differ to some degree, one would also expect their response to the leader to vary.

Bass (1985b) identifies a number of follower personality traits which may have a more general influence on their response to charismatic leaders. It is easier to be perceived as a charismatic leader, he suggests, when followers have highly dependent personalities. Conversely, subordinates who pride themselves on their own rationality, scepticism, independence, and concern for law and precedence are less likely to be influenced by a charismatic leader. He also suggests that subordinates who are egalitarian, self-confident, highly educated, self-reinforcing, and high in status are likely to resist charismatic leaders. Similarly, Yukl (1994) suggests that personal identification with a charismatic leader is most likely to occur with followers who have low self-esteem, a weak self-identity, and a high need for dependence on an authority figure. These followers, he argues, become loyal to the leader, not to any particular attitude or strategy espoused by the leader. If the leader dies or departs, followers will look for a substitute leader to help them understand their hostile environment and feel less anxious about it. On the other hand, Shamir *et al.* (1993) hypothesize that followers will be susceptible to charismatic leadership the more they are motivated by a need for self-expression and the more they have a principled approach to social relations. Furthermore, Conger (1989) points out that many of the studies which found that followers of charismatic leaders were easily persuaded and lacking in self-esteem focused on followers who were disaffected by society, and none of them involved business organizations. He argues that in business settings there is likely to be a broad range of individuals, ranging from the assertive to the servile, and both types can become followers of charismatic leaders. He therefore concludes that it would be wrong to assume that only the insecure will follow a charismatic leader.

One characteristic that may affect followers' general response to charismatic leadership which has been studied within business organizations is the tendency to romanticize leadership. Meindl (1988, 1990) suggests that people who take a romanticized view of leadership (that is, they believe that leaders have a major impact on organizational effectiveness) are more likely to perceive leaders as being charismatic. Supporting this contention, he found correlations between scores on Meindl and Ehrlich's (1988) Romance of Leadership scale and ratings of Ronald Reagan and Lee Iacocca on Bass's (1985b) measure of charisma of 0.44 and 0.53 respectively. In a later study by Ehrlich *et al.* (1990) the relationship was investigated between employees' Romance of Leadership scores and their attributions of charisma to a general manager who was regarded as having been responsible for an abrupt turnaround in the financial and market performance of a small high-technology company. The correlation between the two measures was 0.32, which fell marginally short of significance. Thus there was some evidence of a relationship, but in this case it was not a strong one. However, it is interesting to note that individuals who had had greater contact with the general manager before his appointment to his present position perceived him to be less charismatic.

The influence of the situation on the emergence of charismatic leaders

A number of characteristics of the situation have also been suggested as factors leading to the emergence of a charismatic leader or the perception of charismatic attributes in a leader. According to Weber, the existence of a crisis is necessary for charismatic leadership to occur. This issue has caused deep divisions among subsequent writers on charismatic leadership, some arguing that a crisis is a necessary condition for, or even a root cause of, the emergence of charismatic leadership, and others that it is neither a necessary nor a sufficient cause (Conger and Kanungo 1987). Organization theorists writing on charisma have tended to take a less dogmatic view on this subject. House (1977) hypothesized that a strong feeling of distress on the part of followers is one of the situational factors that interacts with the leader's traits and behaviour to result in charismatic effects, but added that it remained to be established whether this was a necessary condition. For Trice and Beyer (1986), the existence of a social crisis or situation of desperation is by definition one of the components of charisma, but they state that it need not be present to a high degree, only to some minimal degree that has not yet been determined. It seems unlikely that this controversy will ever be satisfactorily resolved, given the enormous potential for disagreement about whether any particular leader is really charismatic or whether any particular situation is really serious enough to constitute a crisis. Nevertheless, a consensus appears to be emerging among organization theorists writing on charisma that, while charismatic leaders often emerge in times of crisis (Bass 1990) and disenchantment with the prevailing social order and psychological distress facilitates the emergence of charismatic leaders (Conger and Kanungo 1987), none of these conditions is necessary for charismatic leadership to occur.

Weber also argued that it was necessary for charismatic leaders to be successful in order to validate their extraordinary gifts. If a charismatic leader failed, then the leader's charismatic authority was likely to disappear. According to Bryman (1992), this seems to be happening in the case of Lee Iacocca who appears to be undergoing a process of 'decharismarization' following recent poor results at Chrysler. Bennis and Nanus (1985) go so far as to suggest that charisma is probably the result of effective leadership rather than the other way around, and that those who are good at it are granted a certain amount of awe by their followers. Some support for this view can be found in the work of Lord and his associates which showed that perceptions of leadership could be influenced by bogus information concerning the performance of the leader's group. This suggests that success and failure are likely to influence perceptions of charismatic leadership even when the leader had little direct influence over the outcomes concerned. Nevertheless, it is questionable whether effective leadership will always result in attributions of charisma. The research of Lord and his associates suggests that the reverse may happen. An effective, but self-effacing leader may find that his or her successes are attributed to other factors. Furthermore, while failure may result in disillusionment with an erstwhile charismatic leader, it is also questionable whether this invariably happens, particularly in the short run. As Lepsius (1986) points out, there are many examples of failed prophesies which are still believed. Following a cause wholeheartedly can involve a considerable investment of emotion, effort, time, resources, credibility and so on, and many followers may, initially at least, find it easier to reinterpret the situation than admit to failure, and the unpleasant corollary that their commitment to the cause had been misguided. A skilful charismatic leader may therefore be able to capitalize on this, claiming that actually the apparent failure will ultimately help them to achieve an even greater success.

Finally, people may be perceived as possessing charismatic qualities because they occupy a particular position. Etzioni (1961) distinguished between 'personal' and 'office' charisma. Personal charisma derives from the qualities which followers ascribe to the leader as a person, regardless of his or her status. Office charisma, on the other hand, accrues from holding some high status position, such as pope, president or queen. In some cases, of course, the person occupying such a position may have personal charisma, as well as that derived from the office.

Theories of charismatic leadership

It will be apparent that in addition to identifying the characteristics of leaders, followers and situations which give rise to charismatic leadership, the material described above also provides a set of discrete, relatively simple explanations of why charismatic leadership occurs. For example, charismatic leaders are able to influence followers because they have dominant personalities, provide attractive solutions to distressing situations, appeal to people who have little capacity for independent thought, and so on. Some theorists, however, have attempted to develop more comprehensive explanations of the psychological and social processes involved in followers' emotional responses to charismatic leaders and attribution of charismatic qualities to them.

Conger (1989), for example, suggests that followers are attracted to charismatic leaders because of their identification with his or her ability. The leader's qualities of strategic insight, unconventionality, dynamism, ability to excite and other traits appear so extraordinary that subordinates are naturally attracted to him or her. This extraordinary figure then becomes a model for success and excellence within the organization, and subordinates quite naturally desire to emulate his or her strengths and values. Furthermore, such leaders use a variety of techniques to empower their subordinates. These include providing opportunities to accomplish difficult or complex tasks, persuading subordinates that they have the capacity to master difficult tasks, staging dramatic events which stir up positive emotions, and acting as a model for subordinates by visibly demonstrating confidence in their own abilities. By such means, Conger suggests, charismatic leaders are able to heighten followers' beliefs in their ability to achieve the leader's vision. Empowerment, according to Conger, is essentially a process of strengthening subordinates' conviction in their own self-efficacy.

Similar ideas are incorporated into a more complex theory concerning the processes involved in charismatic leadership developed by Shamir *et al.* (1993). They suggest that charismatic leadership has its effects by strongly engaging followers' self-concepts and expressive motivation in the interest of the mission articulated by the leader. They argue that people's behaviour is not motivated solely by self-interest, but is also expressive of feelings, aesthetic values and self-concepts. In particular, people are motivated to maintain and enhance their self-esteem and self-worth. Self-esteem is based on a sense of competence, power, achievement or ability to cope with and control one's environment.

Self-worth is based on a sense of virtue and moral worth and is grounded in norms and values concerning conduct.

Shamir *et al.* (1993) suggest that charismatic leaders motivate their followers in the following ways:

- Increasing the intrinsic valence of effort, e.g. by emphasizing the symbolic and expressive aspects of effort – the fact that effort itself reflects important values and that by making effort one makes a moral statement.
- Increasing effort–accomplishment expectancies, by expressing high expectations of followers and confidence in their ability to meet such expectations, thus enhancing followers' feelings of self-esteem and self-worth.
- Increasing the intrinsic valence of goal accomplishment, by articulating a vision and a mission in terms of actions and values which are consistent with the followers' self-concept.
- Instilling faith in a better future, typically by emphasizing vague and distal goals and utopian outcomes, rather than proximal, specific goals and outcomes.
- Creating personal commitment, by recruiting the self-concept of followers, increasing the salience of certain identities and values, and linking behaviours and goals to those identities and values and to a mission that reflects them.

Shamir *et al.* (1993) suggest that these motivational processes are aroused by two main classes of leader behaviour. The first is role modelling. Followers' observations of the leader's behaviour, life style, emotional reactions, values, aspirations, preferences and the like, provide them with an image that helps to define what kinds of traits, values, beliefs and behaviours it is good and legitimate to develop. The second is frame alignment – that is charismatic leaders communicate with followers in such a way that some sets of followers' interests, values and beliefs, and the leader's activities, goals and ideology become congruent and complementary. They accomplish this through the various influence methods described above, and by various other means such as relating their vision to significant historical events, using labels and slogans, providing a vivid image of the future and so on.

Finally, Shamir *et al.* (1993) suggest that such behaviour, through its influence on followers' self-concepts, will stimulate three processes of psychological attachment:

- personal identification with the leader – the desire to emulate or vicariously gain the qualities of the leader;
- social identification with the leader's followers as a distinctive group;
- value internalization – the incorporation of the leader's values with the self as guiding principles.

These processes, it is argued, will produce increased personal commitment to the leader, increased willingness to make personal sacrifices for the collective mission articulated by the leader, increased willingness of followers to perform activities outside their formal job description which benefit the organization, and greater meaningfulness in followers' work and lives.

Shamir *et al.* (1993) note that while personal identification with the leader is consistent with their theory, their main emphasis is on social identification and value internalization. Meindl's (1990) theory of charismatic leadership represents a more extreme version of this viewpoint. Like Shamir *et al.*, he argues that follower responses to charismatic leaders may have their origins in the follower's self-concept. However, he points out that the vast majority of subordinates and followers have little direct contact with and experience of senior executives. He suggests, therefore, that any given individual's charismatic experience is dependent on the experiences of other members of the group. This leads Meindl to the view that the emergence of charismatic leadership is best understood as a social contagion process; that is, the spontaneous spread of emotional or behavioural reactions among a group, analogous to the spread of an infectious disease. There is evidence, Meindl suggests, that there is a facet of the self-concept which is tied to the expression of 'heroic' motives, implying values, attitudes and behavioural orientations which closely resemble many of the elements of charismatic leadership. Heroic motives arise within the context of salient causes that extend beyond the self, but, Meindl claims, are most likely to be aroused under conditions of general ego-threat, such as a severe blow to the self-esteem. Thus, the potential for the contagion of charismatic leadership is made possible by latent heroic motives tied to the self-concept, which are activated by external threats.

Meindl (1990) suggests that the process of social contagion by which charismatic experiences are diffused among followers and subordinates can be thought of in terms of general phases. The initial phase involves the general onset of arousal as experienced by subordinates and followers, and the real or implied presence of a salient leadership figure. Meindl notes that the arousal can arise from a variety of sources, but he does not explore these in detail. However, he states that it provides the latent potential for the contagion of charismatic experiences. In the next phase, the first members join the charismatic movement. These are likely to be drawn from the ranks of marginal group members. Because they are less closely tied to the group and its norms and values, such social isolates are more quickly converted to 'true believers'. The charismatic experience then spreads in snowball-like fashion through the social network. In this process, lower level non-charismatic leaders play a crucial role. As they have sufficient status to influence their group members, they may act as the minions through which the charismatic appeal of higher level leaders is legitimized and accepted. Finally, the charismatic syndrome becomes widely diffused throughout the social system and as a result is given social credibility and becomes the new norm.

Meindl (1990) argues that the social processes which result in the attribution of charismatic qualities to leaders are largely autotomous from the leader's actual traits and behaviours. Thus, when people are exposed to the rhetoric of politicians, preachers and CEOs, their experience and attribution of charismatic leadership may have less to do with what is happening at the podium or pulpit and more to do with what is being witnessed off-stage, in the audience, among individuals who are each other's witnesses.

Meindl's approach to charisma has a number of weaknesses, in that he does not explain in detail why a state of arousal should occur among followers or why a particular charismatic appeal should spread from the fringes through a social system, when so many others fail to do so. Furthermore, the fact that social processes among followers play an important role in the attribution of charisma does not of itself demonstrate that the traits and behaviours of the leader are unimportant and Meindl does not present any independent evidence on this point. Nevertheless, his ideas provide a useful addition to the work of other theorists, such as Lord and his associates, concerning the way in which charismatic qualities may be attributed to senior level members of large organizations by subordinates who have little direct contact with them.

Another process that has been identified in the study of charismatic leadership is the routinization of charisma. Followers give high levels of emotional commitment to leaders to whom they attribute charismatic qualities. However, there is a danger that the excitement generated by the charismatic leader's radical vision may wane as followers become involved in the everyday activities required to maintain the new order produced by the vision. An even greater threat is that the departure or death of the charismatic leader will result in the collapse of the new order, particularly if he or she is the only focus of the charismatic vision. To avoid such problems, the charismatic leader's followers may take steps to routinize the charismatic relationship and thus stabilize the new order. According to Weber (1947), the leader's administrative staff or disciples in particular will be highly motivated to do this, as they recognize that it will serve their ideal and material interests by putting their status on an everyday basis. Such routinization of charisma, Weber suggests, can be achieved by setting up a mechanism for the charismatic leader's successor and for the (restricted) recruitment to the inner cadre of administrative staff. The new system will then have traditional or legal authority, depending on the form it takes, but office charisma may still be attached to the role of the head of the organization.

While Weber's conclusions were drawn mainly from the study of religious and political leaders, similar problems may arise with respect to the absorption of charisma into business organizations (Bryman 1992). Surprisingly, however, the subject has received relatively little study. Some indications of both the types of problems which may arise and the methods which can be used to overcome them can be gained from Trice and Beyer's (1986) longitudinal study of two charismatic leaders of social movement organizations who had somewhat similar missions. They conclude that the successful routinization of charisma is facilitated by the development of an administrative apparatus (from which the leader remains rather aloof) which puts the charismatic leader's mission into practice; transference and transformation of charisma to others within the organization by means of rites, ceremonials and symbols; the incorporation of the charismatic leader's message and mission into a written and oral tradition; and the selection of a successor who serves as a 'reincarnation' of the charismatic leader. However, it would appear that the latter is not absolutely necessary, as in one organization the thorny problem of selecting a successor was avoided by developing a structure which could function well without a strong leader. Rather than having a single leader, the leadership function was invested in a series of interlocking offices or groups.

Interim summary

In summary, if we draw together the various themes which can be found in writings on charismatic leadership, the following picture emerges. Charismatic leadership involves both a highly positive emotional response towards a leader and the attribution of extraordinary qualities to that leader on the part of followers. Such reactions result, at least in part, from the followers' own needs, but probably also reflect to some degree the actual traits and behaviours of the leader concerned. It is also likely that the situation, in the form of a crisis to which the leader presents a radical solution, and a record of successful achievement influence the followers' responses to the leader. Charisma may also be attached to certain high offices within organizations, and may become routinized by followers in order to maintain the new order brought about by the charismatic leader's mission. I am aware that different writers on charisma place a different emphasis on these various elements of charismatic leadership. Some give a central role to the emotional response, others to the follower attributions, yet others to the situation in which the leader emerges, and so on. However, for two main reasons, I think it would be unwise to exclude any of them from consideration.

First, there is evidence to support many of the observations outlined above concerning such elements of the charismatic relationship as the leader's traits and behaviours, the followers' emotional responses and attributions, the role or crises in the emergence of charismatic leaders, and so on. For example, Smith (1982) identified 30 effective charismatic leaders and 30 effective non-charismatic leaders on the basis of nominations from people who were familiar with their work. Questionnaires were then distributed to the subordinates of these 60 leaders asking them to describe the characteristics of the leaders and their responses to them. Smith found that subordinates of charismatic leaders described their leaders as being significantly higher in leader dynamism (empathetic, active, energetic, extroverted, frank, fast, bold, and aggressive) and themselves as being significantly higher in self-assurance and experiencing meaningfulness of work.

Howell and Higgins (1990) studied 25 'champions', middle managers who had successfully introduced innovations within their organizations. They found that such champions were charismatic leaders. They articulated a compelling vision of the innovation which inspired others with its potential. They expressed confidence in others' capabilities to meet the vision. By building commitment, enthusiasm and support round an innovation, they gave a sense of purpose and meaning to those who shared their vision. They gained commitment to the idea by appealing to larger principles or unassailable values about their innovation's potential for fulfilling the organization's dream about what it could be. Finally, the hallmark personality characteristics of champions were extremely high self-confidence in themselves and their mission, strong convictions of the rightness of their beliefs, persistence, energy and risk-taking.

In a laboratory study, Puffer (1990) examined the effects of decision-making style and outcome on attributions of expertise, risk-taking and charisma. 'Charisma' is defined as being attributed with extraordinary personal characteristics. All three attributions are regarded as being components of a global measure of perceived charismatic leadership, based on the work of Conger (1989). Four versions of a case concerned with a general manager who had to make a 'nonroutine, ill-structured, nonprogrammed' decision involving the introduction of a new product in a new market were distributed to samples of managers and students with no managerial experience. In the four cases, the manager was portrayed as using two different decision-making styles – intuitive and technical – and achieving two different outcomes – a net profit and a net loss. Puffer found that an intuitive decision-making style led to attributions of risk-taking, charisma and overall charismatic leadership. On the other hand, leaders who were portrayed as being successful were credited with greater expertise, charisma and overall charismatic leadership. There were also a number of interesting interactive effects. Individuals whose intuitive style was unsuccessful were viewed as having the least expertise. Individuals who employed a successful intuitive style were credited with no more expertise than those with a successful technical style. However, attributions of risk-taking and charisma, as well as the global measure of charismatic leadership, were highest for an intuitive decision-making style, regardless of outcome. Puffer suggests that this may be because attributions of expertise are based primarily on rational criteria, such as the use of analytical techniques, whereas attributions of risk-taking, charisma and overall charismatic leadership are based primarily on emotional or intuitive criteria. Finally, managers made greater attributions of charisma as a personal quality and overall charismatic leadership than did students. Puffer suggests that this may have occurred because managers have greater knowledge of the leadership function and identified more closely with the individual they were rating than did the non-manager observers.

Second, in the case of many of the above elements the whole concept of charisma becomes untenable if they are omitted. It would be unthinkable to describe someone as a charismatic leader, but to follow this statement by saying that nevertheless he or she is not revered by followers, or is seen by followers as being very ordinary, or has no influence over followers, or has no sense of mission, and is totally ineffective. Furthermore, it seems unlikely that the actual characteristics of the person who emerges as the charismatic leader have no influence on the followers' responses. To go this far would be to suggest that when social forces dictate that a charismatic leader is needed, an individual is randomly selected to fulfil this role, irrespective of his or her characteristics and wishes, and any one member of the group, organization or country is just as likely to be perceived as possessing charismatic qualities as any other. Granted that people with some rather strange and perhaps unlikely qualities have emerged as charismatic leaders from time to time, this does seem to be taking social determinism rather further than I am willing to accept.

Nevertheless, including all these disparate elements in the concept of charismatic leadership does raise problems in carrying out objective research into its effectiveness. As pointed out at the beginning of this chapter, charismatic leaders are by definition successful in influencing followers. A leader who is not regarded with awe, trust, devotion and so on is simply not charismatic. Thus, finding that a charismatic leader is regarded with awe, trust and devotion does not tell us whether followers respond in this way because the leader is charismatic, or whether the leader is regarded as being charismatic because the followers respond as they do. Similarly, the fact that a leader is effective in achieving organizational objectives may be due to the leader's charisma or the leader may have charisma attributed to him or her because he or she is successful in achieving these objectives.

The practical implications of much of the research into charismatic leadership are, therefore, less significant than it appears at first sight. The fact that charismatic leaders are successful in influencing followers and achieving organizational objectives may seem to indicate that people in leadership positions should attempt to be charismatic. However, for this to be good advice, we need to know how many leaders who attempt to be charismatic are actually successful, and what are the costs of attempting to be charismatic and failing. For example, it could be that the gains from being a successful charismatic leader are enormous, but few people are able to become a charismatic leader, while the adverse consequences of attempting to be one and failing are much worse than is the case with other types of leadership. On the other hand, it may be very easy to become a charismatic leader and the few who do not succeed may fail no more drastically than other types of leaders. However, studying charismatic leaders or even comparing charismatic leaders with non-charismatic leaders will not demonstrate which of these statements is correct.

What is needed to answer this question is rigorous experimental research which compares the effects of different leadership traits and behaviours on subsequent follower responses. Unfortunately, as Bass (1990) points out, there is a paucity of this type of research relating to charismatic leadership.

Experimental studies of the behaviour of charismatic leaders

However, a small number of experimental studies do exist. Howell and Frost (1989) carried out a laboratory study of charismatic, structuring and considerate leadership, defining each in terms of the leader's verbal and non-verbal behaviour. Those playing the leaders were trained to portray all three leadership styles used in the experiment. When portraying the charismatic style, the leaders articulated an overarching goal, communicated high performance expectations, exhibited confidence in the subordinates' ability to meet these expectations, empathized with the subordinates' needs, projected a powerful, confident and dynamic presence, spoke in a captivating, engaging voice tone, alternated between pacing and sitting on the edge of their desk, leaned toward the participant, maintained direct eye contact, and had a relaxed posture and animated facial expressions.

Considerate leaders exhibited concern for the personal welfare of the participant, engaged in participative two-way conversations, emphasized the comfort, well-being and satisfaction of the participant, were friendly and approachable, spoke in a warm tone of voice, sat on the edge of their desk, leaned towards participants, maintained direct eye contact, and had a relaxed posture and friendly facial expressions (i.e. smiling, positive head nods).

When using a structuring style, leaders explained the nature of the task, decided in detail what should be done and how it should be done, emphasized the quantity of work to be accomplished within the specified time period and maintained definite standards of work performance. They acted in a neutral, businesslike manner towards the participants, being neither warm nor cold, and maintained a moderate level of speech intonation. They sat behind their desks, maintained intermittent eye contact and had neutral facial expressions (i.e. absence of smiling and positive head nods).

The task performed by the participants was an in-basket exercise. It was found that individuals working under a charismatic leader had higher task performance in terms of the number of courses of action suggested and higher quality of performance, higher task satisfaction and lower role conflict and ambiguity in comparison with individuals working under considerate leaders. In addition, individuals with a charismatic leader suggested more courses of action and reported greater task satisfaction and less role conflict than individuals with structuring leaders. The results further indicated that participants felt that they had a better quality of relationship with the charismatic leaders than with the structuring or considerate leaders, despite the latter's exclusive focus on establishing a strong emotional bond with subordinates by conveying warmth, acceptance, support and reassurance.

Howell and Frost (1989) recognize that there are inevitably limitations in the extent to which it is possible to generalize from their study. In particular, their findings are based on a 45-minute exercise. The participants did not formally join an organization and knew that their participation would only last a short while. Thus, the experiment did not take into account either the long-term effects of the leaders' styles or the real-life organizational leader's reward and punishment power over subordinates. To this I would add that there seems no reason to assume that all structuring leaders behave in the neutral fashion portrayed in this study. For example, they could be equally expressive as charismatic leaders in the way they offer rewards and threaten punishments. Nevertheless, the study showed that it was possible to identify certain of the characteristics of charismatic leadership and to train people to exhibit them, thus making it possible to study charismatic leadership under controlled laboratory conditions.

Another experimental study was carried out by Kirkpatrick (1992). Business Studies students carried out a simulated production task based on a printing company. They were briefed for their work by two professional actors, one male and one female, who played respectively the CEO and president of the company. Their presentations were varied in terms of both content (what the leader said) and process (how the leader said it). The content of the presentations varied with respect to whether or not the leaders articulated a vision and whether or not they described the task strategies necessary to achieve it. The process element was varied with respect to whether the leader used an enthusiastic communication style or not.

The effects of the leaders' presentations were assessed in terms of the subjects' quantity and quality of production and their attitudes towards and perceptions of the leaders. Kirkpatick found that in the vision condition there were significantly fewer errors and eight of the thirteen attitude and perception variables were affected. These were enthusiasm for the task, enthusiasm for the vision, congruence between the leader's and followers' beliefs and values, trust in the leader, liking for the leader, leader regarded as more charismatic, intellectual stimulation and inspiration. In the task strategy condition, both quality and quantity of production were significantly higher, as were task satisfaction, willingness to work for the leader, intellectual stimulation and task clarity. In the enthusiasm condition, there were no significant effects on either quantity or quality of production and the only attitude and perception variables affected were liking for the leader and leader regarded as charismatic. The only attitude and perceptual variables not directly affected by any of the presentation styles were the two mood states of anxiety and energy. However, anxiety was affected by combinations of vision and task strategy and of vision and enthusiasm. Finally, exploratory analysis indicated that the positive effects of vision and task strategy were mediated by the subjects' self-set goals and self-efficacy. The vision–performance quality link was completely mediated by quality goals, quality self-efficacy and goal commitment for quality and the task–strategy–performance quantity link was partially mediated by quantity goals and quantity self-efficacy. Kirkpatrick therefore concludes that in order for high performance to exist, the leader's actions must result in the followers setting themselves difficult goals and having high self-efficacy.

Such experiments provide support for the idea that charismatic leadership is not purely an attributional phenomenon. Certain behaviours which are commonly thought to be associated with charismatic leadership can bring about (as opposed simply to being the result of) favourable outcomes in terms of subordinates' emotional reactions, attributions, perceptions and performance. Nevertheless, studies of charismatic leadership within organizations suggest that the very characteristics which can make charismatic leaders so successful can sometimes also have adverse consequences for their subordinates, for the achievement of their mission and for the organizations for which they work.

Organizational effects of charismatic leadership

Conger (1989) points out that there are risks as well as positive outcomes associated with charismatic leadership. He states that there are potential problems with each of the elements which distinguish charismatic from other types of leader – their vision, their articulation of goals and the management practices which they use to achieve their visions. Charismatic leaders' whole-hearted commitment to their vision may lead them to concentrate narrowly on fulfilling their personal goals, with the result that they ignore the needs of the organization, make unrealistic assessments of the demands of the market and the resources needed to achieve the vision, and fail to recognize environmental changes necessitating a change in the vision. They may use their communication skills to manipulate people, claiming responsibility for others' accomplishments, making exaggerated claims for their vision, suppressing negative information, dissociating themselves from their failures, and so on. They may also manage their relations with their peers and superiors badly, act autocratically towards their subordinates, create inter-group rivalry which disrupts the organization, create dependence among their followers, and so on. In each case, Conger is able to give examples of these types of behaviour on the part of leaders who are widely regarded as being charismatic. He notes that while some of these problems are common to many leaders, charismatic or not, they are likely to occur in a more extreme form among the charismatics. For example, given their ability to persuade, they are more likely to secure continued commitment to failing goals than the average leader.

Similarly, Bryman (1992) points out that charismatic leadership is not always something which benefits an organization. Charismatic leaders' arrogance about their own special abilities can lead to folly, their vision may become an unshakeable obsession leading to catastrophe, or they may become autocratic, using their power over people as a means of getting their own way, regardless of the views of others. Indeed, Bryman suggests (p. 42) that 'charismatic leaders often do become autocratic, which can have deleterious effects upon their followers'. In this respect, it is interesting to note the different emphasis placed on the concept of 'empowerment' by writers on self-management and charisma. Proponents of self-management see empowerment as a process of giving people more autonomy, so that they may have more control over their working lives. Proponents of charismatic leadership on the other hand describe empowerment as benefiting followers by giving them a greater sense of power, so that they have greater confidence in their ability to achieve the charismatic leader's vision. Admittedly, it is sometimes suggested that charismatic leaders also empower people by giving them more autonomy. However, writers on charismatic leadership use the term empowerment in this sense much less frequently, and when it is used in this sense it is poorly integrated into their overall theory of charisma. This is hardly surprising, as there seems no logical reason why charismatic leaders should be any more willing to allow followers greater autonomy than any other type of leader. Indeed, if their strongly held vision includes prescriptions concerning the ways in which people should behave and the values which they should express, the followers of charismatic leaders could find themselves with much less autonomy rather than more.

The fact that charismatic leadership can have adverse as well as beneficial effects has led some writers to suggest that there are two different types of charismatic leader. Based on McClelland's (1975) work on the need for power, Howell (1988) distinguishes between socialized and personalized charismatic leaders. She proposes that for socialized charismatic leaders the primary focus of the power motive is the communication of higher order values: understanding of others, tolerance and serving the common good. They articulate goals that originate from followers' fundamental wants, recognize followers' needs in order to help them develop in their own right and stimulate followers intellectually. Consequently, socialized charismatic leaders make followers feel stronger and more in control of their own destinies, creating autonomy and empowerment. By contrast, according to Howell, the primary focus of the power motive for personalized charismatic leaders is to exert dominance and submission over others. They articulate goals that originate from their own private motives or intentions and recognize followers' needs only to the degree necessary to achieve their own goals. Consequently, they evoke feelings of unquestioning trust, obedience and loyal submission, creating follower dependence and conformity.

Avolio and Gibbons (1988) also distinguish between different types of charismatic leader. They suggest that 'pure' charismatics are not concerned with the development of others and indeed may find followers' desire for autonomy a threat to their own leadership and hence intentionally keep followers from developing. By contrast, the charisma of the transformational leader is regarded as the emotional fuel that energizes and transforms followers into leaders. On the other hand, Shamir et al. (1993) do not distinguish between 'good' or 'moral' and 'evil' or 'immoral' charismatic leadership. In their view, the motivational techniques used by charismatic leaders can lead to blind fanaticism in the service of megalomaniacs and dangerous values, no less than to heroic self-sacrifice in the service of a beneficial cause. They therefore conclude that the risks involved in following charismatic leaders are at least as large as the promises. Similarly, for Conger and Kanungo (1988c), the notion of a personalized and 'pure' charismatic leader versus a transformational charismatic leader is primarily a matter of opinion at this time. Hard empirical evidence is required before the distinction can be accepted with any confidence. While we might sort charismatic leaders into 'good' and 'bad' groupings, this distinction is simply a matter of our own value system.

As our knowledge concerning charismatic leadership is largely based on research which does not differentiate between different forms of charisma, it is impossible to say with any degree of certainty which of these views is correct. However, it is worth noting that charismatic leaders always seem to claim that they are doing things for the benefit of their followers and the followers always seem to believe that they are, so it may be very difficult to distinguish between positive and negative charismatics in practice.

Two further limitations of theories of charismatic leadership are identified by Bryman (1992). First, there is a tendency to focus on senior executives when talking about charismatic leadership within organizations. Most of the research on charismatic leadership within organizations has been concerned with higher level managers and most of the examples used as illustrations have been concerned with CEOs and other senior executives. To some extent, this may be realistic. Bass (1990) claims that charismatic leadership can exist at any organizational level. At lower levels within organizations, however, a manager is likely to find it much more difficult to introduce a radically new vision concerning the mission of the particular part of the larger organization for which he or she is responsible. As Bryman points out, for all the talk of empowering subordinates and converting followers into leaders, there has been little discussion of how an organization would be pulled together if it had many leaders pursuing their own personal visions. This is particularly true in hierarchical relationships. Two peers who have radically different visions may find it difficult to co-operate, but a charismatic senior manager is unlikely even to tolerate a subordinate whose vision differs radically from his or her own.

Second, Bryman notes that most of the research concerning charismatic and related forms of leadership smacks of the 'one best way' thinking which characterized the early trait and behavioural style approaches before the emergence of situational theories of leadership. As we have seen, it is sometimes argued that charismatic leadership is more likely to emerge in times of crisis or psychological distress, and is likely to be more successful in influencing followers with certain types of personality. Nevertheless, there does not exist a well-developed, research-based situational theory of charismatic leadership of comparable complexity to the situational style theories of Fiedler, House, Vroom, Misumi, and so on, described in Chapter 4.

Trice and Beyer (1993) argue that, for a number of reasons, cultivating charisma may not be practical in most business and other work organizations. First, genuine charisma is rare. One or another of the factors which produce charisma may be relatively common, but the coming together of all of them is not. Second, charismatic leadership is risky, being at base irrational. The attraction to a charismatic vision is based on emotional anxieties provoked by a sense of crisis and in this state people may be attracted to foolish or bad ideas. Third, its results are unpredictable and may not be what the relevant authorities envisaged or wanted. Fourth, it is a transitory phenomenon and without routinization the fervour of followers cools and the situation reverts to the status quo. Furthermore, Trice and Beyer suggest that the need for charisma has been exaggerated. They argue that the current emphasis on charisma, which is a force for drastic and revolutionary change, seems misplaced, because continual change would amount to chaos. A succession of different change-oriented leaders, each of whom espouses new and different ideas, seems likely to produce so much ambiguity and conflict that members will have difficulty making sense of what is going on. Thus, managers need to know how to maintain and integrate the cultures of their organizations as much as, and perhaps more than, they need to know how to change them.

Finally, it is worth noting that there is a risk involved in attempting to be a charismatic leader which does not apply in the case of other types of leadership. It is possible gradually to change one's leadership behaviour with respect to other forms of leadership, modifying one's behaviour as one goes along on the basis of the positive or negative feedback received. Thus one could gradually become more considerate, gradually increase one's skills, gradually allow more autonomy, and so on. Indeed, many writers would argue that such changes not only can but should be introduced gradually. Charisma is much more an all-or-nothing matter. It is more difficult to imagine someone saying: 'As from tomorrow I am going to be a little bit more charismatic and see what response I get.' In effect, being charismatic is a gamble, and not one which involves small bets. One virtually has to bet all one has, and the returns can be enormous, but so too can the losses.

TRANSFORMATIONAL LEADERSHIP

The concept of transformational leadership is closely related to that of charismatic leadership, but is somewhat broader in scope. The initial impetus for the study of transformational leadership came from the work of Burns (1978). Based on the study of major political leaders, Burns distinguished between two types of leadership, transactional and transforming. Transactional leaders influence the behaviour of their followers by exchanging one thing for another; for example, jobs for votes, subsidies for campaign contributions, hospitality to another person in exchange for willingness to listen to one's troubles, and so on. The transforming leader seeks instead to satisfy higher needs and engages the full person of the follower. The result, according to Burns, is a relationship of mutual stimulation and elevation which converts followers into leaders and may convert leaders into moral agents. In other words, the leader and the led have a relationship not only of power but of mutual needs, aspirations and values.

Burns (1978) regards transforming leadership as being more powerful than transactional. In a transactional relationship, the leader and followers recognize their mutual interests, but the relationship does not go beyond this. They have no enduring purpose that holds them together and hence may go their separate ways. The transforming leader, on the other hand, engages followers in such a way that they raise one another to higher levels of motivation and morality, thus binding them together in a mutual pursuit of a higher purpose.

Burns' ideas on transactional and transforming leadership were later taken up by Bass (1985a) and applied to the study of organizational leadership. Bass defines the transactional leader as one who:

1 recognizes what it is we want to get from our work and tries to see that we get what we want if our performance warrants it;
2 exchanges rewards and promises of reward for our effort;
3 is responsive to our immediate self-interests if they can be met by our getting the work done.

These three processes clarify how subordinates' needs and wants will be satisfied if they achieve designated outcomes. In addition, by clarifying the subordinates' role and task requirements, transactional leaders give subordinates confidence that they can reach the designated outcomes if they expend the necessary effort. This provides the motivation to expend the effort required to attain the desired outcomes and, providing they also have the capability to perform as required, results in subordinates achieving the expected level of performance.

By contrast, the transformational leader is one who motivates us to do more than we originally intended to do. According to Bass, such a transformation can be achieved in any one of three interrelated ways:

1 By raising our level of awareness, our level of consciousness about the importance and value of designated outcomes, and ways of reaching them.
2 By getting us to transcend our own self-interest for the sake of the team, organization or larger polity.
3 By altering our need level on Maslow's (1943) Need Hierarchy and expanding our portfolio of wants and needs.

These three processes, according to Bass, combine to raise the value of designated outcomes for followers. In addition, confidence-building by transformational leaders elevates the followers' subjective probabilities of success in attaining the designated outcomes. Together, these changes increase motivation to attain such designated outcomes above the level which can be achieved by transactional leadership alone, resulting in extra effort and performance beyond expectations. The interrelationship between transformational and transactional leadership is shown in Figure 9.1. Note that transformational and transactional leadership are seen as complementary rather than as alternatives.

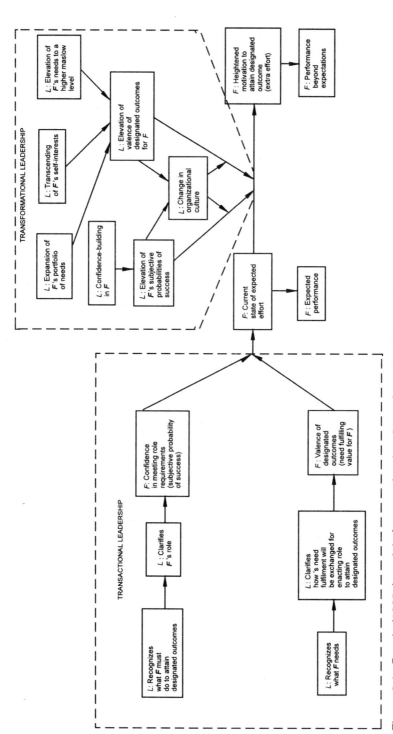

Figure 9.1 Bass's (1985a) model of transactional and transformational leadership

Note: L = leader; F = follower

Source: Avolio and Bass 1988.

As Bass and Avolio (1990a) put it, transformational leadership builds from the transactional base to augment leadership effectiveness.

According to Bass (1985a), this is one of the ways in which his view of transformational leadership differs from Burns's concept of transforming leadership. Burns saw transforming and transactional leadership as being at the opposite ends of a single continuum. For Bass, on the other hand, leaders are both transformational and transactional. While conceptually distinct, transformational and transactional leadership are likely to be displayed by the same individuals in different amounts and intensities and perhaps also in different situations. Bass also notes that his views on the morality of transformational leaders differ significantly from those of Burns. Burns saw transforming leadership as being invariably elevating, benefiting both the individual follower and society as a whole. Bass, on the other hand, accepts that transformational leaders also can be immoral, brutal and aggressive, moving their followers downward in Maslow's Hierarchy, and incurring costs rather than benefits for all concerned.

Having defined transformational and transactional leadership, Bass (1985a) then developed the Multifactor Leadership Questionnaire (MLQ) in order to provide a measure of the extent to which different leaders employed these two approaches to influencing the motivation and performance of subordinates. The questionnaire (in its original form) yields scores on five aspects of leadership. Three factors, charisma, individualized consideration and intellectual stimulation, are regarded as being aspects of transformational leadership, while the remaining two, contingent reinforcement and management-by-exception, are regarded as being aspects of transactional leadership. Charisma is primarily concerned with the extent to which the leader inspires the enthusiasm, faith, loyalty, respect, pride, trust, optimism, and so on of subordinates, but also includes other elements such as acting as a model, having a sense of mission, providing a vision and being a symbol of success and accomplishment. Individualized consideration consists of treating each subordinate differently according to his or her particular needs and capabilities. Intellectual inspiration is the arousal and change in followers of problem awareness and problem solving, of thought and imagination, and of beliefs and values, rather than arousal and change in immediate action. Charisma is the most important factor in transformational leadership. However, the three factors are correlated and therefore it is possible to regard transformational leadership as a leadership style in its own right.

Bass regards both contingent reward and management-by-exception as forms of contingent reinforcement. Contingent reward involves letting subordinates know what standards of performance are expected of them and what rewards they will receive if these standards are met and then ensuring that subordinates receive such rewards if their performance warrants it. When using management-by-exception, on the other hand, the leader intervenes only when something goes wrong. No action is taken when subordinates are meeting performance standards, but if performance falls below acceptable levels, the leader responds punitively, by such means as giving negative feedback, expressing disapproval, issuing reprimands, imposing fines, suspension without pay and dismissal.

Research using the MLQ has consistently supported the propositions that: (a) charismatic leadership is highly associated with leadership success and effectiveness; and (b) transformational leadership is superior to transactional (see Bass 1985a; Bass 1990; Bass and Avolio, 1993). For example, Bass (1985a) found that ratings of their immediate superior's charisma by 104 US Army officers correlated 0.85 with their ratings of the superior's effectiveness and 0.91 with their ratings of their satisfaction with the superior's leadership behaviour. According to Bass (1990), the effectiveness of transformational leadership has been shown in extensive surveys of over 1,500 managers, team leaders, administrators and army officers, as well as in more intensive studies of methodist ministers, school principals and world-class industrial, military and political leaders. Subordinates who describe their leaders as being more trans-formational are more likely to say that their organizations are highly effective. They regard such leaders as having better relations with higher-ups and making more of a contribution to the organization than those who are described only as transactional. They also say that they exert a lot more effort for such transformational leaders. When leaders are seen as being only transactional, organizations are seen as being less effective, particularly if most leaders practise passive management-by-exception. Subordinates also say that they exert much less effort for such leaders.

However, such research must be treated with considerable caution. First, in most cases, the ratings of leadership behaviour, the leader's effectiveness and subordinates' satisfaction were all given by the same people, the leader's immediate subordinates. However, it has been shown that people in a good mood tend to rate other people more favourably than those in a bad mood (see Bower 1991). Thus, subordinates' assessments of their leader's behaviour and effectiveness and their own satisfaction with the leader's behaviour could all be distorted in the same direction by their overall job satisfaction or satisfaction with life in general.

Second, as we saw from the studies of implicit theories of leadership reported in Chapter 8, knowledge of a leader's success or failure can influence how favourably or unfavourably he or she is assessed. Thus, an association between being described as transformational and being effective may result because actually being a transformational leader results in greater effectiveness or because effective leaders are perceived as being more transformational, irrespective of their actual behaviour.

Third, Bass's (1985a) original version of the MLQ heavily loads the dice in favour of transformational leadership and against transactional leadership. The scale for charisma contains such items as:

● Makes everyone around him/her enthusiastic about assignments.

- I have complete faith in him/her.
- Is a model to follow.

It seems unlikely that such a person would also be described as ineffective and a source of dissatisfaction.

By contrast, the scale for contingent reward contains such items as:

- Tells me what to do if I want to be rewarded for my efforts.
- There is close agreement between what I am expected to put into the group effort and what I can get out of it.
- Gives me what I want in exchange for showing my support for him/her.
- Talks a lot about special commendations and promotions for good work.

Such items merely describe the leader's behaviour. Unlike the charisma items, they do not imply that the leader's behaviour has a favourable impact on the subordinates' attitudes and motivation. In some cases, the contingent reward items do not even imply that the leader actually fulfils the promises he or she makes. Interestingly, 'He/she carries out the promises he/she makes' was considered for inclusion in the MLQ but discarded because it did not differentiate between transformational and transactional leadership. It might, however, have helped to distinguish between effective and ineffective contingent reward behaviour.

Furthermore, the characteristics ascribed to management-by-exception constitute the very worst imaginable approach to contingency management. Contingent reinforcement theorists have always stressed that reinforcement should be timely. That is, it should occur as soon after the behaviour concerned as possible. Negative feedback can be extremely helpful if it prevents someone from making an error. Similarly, punishment applied soon after the behaviour in question can be an effective way of preventing minor infringements from escalating into major offences. However, both require the monitoring of performance and taking early corrective action rather than ignoring the situation until something goes seriously wrong. Thus, making pronouncements about the effectiveness of transactional leadership as a whole could be very misleading, as it includes both effective and ineffective approaches to contingency management.

Based on such criticisms, both the MLQ and the theory of transformational and transactional leadership have been revised. A new version of the MLQ (Form 5R) measuring seven leadership dimensions was developed (Bass and Avolio 1990b). In six of the scales, most of the items are behaviours. In the scale that measures charisma (retitled 'idealized influence' in later versions), however, most of the items are attributions. That is, they describe the followers' response to the leader (e.g. 'Has my trust in his or her abilities to overcome any obstacle'). Hunt (1991) finds this approach unsatisfactory. What is needed, he states, is a clear and consistent conception of whether transformational leadership is a leader behaviour or subordinate response to a behaviour, and then consistent use in the measuring instruments. Bass and Avolio (1993), on the other hand, argue that including attributional items in the charisma scale is necessary, since this factor represents in part how frequently followers identify with their leader. Their view is that charisma is undoubtedly both a behaviour and an attribution, because it requires a particular emotional reaction to be identified as such. However, they accept that it is important to differentiate between 'attributed' and 'behavioural' charisma and this is reflected in later, experimental versions of the MLQ. The MLQ Form 10 has only behavioural items for each of the leadership dimensions including charisma (e.g. 'Transmits a sense of mission' and 'Uses symbols and images to get his or her ideas across', rather than 'Makes me feel proud to be associated with him or her'). Yet another version, the MLQ5X, which is intended to replace the MLQ5R and is currently being validated, has separate scales for attributed charisma and idealized influence, the latter being assessed entirely by behavioural items.

In the most recent version of the theory, known as the Full Range of Leadership Model, Bass and Avolio (1994) identify eight aspects of leadership: four transformational, three transactional and one non-leadership. The four transformational aspects, referred to as the Four Is, are idealized influence, inspirational motivation, intellectual stimulation and individualized consideration. Intellectual stimulation and individualized consideration are defined in much the same way as before. The concept of idealized influence replaces charisma in the earlier model. It involves leaders becoming role models for their followers. They are admired respected and trusted. They consider the needs of others over their own personal needs, share risks with followers, are consistent rather than arbitrary, demonstrate high standards of ethical and moral conduct and avoid using power for personal gain. Inspirational leadership also includes elements of charisma from the original model. It involves behaving in ways that motivate and inspire those around them by providing meaning and challenge to their followers' work. As a result, team spirit is aroused and enthusiasm and optimism are displayed.

Contingent reward is also defined in much the same way as the original model, but management-by-exception is subdivided into two types. Using active management-by-exception, the leader actively monitors deviances from standards, mistakes and errors in the followers' assignments and takes corrective action as necessary. Passive management-by-exception, on the other hand, implies waiting passively for deviances, mistakes and errors to occur and then taking corrective action. Finally, there is the *laissez-faire* style, which is the avoidance or absence of leadership.

According to Bass and Avolio (1994), every leader displays each style to some degree. However, the optimal profile is regarded as being one in which the leader displays the Four Is style most frequently, the contingent reward style somewhat less frequently, followed in order of decreasing frequency by active management-by-exception, passive management-by-exception and finally the *laissez-faire* style. This profile is shown in Figure 9.2. The depth of each box represents how frequently an individual displays a particular style of leadership,

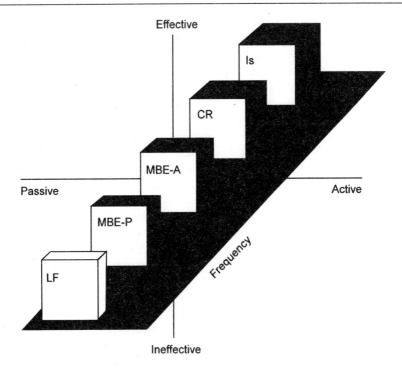

Figure 9.2 Optimal profile in terms of the Full Range of Leadership Model
Source: Bass and Avolio 1994

the active dimension helps to clarify the style and the effectiveness dimension broadly represents the impact of the leadership style on performance. Bass and Avolio (1993) state that a clear hierarchy emerges when ratings of effectiveness of performance, satisfaction with the leader and the leader's use of transformational and transactional leadership are obtained from a single source, such as the leader's subordinates. Based on 17 studies carried out up to 1990, they conclude that correlations with effectiveness and satisfaction typically range from 0.6 to 0.8 for transformational leadership (usually highest for charisma), 0.4 to 0.6 for contingent reward (depending on whether it is promises or rewards), −0.3 to + 0.3 for management-by-exception (depending on whether it is passive or active), and −0.3 to −0.6 for *laissez-faire* leadership (uniformly seen as being ineffective, highly dissatisfying to followers, and one of the more undesirable forms of leadership). Bass and Avolio admit that in the many instances where ratings of leadership and effectiveness were obtained from the same source, the positive relationship between transformational leadership and rated effectiveness was shown to be inflated. Nevertheless, they state that although the relationships were lowered when corrections for this inflation were made, they remained positive and significant, and the hierarchical relationship between transformational and transactional leadership was unchanged. Furthermore, according to Bass (1994), the same hierarchical relationship has been found in more recent research studies using the newer versions of the MLQ.

Nevertheless, Bass and Avolio's revised theory of transformational and transactional leadership still has a number of limitations. Despite its name, and despite including more leadership styles than the original version, the new theory does not include the full range of leadership styles. It will be apparent from the definition of idealized influence that the new theory has reverted to Burns's original conception of the charismatic leader as embodying moral leadership. Indeed, Avolio (1994) states that one of the reasons for preferring the term idealized influence is that it excludes those who use their influence for undesirable purposes. However, this means that the model now does not include the type of charismatic leadership described by Howell (1988) as 'personalized' and by Avolio and Gibbons (1988) as 'pure' as opposed to transformational. This has practical as well as theoretical problems, because it is questionable whether those using the MLQ can necessarily tell the difference between the two. Hogan *et al.* (1990) suggest that there are certain identifiable kinds of people with flawed personalities who initially appear to have desirable leadership characteristics, but who ultimately have a negative impact on the organization. For example, narcissists may appear self-confident and assertive, characteristics which are associated with charismatic leadership, while using their well-developed social skills to disguise the fact that they are also manipulative and exploitative. Thus, someone who is assessed on MLQ as employing idealized influence could later turn out to be a charismatic with distinctly negative qualities and effects.

There is also the question, raised earlier, about the effectiveness with which managers use contingent reward. Howell and Avolio (1993) carried out a study of 78 managers representing the top four levels of management in a large Canadian financial institution. As expected, charisma, intellectual stimulation and individualized consideration predicted business unit performance over a one-year interval while both active and passive management-by-exception were negatively related to business unit performance. However, contrary to expectations, contingent reward was also negatively related to business unit performance. Howell and Avolio suggest that one explanation of this unexpected finding may be that if managers transact with followers but do not consistently fulfil their agreements, they may be viewed as contingent reward leaders who are less effective. Thus, it may be that in order to provide a more comprehensive 'full-range' model it would be necessary to include two types of charisma, idealized and exploitative, and two types of contingent reward behaviour, fulfilled and unfulfilled, as well as two types of management-by-exception. As Bass (1994) and Avolio (1994) point out, leaders who empower subordinates allow them to make their own decisions without interference. Thus, there could even be a positive type of *laissez-faire* leadership. However, where all these different styles would fall on Bass and Avolio's effectiveness dimension is a matter of conjecture.

A second limitation of the Full Range of Leadership Model is that less attention is paid to the role of situational variables. In his original theory of transformational leadership, Bass (1985a, b) noted that individual differences among followers influenced their response to charismatic leaders and that certain contextual factors may facilitate the emergence of charismatic leadership. These issues are not considered by Bass and Avolio (1994: 5–6). They simply state that the research evidence shows transformational leaders to be 'more effective and more satisfying as leaders than transactional leaders, although the best of leaders frequently do some of the latter but more of the former'. They do not suggest whether this balance might vary due to situational factors and if so how. Nevertheless, there is evidence which suggests that situational factors do influence the effectiveness of transformational as well as transactional leadership. Avolio and Howell (1992) obtained measures of perceived locus of control, willingness to take risks and motivation to innovate from 76 senior executives and their immediate subordinates in a large Canadian financial institution. They found that the impact of both transformational and transactional leadership on unit performance over a one-year period was moderated by all three personality variables in the case of both managers and subordinates and by the similarity between leaders' and followers' scores on these personality dimensions. Similarly, Howell and Avolio (1993) found that the causal relationships between transformational leadership behaviours and unit performance were moderated by the level of support for innovation within the leader's unit, but the nature of the moderating effect varied between charisma, individualized consideration and intellectual stimulation.

In summary, research by Bass and his associates shows that transformational leadership behaviours have beneficial effects on subordinates' performance and satisfaction. Early research studies suggested that these effects were large, but as we have seen this research suffered from a number of methodological and conceptual weaknesses which undoubtedly exaggerated the effectiveness of transformational leadership. In order to establish how large an effect transformational leadership behaviours have, how consistent these effects are and what is the strength of these effects in relation to other types of leadership behaviour, evidence from more rigorous research studies is required. In particular, there is a need for more studies which, like those of Avolio and Howell (1992) and Howell and Avolio (1993), do not confuse attributed and behavioural charisma, use independent measures of job performance, employ longitudinal designs which allow the effects of leadership behaviour on subsequent performance to be studied, and take into account individual differences among subordinates and other contextual variables. In addition, there is a need for more studies which compare transformational leadership with the use of both good and poor reinforcement methods. Until such research evidence is available it is impossible to say how effective transformational leadership is with any degree of certainty.

TRAINING IN CHARISMATIC AND RELATED FORMS OF LEADERSHIP

There is considerable disagreement about both the feasibility and the desirability of training people to be charismatic leaders. Trice and Beyer (1993) state that training in charismatic leadership is problematic. It is a complex social process involving, among other things, leaders with genuinely exceptional qualities and situations of crisis. They argue that the genuinely exceptional qualities include enduring traits which cannot be quickly assumed or feigned and that deliberately stimulating perceptions of crisis is a risky business which may leave the organization worse off than it was before charisma was attempted. In general, Trice and Beyer state, those who advocate the training of managers to be charismatic seem to wish away the crucial issue of how all the elements of charisma fit together.

Similar reservations are expressed by Roberts and Bradley (1988). They argue that charisma cannot be created at will. Its emergence depends on a complex interaction of contextual, structural, relational and personal factors, rather than on any one of these factors alone. Thus people who are charismatic in one set of circumstances may not be charismatic in another. This means that there are severe limits to efforts aimed at the deliberate creation of charisma. Furthermore, they question whether charisma is a desirable way of doing things even if it could be deliberately created: 'At present, we have neither a theory to predict outcomes nor any practical understanding to ensure "good" and prevent "bad" charisma . . . . Do we really want to deliberately risk unleashing its darker side?' (Roberts and Bradley 1988: 272–3).

On the other hand, Sashkin (1988) argues that, within the limits of certain personal capacities (which may themselves prove to be modifiable), leaders can be more visionary and more transformational, if they so choose. For example, leaders can be trained about the nature of vision, in the skills for implementing visions, in how to develop an organizational philosophy, in empowering skills, and so on. Similarly, Conger and Kanungo (1988b) believe that if the elements of the charismatic influence process are identified in clear operational terms, then it is possible to train leaders to become more effective influence agents. Thus, while it would be naive to assume that managers everywhere can be transformed into highly charismatic leaders, it is quite reasonable to assume that through teaching more effective strategy-making, more effective speaking skills, greater use of empowering management practices, and more unconventional approaches to problem-solving, we can enhance the effectiveness of managers in leadership roles. They admit that transforming ordinary managers into highly charismatic leaders may sometimes be dysfunctional, in that they may attempt to engender a greater dependence on themselves than is necessary. However, Conger and Kanungo argue that many of the charismatic leader's qualities of strategic vision, entrepreneurship, commitment to and passion for making things better, communication skills, and environmental sensitivity are qualities desperately needed by business today. They therefore feel that the potential benefits of training charisma far outweigh what they believe would be rare occurrence of misuse of such training.

Conger (1989) states that it is possible to teach much of the behaviour associated with the charismatic leader. However, he points out that whether one will become a charismatic leader as a result of such training is another matter. Due to differences in basic skills, motivation, circumstances and so on, it is debatable whether everyone could become charismatic. Conger therefore suggests that it might be more useful to approach the issue of training charismatic leadership, not from the perspective of creating an army of charismatic leaders but rather with the goal of enhancing the general leadership skills of managers. We might then draw lessons from the strategy skills of charismatic leaders to enhance a manager's strategic abilities – in other words, use these leaders as teachers in areas where managers are weakest.

Bass and Avolio (1990a) have developed a training programme for the development of transformational leadership, based on three-day basic and advanced workshops. In the basic workshops, trainees learn about the Full Range of Leadership Model and explore its implications in case discussions and exercises. Each trainee also draws up self-development plans based on his or her MLQ scores and feedback from other trainees. In the three months between the basic and advanced workshops, participants are provided with key readings, encouraged to discuss their development plans with their boss and asked to prepare a statement about an organizational problem which they are currently confronting. Followers, co-workers and/or the boss are also asked to evaluate the trainee's leadership style using the MLQ. This material is discussed in the advanced workshops and a revised development plan drawn up. Following further group exercises, each trainee develops a video depicting a personalized vision of the future which includes how they will align their own, their followers' and their organization's interests. According to Bass and Avolio, the evaluation data so far available have provided evidence of the effectiveness of this approach to leadership training. In one organization, followers rated their leaders as being significantly more effective after training than before. In another, a trained group of managers showed a significant improvement in productivity, absenteeism and turnover in their units compared with an untrained control group.

CONCLUSIONS

It is impossible to come to any clear-cut conclusions concerning the nature and effects of charismatic and related forms of leadership. One reason is that there are widely differing views about what constitutes charisma. Some writers, such as Trice and Beyer (1986), insist that we should continue to adhere to Weber's concept of charisma in all respects. Based on an analysis of Weber's writings, they conclude that his conception of charisma had five components: an extraordinarily gifted person; a social crisis or situation of desperation; a set of ideas providing a radical solution of the crisis; a set of followers who are attracted to the exceptional person and come to believe that he or she is directly linked to transcendent powers; and the validation of that person's extraordinary gifts and transcendence by repeated success. Trice and Beyer reject the idea that any one or two of these components – even when present to an exceptional degree – are sufficient to constitute charisma. All must be present in at least some degree for charisma to emerge and endure.

However, other theorists disagree. For example, Bass and Avolio (1993) argue that by relaxing the criteria set forth by Weber for what is considered to be charisma, operationalizing it, measuring it, and including it as one of four dimensions of transformational leadership, it has been possible to learn a great deal more about transformational leadership and charisma. In particular, they argue, we have been able to develop a much better understanding of the behaviours exhibited by such leaders, key personality characteristics underlying such behaviours, and their impact on how leaders develop. In so doing, however, Bass and Avolio have turned charisma into something akin to a leadership style, which Trice and Beyer specifically reject. Such differences provide the context for the disagreements described above concerning whether charisma can be trained. The argument is one of definition. It is not about whether certain behaviours associated with charismatic leadership can be trained, but is concerned with whether exhibiting such behaviours would alone be sufficient to justify describing someone as being charismatic. As Bass (1994) pointed out, inspirational leadership differs from charismatic leadership in terms of training. It is probably easier to be a bit more inspirational than a bit more charismatic.

Another major area of disagreement is the question of whether there are different types of charisma, 'good' and 'bad'. It seems that some writers on charismatic and transformational leadership have a need to discover a form of leadership which is not only effective, but which can be advocated as being admirable, a force for good. This motivation can be seen in other areas of leadership theory, but it seems particularly strong among certain of the theorists in the area of charismatic and transformational leadership. For example, Avolio (1994) sees the hierarchy in the Full Range of Leadership Model as being a moral hierarchy as well as one of effectiveness. Transformational leaders have attained a higher level of morality than other types, and cannot by definition be unethical. Other theorists, as we have seen, ·regard the skills of charismatic leadership as being essentially neutral, capable of being used for good or evil. For what they are worth, my own sympathies lie with the latter viewpoint. It seems that most tools which human beings are capable of using can be applied for good or evil, depending on the person involved. Thus, whether the effects of charisma are good or bad depends not on the type of charisma, but on the motives and emotional stability of the charismatic leader. However, a consensus has not yet emerged on this issue. Thus, pronouncements on the nature and effects of charismatic leadership are again as much a matter of definition as one of empirical research.

A second reason for our inability to come to clear-cut conclusions concerning charismatic and related forms of leadership is that much of the research is not sufficiently rigorous to allow us to do so. As we have seen, charismatic leadership is a particularly difficult area in which to carry out empirical research. Even if we do not insist that charisma must have all five of Trice and Beyer's (1986) components, it is still difficult to imagine a charismatic leader who is very ordinary, is regarded with indifference by his or her followers and is widely considered to be a failure. Thus, to find that certain personal characteristics are associated with positive responses from followers and with organizational effectiveness tells us little about the causal relationships involved. Is the leader successful because he or she is self-confident, or self-confident because of past successes? Do followers regard charismatic leaders with awe because of their personality characteristics or attribute these personality characteristics to such leaders because they are in awe of them? Does charismatic leadership result in the leader being successful or does success result in the leader being perceived as charismatic? Are dependent people more likely to follow charismatic leaders or does following charismatic leadership foster dependency?

In order to answer such questions with any degree of confidence, it is necessary to find some way of breaking into the causal chain and establishing the consequences of specific variables, and the research methods most commonly used in the study of organizational behaviour are inadequate for this purpose. Deriving correlations from questionnaire data obtained at a single point in time from the same respondents cannot provide information about the direction of causality. Furthermore, there is the risk that the respondents' general attitude towards the leader concerned will lead them to respond to all items on the questionnaire in a similar way, producing spurious or inflated correlations between variables. Thus, more sophisticated research techniques are required. Experimental studies such as those of Howell and Frost (1989) and Kirkpatrick (1992) are particularly useful in this respect as they allow us to establish the effect of specific leader behaviours on subsequent subordinate responses, thus permitting the establishment of causal relationships. In future research, such simulation studies could also be used to study other elements of charisma, such as the moderating effect of subordinate personality characteristics on subordinate responses to the leader, the effects of perceived success or failure on perceptions of the leader and so on.

Inevitably, the greater control over key variables which is possible in laboratory experiments is gained at the expense of artificiality and the short time-span of the study. To provide more realistic data, therefore, it would be useful to conduct longitudinal studies of charismatic leadership in real-life organizations. If measures could be obtained of such variables as the personality characteristics and typical behaviour patterns of leaders, the characteristics of followers, subordinate responses to the leader, the leader's organizational environment, and the leader's effectiveness at different stages in his or her career, then this would permit conclusions to be drawn about causal relationships with greater confidence than is possible with much of current research into charisma.

To reiterate our earlier conclusions, therefore, research into charismatic and related forms of leadership shows that they can have positive effects on subordinates' responses and organizational effectiveness. Until more rigorous evidence is available, however, it is impossible to say with any degree of certainty how large these effects are, under what circumstances they occur and how exactly they are produced.

Chapter 10

Conclusions

Having reached the end of this account of leadership theory and research, we are now in a position to identify what conclusions can be drawn, evaluate what has been achieved and suggest areas in which future research would yield greatest dividends. To the practising manager, the picture presented in the preceding nine chapters may be a disappointing one. Most research findings, even when significant, account for a relatively small amount of the variance in subordinates' work performance and satisfaction. Similarly, there are a great many alternative approaches to leadership theory, the different theories within any one approach often contradict each other, and none is without flaws or limitations.

Even leadership theorists themselves disagree about how optimistic we should be about the state of leadership theory. For example, McCall and Lombardo (1978) suggested that a sense of frustration and disappointment pervaded the study of leadership.

> Students of leadership – academics and practitioners alike – have no doubt discovered three things: (1) the number of unintegrated models, theories, prescriptions, and conceptual schemes of leadership is mind-boggling; (2) much of leadership literature is fragmentary, trivial, unrealistic, or dull; and (3) the research results are characterized by Type III errors (solving the wrong problems precisely) and by contradictions.
>
> (McCall and Lombardo 1978: 3)

Similarly, Quinn (1984: 10) says of the study of leadership: 'Despite the immense investment in the enterprise, researchers have become increasingly disenchanted with the field. The seemingly endless display of unconnected empirical investigations is bewildering as well as frustrating.'

Fiedler and House (1988), however, are much more optimistic. They argue that, even if differences in leadership behaviour do account for a relatively small proportion of the variance in performance, perhaps as low as 10 to 15 per cent, this does not mean that the leader's contribution is negligible. Most managers, as they rightly point out (p. 83), 'would give their eye teeth for this extra 10 to 15 per cent of the variance'. Furthermore, Fiedler and House have little doubt that leadership research has resulted in 'an accumulation of substantial knowledge'. In support of this contention they cite (pp. 87–8) nine 'well-established conclusions about leadership which . . . constitute important contributions to our knowledge':

1 Two major categories of leader behaviour have been identified, one concerned with interpersonal relations (e.g. consideration) and the other with task accomplishment (e.g. structuring).
2 There is no one ideal leader personality. However, effective leaders tend to have a high need to influence others and to achieve, and they tend to be bright, competent and socially adept, rather than stupid, incompetent and social disasters.
3 Leader–follower relations affect the performance, satisfaction, motivation, self-esteem and well-being of followers.
4 Different situations require different leader behaviours. These are the behaviours required to compensate for deficiencies in the followers' environment and abilities.
5 Attributions play an important part in the leadership process.
6 Intellectual abilities and experience contribute to performance only under selected conditions. Whether leader intelligence or experience is required is determined by the task and the environment.
7 Charismatic or transformational leadership is not a mysterious process, but is the result of clearly identifiable behaviours.
8 There is considerable evidence in support of several leadership theories.
9 Several leadership training methods have been subjected to rigorous evaluations.

Fiedler and House admit that we do not yet have a single overarching theory of leadership, and we are not likely to achieve one for some years. However, they point out that the same could be said of theories of depression, motivation, schizophrenia, microbiology, tectonic plates, and the origin of the common cold, to mention but a few. Their argument may have some validity when comparing the progress made in the different areas of study from the academic point of view. However, the study of leadership is different from most of the other fields which they cite in at least one important respect. In a practical sense, the aim of leadership research and theory is to help leaders to lead more effectively, and to do this they need to understand the implications of such research and theory. By contrast, the cold sufferer does not need the same understanding of the common cold to select a cold remedy, nor does the householder living on a fault line need the same level of understanding of tectonic plates to implement earthquake precautions.

Thus, the list of contributions of leadership research drawn up by Fiedler and House (1988) is encouraging in the sense that it shows that progress is being made in a variety of areas (even though other researchers might question precisely how 'well-established' they actually are). However, the fact that they are derived from a variety of different theoretical frameworks and thus constitute a relatively fragmented and disparate list of findings does reduce their value to a leader wishing to learn how to lead more effectively. As expressed in Fiedler and House's list, the items are far too brief to provide a reliable guide to action. A great deal more detailed information would be required to make them adequate for this purpose. Put simply, this is an awful lot of information to expect managers to remember, when they have other things to do during their working lives apart from studying leadership theory. McCall and Lombardo may not be exaggerating very much when they ask:

> Can anyone imagine a manager considering which variable or groups of variables are appropriate to a particular situation? 'Let's see, I have to interact with Mary and Bill, so conditional models 83, 112, and 199 seem the way to go.'
>
> (McCall and Lombardo 1978: 7)

Mintzberg (1982), on the other hand, is more concerned about the content of leadership research and theory rather than the amount. Faced with the task of writing an overview of the leadership symposium by Hunt *et al.* (1982), he sent copies of eight of the contributions to Bill and Barbara, two of his manager friends. Barbara expected something quite germane to her concerns about leadership, and, in her opinion, she did not get it, while Bill was positively angered by the material. Mintzberg (p. 248) notes that 'these are two well-educated, bright, articulate people who can handle concepts. If you cannot get through to Bill and Barbara, then I firmly believe that you have no chance of getting through to any important segment of the leadership community out there.' Mintzberg entitled his commentary 'If you are not serving Bill and Barbara, you're not serving leadership'. From their comments, it does not look as though we are.

However, it is necessary to keep assessments of the progress made in the study of leadership in perspective. Without wishing to minimize the short-comings of leadership theory, many of which are discussed in the present book, it could be argued that the work of leadership researchers and theorists should be judged not only in terms of what they have achieved but also in relation to the difficulty of what they have set out to achieve. Perhaps one of the reasons for the feelings of disappointment and frustration experienced by some leadership researchers and theorists at what they regard as the slow progress in the study of leadership is the fact that leadership theorists have consistently underestimated the sheer enormity of the task they have set themselves. The study of leadership is part of the general area of study known as the behavioural sciences. The aims of science, according to Allport (1942), are to give us an understanding, a power of prediction, and power of control beyond that which can be achieved through unaided common sense. Although definitions of psychology vary, it can in its broadest sense be regarded as the study of thoughts, feelings and behaviour. Thus the aims of a science of psychology are to achieve understanding, prediction and control of thoughts, feelings and behaviour, beyond that which can achieved by unaided common sense. It will be noted that this is very similar to Wright and Taylor's (1994) definition of leadership given in Chapter 1. In other words, leadership theorists and researchers are attempting to achieve within organizations much the same objectives as psychologists are attempting to achieve with respect to humankind in general.

There are, of course, large areas of psychology which have little or no relevance to the study of leadership. Examples include physiological psychology and clinical psychology. Nevertheless, there are a considerably larger number of areas which are relevant. Leadership involves interaction, either direct or indirect, between people. When such interactions take place, how one person responds to another depends on a wide variety of factors. Even a relatively superficial list would include how they perceive one another, how they communicate with one another, their verbal behaviour and non-verbal behaviour, their needs, their expectations, their emotions, their intelligence, their experience, their personality, their attitudes and values, the extent to which they are under stress, their stress tolerance, their interpersonal and other skills, and their use of and response to reward and punishment. In addition, there is a wide variety of sociological factors which will influence the outcomes of the interaction, such as social norms, social class, gender and cultural background, as well as the numerous environmental factors noted in Chapter 4.

In effect, then, the task which leadership researchers and theorists have set themselves is to incorporate most of the subjects taught within the subject of psychology and large parts of sociology within a single theoretical framework. When writing textbooks or giving a series of lectures, it is possible to examine such factors in different chapters or different lectures. Real life does not lend itself to such a convenient isolation of different factors influencing an interaction. When people interact, all these factors influence the outcomes of the interaction simultaneously. Furthermore, they all interact and influence one another. Motives affect perception, perception affects attitudes, attitudes affect non-verbal behaviour, and so on. No one leadership study can hope to incorporate more than a small proportion of the variables outlined above. Viewed in this light, the fact that the results of leadership research account for only a relatively small portion of the variance in performance and satisfaction is hardly surprising. Given the number of uncontrolled variables involved, it is, perhaps, rather more surprising that they manage to account for any significant part of the variance at all.

One cannot help feeling, therefore, that early leadership theorists were incredibly naive in their belief that they could understand and predict followers' reactions to leaders in terms of a set of isolated personality characteristics or a small number of behavioural categories. Furthermore, while modern leadership theorists have, in general, produced much more complex models, one is sometimes left with the impression that they too either do not realize or do not wish to admit to the magnitude of the task before them. Fiedler and House

(1988), for example, say that we are not likely to achieve a single, over-arching theory for some years. If the above analysis is correct, a single, overarching theory of leadership would require an advance in knowledge of much the same magnitude as the production of a single, comprehensive theory of the behavioural sciences. Most behavioural scientists would, I think, regard that as being rather more distant than 'some years' away.

The second half of Allport's (1942) definition of the aims of science is also of considerable relevance to leadership theorists. With their unaided common sense, but without the help of leadership theory, many leaders have been reasonably successful and some very successful in influencing the beliefs, feelings and behaviour of their followers. Thus, in a practical sense, the task before leadership theorists and researchers is not simply to help leaders to be successful and effective. It is to help leaders to be more successful and effective than they would be anyway without the help of leadership theory. In other words, leadership theorists and researchers are not by any means starting from a situation in which the people whom they are trying to help have no knowledge or expertise. They are attempting to improve something which people have for the most part been reasonably good at over the centuries. This too increases the magnitude of the task.

If this analysis of the problem facing leadership theorists and researchers is correct, what should they do in order to fulfil their objectives more successfully? From the practical point of view, the answer may not be more and more complex theories which attempt to take into account a wider variety of variables and interactions influencing leadership performance. This is not to say that such theories are of no value. They are undoubtedly one of the ways forward for leadership research. I do not agree with Mintzberg's pronouncement that you are not serving leadership if you are not directly serving leaders. There is a need for studies of the complex processes which take place in relationships between leaders and followers, and for theories and models which attempt to account for such complex processes. Even though such studies and theories may not have immediate implications for the leaders themselves, they may help leadership researchers and theorists to understand leadership better, or at least to become more aware of the limitations of their knowledge or research methods. Furthermore, there is a need for a dialogue between those working in the field of leadership research and theory while they attempt to refine their knowledge of the complex processes involved, and inevitably this dialogue may not always be readily understood by outsiders. Ultimately, however, if the work of leadership researchers and theorists is to be of practical value, a distillation of such research findings and theoretical models into a form which is useful to the leaders themselves is required. This does not mean the reduction of such material to the level of the simple, superficially plausible prescriptions sometimes found in popular texts and articles. Such advice often works well some of the time, but because it ignores the very real complexities of leader–follower relations, it can also be irrelevant, inappropriate, and even disastrous on other occasions. What is required instead, therefore, is an approach which pays due attention to the complexity of the situations which leaders face, but at the same time provides applicable methods of improving leadership performance.

Having come to the study of leadership from a background in interpersonal skills training, this has inevitably influenced my views on how this problem should be approached. It seems to me that an appropriate balance between recognizing the complexities of the process involved in leadership and giving practical advice on how to improve leadership performance can be achieved by treating leadership as a set of interpersonal skills which can be developed through practice with feedback and guidance from a skilled tutor. As Mintzberg puts it:

> Cognitive learning no more makes a manager than it does a swimmer. The latter will drown the first time he jumps into the water if his coach never takes him out of the lecture hall, gets him wet, and gives him feedback on his performance. In other words, we are taught a skill through practice, plus feedback, whether in a real life or a simulated situation. Our management schools need to identify the skills managers use, select students who show potential in these skills, put the students into situations where these skills can be practiced, and then give them systematic feedback on their performance.
>
> (Mintzberg 1975: 61)

A similar point is made by Hunt and Boal (1992) in their review of Manz and Sims' book *SuperLeadership* (1989). In their preface, Manz and Sims quote the well-known saying, 'Give a man a fish, and he will be fed for a day; teach a man to fish, and he will be fed for a lifetime.' The important question from Hunt and Boal's point of view is whether the book tells the reader *about* fishing or does indeed teach the reader *how* to fish. Although the book provides some examples and illustrations of how one can perform leadership activities, their conclusion is that the book does a fine job at consciousness raising *about* fishing, but reading it does not make one a fisherman. This is not a criticism that applies specifically to Manz and Sims' book, which is, in fact, more practical than most. Much the same can be said of most of the literature on leadership theory. While it tells us a great deal about leadership, for the most part it does not describe precisely how to lead.

The practice of interpersonal skills training, on the other hand, has traditionally concentrated on the development of specific skills which will help the trainee to cope more effectively in particular situations. Its application to leadership development, therefore, provides a welcome element of learning how as well as learning about. It also helps to reduce the problems of the complexities of leadership processes mentioned earlier. As we have already noted, leadership development does not start from a base line of zero knowledge and expertise. People in leadership positions will inevitably already have some ability as a leader and some will have a great deal. However, they will differ not only in how much they know, but in what they know. Two people could be equally good as leaders, but their expertise could lie in different areas. Thus, they do not need to know the whole of leadership theory in order to improve their leadership effectiveness. What they need to know is what particular skill or skills they could develop next which would most help them to improve their leadership performance. Furthermore, this is likely to be different for each trainee. A skilled tutor can, therefore, help trainees to identify what skills they most need to develop next and give them an opportunity to practise them (Randell 1981). It follows that the leadership skills trainer needs to understand as much as possible of the complexities of leadership processes in order to ensure the relevance and validity of the guidance which he or she gives. The trainee, on the other hand, needs an integrating framework which will help to make sense of such advice, but does not require the same depth of knowledge concerning leadership theory and research as the trainer.

What is needed to increase our confidence in the validity of such advice, however, is more research into specific leadership behaviours and skills. Extensive research has been carried out in relation to certain more specific behaviours, such as goal setting, and research into other specific behaviours, such as rewarding, punishing and performance monitoring has increased in recent years. Nevertheless, the amount of research carried out into specific leadership behaviours is much smaller than that devoted to more abstract conceptualizations of leadership behaviour such as leadership styles. I am not arguing that the study of leadership styles is unimportant or should cease. The context within which the specific leadership behaviours take place will undoubtedly have an effect on the way in which subordinates respond to them, as Misumi (1985) and Wright (1993) (see pp. 77 and 124, this volume) point out. Thus, for example, advice or criticism could have a different effect depending on whether they occur during an interaction in which the manager behaves in a largely autocratic or democratic manner. However, I do feel that, given the marked difference in the amount of research evidence concerning specific leadership behaviours as opposed to leadership styles, it would be of considerable benefit if this balance could be redressed by carrying out much more research into specific leadership behaviours. In particular, it would be useful to have more information on the way in which sequences of behaviours influence what is achieved in manager–subordinate interactions, as opposed to simply studying the relationship between the extent to which particular behaviours are used and success or failure (Callaghan and Wright 1992).

Another, much neglected area in which further research is required is the study of the relationship between the emotions and leadership. While the emotions were a major area of study in general psychology during the early decades of this century, research and theory on the emotions declined dramatically after the 1920s. A similar neglect of the subject occurred in the study of organizational behaviour (OB). Most OB textbooks, for example, contain only one or two references to the subject, whereas whole chapters are devoted to such topics as motivation and leadership. During the 1980s, however, there was a major resurgence of interest in the emotions in general psychology, and more recently a growing number of researchers and theorists have begun to take an interest in the role of the emotions within organizations (see, for example, Hosking and Fineman 1990; Fineman 1991, 1993; Baverstock 1993, 1994; Ostell, under review; Baverstock and Wright, under review).

The neglect of the part played by emotions in organizational life is particularly surprising in the study of leadership. Followers' reactions to leaders are by no means solely influenced by coldly calculative considerations. Leaders arouse joy, fear, excitement, anger, contentment, sadness, frustration, disgust, shame, and so on. One area of leadership research and theory in which the role of the emotions in followers' reactions to leaders has been recognized is the study of charismatic and transformational leadership. Bass (1985a), for example, refers to charisma and inspirational leadership as the emotional component of leadership. In practice, however, the range of emotional responses considered in such theories is relatively narrow. Some theorists insist that transformational leaders can only have benign effects, and while others accept that charismatics may deliberately arouse negative emotions, they tend for the most part to concentrate upon the desirable sentiments such as trust, loyalty, reverence, devotion, admiration, and the like. Such primary emotions as anger, fear, anxiety, sadness, disgust, happiness, contempt, joy, guilt, shame, surprise and envy are largely ignored. Furthermore, recognition of the importance of the emotions in transformational leadership should not lead us to underestimate their significance in transactional leadership. For example, a subordinate given a well-deserved pay rise may experience pleasure, another given unwarranted negative feedback may feel anger, a third failing to meet a deadline may experience anxiety and so on.

Elsewhere in leadership theory, virtually the only 'affective' reaction to be considered is job satisfaction, which is widely used as a criterion of successful leadership. However, this is a very broad category of response. Excitement and contentment could yield similar levels of job satisfaction, and anger, depression and anxiety similar levels of dissatisfaction. However, the types of leader behaviour which produce such emotional reactions and the ways in which followers experiencing such reactions respond are likely to be very different. Given that the experience of such reactions as excitement and contentment, and of anger, depression and anxiety are likely to have quite different organizational effects, it would be very beneficial to have more evidence from well-controlled studies concerning which types of leadership behaviour produce such emotional reactions and what effect they have on organizational behaviour.

Other areas in which further research would be beneficial in order to clarify issues in relation to specific areas of study discussed in earlier chapters include the following.

1 The data on how managers spend their time reported in Chapter 2 come from the past four decades. During the latter part of this period in particular

there have been major changes in the working environment. In many sectors of the economy considerable 'downsizing' has taken place. In addition, various forms of self-management, such as empowerment and self-managing teams have been introduced. Often these two processes have been implemented at the same time, with self-management permitting the elimination of a whole supervisory layer within an organization. Inevitably, such changes will have a major impact on the nature of managerial work. Pushing the responsibility for decision-making downwards in organizations will have significant effects on the type of activities performed at different levels within organizations. In theory, delegating more routine decisions to subordinates could enable managers to generate more free time for strategic thinking and planning. On the other hand, if (a) their bosses are also delegating their routine decision-making downwards; and/or (b) downsizing has resulted in a marked increase in the workload of the remaining members of staff, then any free time could rapidly be filled and managers could find themselves under even more pressure of work than before. It would be useful, therefore, to have more recent data on how managers spend their time and the content of managerial work in order to establish how these have been affected by such processes as empowerment, self-managing teams and downsizing.

2 Despite the assertions of such authorities as Bass (1990) and Fiedler and House (1988) that leadership research has revealed two basic leadership dimensions, this appears to be an oversimplification. Four basic leadership dimensions are identified at the beginning of Chapter 4, and indeed the later versions of House's own Path–Goal Theory described later in Chapter 4 identify four leadership dimensions. A great many other systems for describing leadership styles exist, often overlapping in some respects, but differing in emphasis in others. Given that the early style classification systems have proved to be oversimplifications, perhaps the time has come to have a new look at what styles are needed to provide a valid description of leadership behaviour at higher levels of abstraction.

While leadership styles on their own may not provide an adequate guide to action, they are nevertheless useful as overarching concepts which integrate and make sense of more specific leadership behaviours. However, we do not know whether the style models currently employed are the most useful for this purpose. For example, Lindell and Rosenqvist (1992) recently carried out an analysis of leadership behaviour in Sweden and identified a separate dimension of development-oriented behaviour in addition to the traditional task- and relationships-oriented dimensions. They suggest that development-oriented management behaviour is particularly appropriate for the increased turbulence of the business world today. Thus, another look at leadership styles might produce a more comprehensive styles model which could replace and integrate the various different styles models currently found in leadership literature and research.

There is also a need for more research into curvilinear relationships between leadership styles and outcome variables. Very few studies or theories even mention intermediate positions on styles dimensions. Blake and Mouton had a 5:5 style, but argued that it was suboptimal compared with the 9:9 style. Most situational style theorists merely state that the leader should, say, be task-centred or not, or relationships-oriented or not, and do not discuss the possibility that being moderately task- or relationships-oriented might be an effective style in some situations. The only major exception is Vroom and Yetton's normative model where varying degrees of participation are identified as being appropriate in different situations.

Taking both the above points into account, it may well be that a typology of leadership styles rather than a set of dimensions could be a useful way of describing leadership behaviour in general terms. For example, one style type could be an approach which is high on task orientation, low on relationships orientation and moderate with respect to participation, while another could be moderate on task orientation, moderate on relationships orientation and high on participation, and so on. This would allow for both interactions between style dimensions and intermediate positions on dimensions, while keeping the descriptions of the types of behaviours concerned within reasonable bounds.

3   The work of McClelland and Miner has shown that it is possible to identify clusters of personality traits which are associated with successful leadership in different situations. Similarly, Fiedler's work shows that the relationship between intelligence and leadership effectiveness varies in different situations. However, further research is required to establish whether a more comprehensive situational trait theory of leadership can be developed. In particular, it would be useful to investigate whether the incorporation of additional personality traits such as dominance, introversion and extraversion, emotional stability, and so on, and other intellectual abilities, such as creativity, would increase the predictive validity of such a model.

4   The two areas of leadership theory which have aroused greatest interest and enthusiasm in recent years are the various forms of self-management (e.g. empowerment, self-managing teams, etc) and charismatic and other inspirational forms of leadership. Progress in both areas has followed a pattern which is familiar in the study of organization behaviour. Initial results were very impressive, but later experience suggests that the approach may not be as effective and, in the case of self-management, as problem-free as it at first appeared. In both cases, more research is needed to establish more clearly what effects implementing the theory and recommended practices have, how strong these effects are, whether they vary in different circumstances, and if so how, and what significant drawbacks, if any, they have. In the areas of both self-management and charismatic leadership, the type of research required to fulfil these ends is very similar. In both cases, there is a need for:

1 More rigorously designed studies, particularly those using experimental or quasi-experimental designs.
2 More longitudinal studies, to establish long-term effects.
3 More studies of failure.
4 More studies of the effects of individual differences among subordinates/followers/employees on the way they respond to the approach in question.
5 More studies of other contextual factors, e.g. type of organization, work, etc. on the effectiveness of the approach.
6 More studies of the effects of cultural differences on the results obtained.

5 The latter point is worth taking up as a separate issue. There is ample evidence that cultural factors influence responses to leadership styles (Bass 1990) and verbal and non-verbal behaviour (Wright 1994). Nevertheless, the potential for variations between different cultures is very large, as we saw in Chapter 5, and work in this area has no more than scratched the surface. Although less research has been carried out into the effects of cultural factors on responses to other aspects of leadership, such as the personality characteristics of leaders, empowerment, self-managing teams and charismatic leadership, it seems likely that they too are influenced by the cultural background of the followers concerned. For example, Hofstede (1991) suggests that motivation theories such as those of Maslow and Herzberg which emphasize growth and the fulfilment of higher order needs reflect the (US) culture in which the authors grew up, do not necessarily apply in other parts of the world, and may not even be representative of other cultural groups within the USA. Given that such theories provide much of the theoretical underpinning for the concept of self-management, it seems likely that responses to self-management might also differ widely in different parts of the world. Similarly, as Full-Range Leadership Training is applied in different parts of the world, it may become apparent that modifications are necessary to cater for cultural differences. For example, Hartanto (1994) suggests that in Indonesia individualized consideration can be effective, but it can also have adverse effects if it produces dependency.

It follows that the more the nationality, ethnic background, social class, gender and so on of leaders and followers differ from those of the people who were studied in a particular piece of leadership research, the greater the danger that the findings do not apply in their case. There is, therefore, a need for much more cross-cultural research with respect to all aspects of leadership.

So much for the future of leadership research and theory. What have we learned so far which can help leaders to lead more effectively? In a negative sense, we have learned that there is no one best way of behaving and no one best combination of personality traits which will invariably produce leadership effectiveness and success. More positively, we have learned that there are a number of general patterns of leadership behaviour, or leadership styles, which vary in a number of ways, including the extent to which there is shared decision-making, emphasis on task performance and consideration for subordinates' needs. The effectiveness of such styles has been shown to be dependent upon a wide variety of situational factors, including those relating to the leader's personality, power and authority, the personality, ability and experience of followers, the type of task, organizational structure and culture, and so on. Many of the specific behaviours and micro-skills which go to make up these leadership styles or approaches have been identified and research in this area is revealing more about their relationships to leadership success and effectiveness. In addition, variations in the leadership styles, specific behaviours and micro-skills associated with leadership effectiveness in different cultures are beginning to be established.

Theories concerning the relationships between personality traits and leadership success and effectiveness are less well developed. However, it has been established that there are clusters of traits which are related to leadership success and effectiveness in different situations. It has also been shown that perceptions of leadership traits and behaviour are influenced by factors other than the leader's actual traits and behaviour (e.g. the leader's apparent success and the extent to which he or she fits a leadership prototype held by the observer). This has considerable implications for our perception of leadership potential.

The work on substitutes for leadership suggests that certain factors within organizations may render leadership either less necessary or impossible. The latter may have adverse effects as far as the organization is concerned, because it leaves a leadership vacuum which allows maladaptive behaviour to take place unchecked. The former may have beneficial effects, in that it can reduce the need for leadership by enabling subordinates to manage themselves. Work in the area of self-management suggests that it is possible to reduce the number of supervisory posts required by the introduction of such concepts as empowerment and self-managing teams. Furthermore, although there are potential drawbacks to such approaches, the evidence so far suggests that in general they can have beneficial effects on both job satisfaction and work performance. However, it appears that the effective operation of self-management systems requires more sophisticated types of leadership, rather than reducing the need for leadership.

Finally, after many years of neglect, we are now beginning to develop a much better understanding of charismatic leadership. There is still disagreement about whether it is possible to develop 'full-blown' charismatic leaders, and whether this would be desirable even if we could. However, many of the inspirational techniques used by charismatic leaders have been identified and it appears that these can be trained in at least some degree. Although work in this area has begun only recently, it does suggest that, by means of such training, it may be possible to gain some of the benefits of charismatic leadership without necessarily unleashing the potentially negative consequences of the classic charismatic demagogue.

In Chapter 5 it was suggested that leadership involves reacting adaptively to the relatively unpredictable. There are far too many variables involved in any one leadership situation to produce simple laws concerning types of behaviour which will invariably be effective. Reacting adaptively means selecting the ways of behaving which are most likely to be effective in particular situations and if, due to unforeseen circumstances, the choice turns out to be less appropriate than one would have wished, finding alternative ways of behaving which are more likely to achieve one's objectives. This requires having a knowledge of different leadership behaviours and the ability to perform them well, the ability to recognize different leadership situations, and a knowledge of which behaviours are most appropriate in the situation in question. It is one of the great unfairnesses of life that some people, using their natural abilities and unaided common sense, seem to be able to perform such complex behaviours well without the need of any additional training, while the rest of us have consciously to work on our leadership skills if we wish to improve our performance as leaders. Nevertheless, whatever our initial level of ability may be, we can all become better leaders. We can increase the range of leadership behaviours we can perform, improve our skill in performing such behaviours, develop our awareness of the different situational factors which influence the effectiveness of different leadership behaviours and of the factors which influence our perception of these situations. This book has attempted to provide a knowledge of the basic concepts which will enable a start to be made on this difficult but rewarding task.

Bibliography

Adams, J. S. (1963) 'Toward an understanding of inequity', *Journal of Abnormal and Social Psychology* 67(5): 422–36.

—— (1965) 'Inequity in social exchange', in L. Berkowitz (ed.) *Advances in Experimental Social Psychology, Vol. 2*, New York: Academic Press.

Adams, J. and Yoder, J. D. (1985) *Effective Leadership for Women and Men*, Norwood, NJ: Ablex.

Adorno, T. W., Frenkel-Brunswick, E., Levinson, D. J. and Sanford, R. N. (1950) *The Authoritarian Personality*, New York: Harper & Row.

Alban Metcalfe, B. M. (1982) *Microskills of Leadership*, unpublished PhD thesis, University of Bradford Management Centre.

—— (1984) 'Microskills of leadership: A detailed analysis of the behaviors of managers in the appraisal interview', in J. G. Hunt, D. M. Hosking, C. A. Schriesheim and R. Stewart (eds) *Leaders and Managers: International Perspectives on Managerial Behavior and Leadership*, New York: Pergamon.

Allport, G. W. (1942) *The Use of Personal Documents in Psychological Science*, New York: Social Science Research Council.

Anonymous (1976) 'Job enrichment: An assessment of the Volvo experiment', *European Industrial Relations Review*, 36, December: 4–6.

Argyle, M. (ed.) (1981) *Social Skills and Work*, London: Methuen.

Arvey, R. D., Davis, G. A. and Nelson, S. M. (1984) 'Use of discipline in an organization: A field study', *Journal of Applied Psychology* 69(3): 448–60.

Arvey, R. D. and Jones, A. P. (1985), 'The use of discipline in organizations: A framework for future research', in L. L. Cummings and B. M. Staw (eds) *Research in Organizational Behavior, Volume 7*, Greenwich, CT: JAI Press.

Avolio, B. J. (1994) 'Evaluation of Full Range Leadership Training in transformational and transactional leadership in the United States and Canada', paper presented at 23rd International Congress of Applied Psychology, Madrid, July.

Avolio, B. J. and Bass, B. M. (1988) 'Transformational leadership, charisma, and beyond', in J. G. Hunt, B. R. Baliga, H. P. Dachler and C. A. Schriesheim (eds) *Emerging Leadership Vistas*, Lexington, MA: Lexington Books.

Avolio, B. J. and Gibbons, T. C. (1988) 'Developing transformational leaders: A life span approach', in J. A. Conger and R. N. Kanungo (eds) *Charismatic Leadership: The Elusive Factor in Organizational Effectiveness*, San Francisco: Jossey-Bass.

Avolio, B. J. and Howell, J. M. (1992) 'The impact of leadership behavior and leader–follower personality match on satisfaction and unit performance', in K. E. Clark, M. B. Clark and D. P. Campbell (eds) *Impact of Leadership*, Greensboro, NC: Center for Creative Leadership.

Ball, G. A., Trevino, L. K. and Sims, H. P. (1992) 'Understanding subordinate reactions to punishment incidents: Perspectives from justice and social affect', *Leadership Quarterly*, 3(4): 307–33.

Bandura, A. (1977) *Social Learning Theory*, Englewood Cliffs, NJ: Prentice-Hall.

Baron, R. A. (1990) 'Countering the effects of destructive criticism: The relative efficiency of four interventions', *Journal of Applied Psychology* 75(3): 235–45.

Barrick, M. R. and Mount, M. K. (1991) 'The big five personality dimensions and job performance: A meta-analysis' *Personnel Psychology*, 44(1): 1–26.

Bass, B. M. (1985a) *Leadership and Performance Beyond Expectations*, New York: Free Press.

—— (1985b) 'Leadership: Good, better, best', *Organizational Dynamics* 13(3): 26–40.

—— (1990) *Bass and Stogdill's Handbook of Leadership: Theory, Research and Managerial Applications*, 3rd edn, New York: Free Press.

—— (1994) 'Introduction to symposium on The Avolio/Bass Full-Range of Leadership Training: Applications in Austria/Germany, Indonesia, Italy, Spain and the U.S./Canada', 23rd International Congress of Applied Psychology, Madrid, July.

Bass, B. M. and Avolio, B. J. (1990a) 'Developing transformational leadership: 1992 and beyond', *Journal of European Industrial Training* 14(5): 21–7.

—— (1990b) *Manual for the Multifactor Leadership Questionnaire*, Palo Alto, CA: Consulting Psychologists Press.

—— (1993) 'Transformational leadership: A response to critiques', in M. M. Chemers and R. Ayman (eds) *Leadership Theory and Research: Perspectives and Directions*, San Diego, CA: Academic Press.

—— (1994) 'Introduction', in B. M. Bass and B. J. Avolio (eds) *Improving Organizational Effectiveness Through Transformational Leadership*, Thousand Oaks, CA: Sage.

Baverstock, S. M. A. (1993) 'Managing emotion at work: A study of manager–subordinate interactions', paper presented at the British Academy of Management Conference, 'The Crafting of Management Research', Milton Keynes, September.

—— (1994) *Managing the Emotions of Others in the Workplace*, unpublished PhD thesis, University of Bradford Management Centre.

Baverstock, S. M. A. and Wright, P. L. (under review) 'Verbal behaviour associated with effective emotion-handling in interpersonal interactions at work'.

Beekun, R. I. (1989) 'Assessing the effectiveness of sociotechnical interventions: Antidote or fad', *Human Relations* 42(10): 877–97.

Bennis, W. G. and Nanus, B. (1985) *Leaders: The Strategies for Taking Charge*, New York: Harper & Row.

Bettin, P. J. and Kennedy, J. K. (1990) 'Leadership experience and leadership performance: Some empirical support at last', *Leadership Quarterly* 1(4): 219–28.

Blake, R. R. and McCanse, A. A. (1991) *Leadership Dilemmas – Grid Solutions,* Houston, TX: Gulf.

Blake, R. R. and Mouton, J. S. (1964) *The Managerial Grid*, Houston, TX: Gulf.

—— (1978) *The New Managerial Grid*, Houston, TX: Gulf.

Blank, W., Weitzel, J. R. and Green, S. G. (1990) 'A test of the Situational Leadership Theory', *Personnel Psychology* 43(3): 579–97.

Bower, G. H. (1991) 'Mood congruity and social judgements', in J. P. Forgas (ed.) *Emotion and Social Judgments*, Oxford: Pergamon.

Bryman, A. (1992) *Charisma and Leadership in Organizations*, London: Sage.

Bucklow, M. (1966) 'A new role for the work group', *Administrative Science Quarterly*, 11(1) 59–78.

Burns, J. M. (1978) *Leadership*, New York: Harper & Row.

Burns, T. (1954) 'The directions of activity and communication in a departmental executive group: A quantitative study in a British engineering factory with a self recording technique', *Human Relations* 7(1): 73–97.

Calkins, R. D. (1952) 'The decision processes in administration', *Business Horizons* 2(3): 19–25.

Callaghan, C. A. (1991) 'Verbal Leader Behaviour in manager–subordinate interactions', unpublished PhD thesis, University of Bradford Management Centre.

Callaghan, C. A. and Wright, P. L. (1992) 'Observing leaders at work: An alternative approach to the study of managerial leadership', paper presented at the British Academy of Management Conference, 'Management into the 21st Century', University of Bradford, September.

—— (1994) 'Verbal leader behaviour in appraisal interviews: An observational study', paper presented at the Occupational Psychology Conference of the British Psychological Society, Birmingham, January.

Campbell, J. P. (1977) 'The cutting edge of leadership: An overview', in J. G. Hunt and L. L. Larson (eds) *Leadership: The Cutting Edge*, Carbondale, IL: Southern Illinois University Press.

Carlson, S. (1951) *Executive Behaviour: A Study of the Work Load and the Working Methods of Managing Directors*, Stockholm: Strömbergs.

Choran, I. (1969) *The Manager of a Small Company*, unpublished MBA thesis, McGill University, Montreal.

Coch, L. and French, J. R. P. (1948) 'Overcoming resistance to change', *Human Relations* 1(1): 512–32.

Cohen, S. G. and Ledford, G. E. (1994) 'The effectiveness of self-managing teams: A quasi-experiment', *Human Relations* 47(1): 13–43.

Conger, J. A. (1989) *The Charismatic Leader: Behind the Mystique of Exceptional Leadership*, San Francisco: Jossey-Bass.

Conger, J. A. and Kanungo, R. N. (1987) 'Toward a behavioral theory of charismatic leadership in organizational settings', *Academy of Management Review* 12(4): 637–47.

—— (1988a) 'The empowerment process: Integrating theory and practice', *Academy of Management Review* 13(3): 471–82.

—— (1988b) 'Training charismatic leadership: A risky and critical task', in J. A. Conger and R. N. Kanungo (eds) *Charismatic Leadership: The Elusive Factor in Organizational Effectiveness*, San Francisco: Jossey-Bass.

—— (1988c) 'Conclusion: Patterns and trends in studying charismatic leadership', in J. A. Conger and R. N. Kanungo (eds) *Charismatic Leadership: The Elusive Factor in Organizational Effectiveness*, San Francisco: Jossey-Bass.

Cornelius, E. T. and Lane, F. B. (1984) 'The power motive and managerial success in a professionally oriented service organization', *Journal of Applied Psychology* 69(1): 32–9.

Cummin, P. (1967) 'TAT correlates of executive performance', *Journal of Applied Psychology* 51(1): 78–81.

Dansereau, F., Graen, G. and Haga, W. J. (1975) 'A vertical dyad linkage approach to leadership within formal organizations: A longitudinal investigation of the role making process', *Organizational Behavior and Human Performance* 13(1): 46–78.

Davis, L. E. (1966) 'The design of jobs', *Industrial Relations* 6(1): 21–45.

Dessler, G. (1973) 'An investigation of the path–goal theory of leadership', unpublished PhD dissertation, City University of New York, Bernard M. Baruch College.

Dorfman, P. W. and Howell, J. P. (1988) 'Dimensions of national culture and effective leadership patterns: Hofstede revisited', *Advances in International Comparative Management* 3: 127–50.

Ehrlich, S. B., Meindl, J. R. and Viellieu, B. (1990) 'The charismatic appeal of a transformational leader: An empirical case study of a small, high-technology contractor', *Leadership Quarterly* 1(4): 229–48.

Emery, F. E. (1959) 'Characteristics of socio-technical systems', Tavistock Institute of Human Relations, Document No. 527, excerpts reprinted in L. E. Davis and J. C. Taylor (eds) (1972) *Design of Jobs*, Harmondsworth, Middlesex: Penguin.

Etzioni, A. (1961) *A Comparative Analysis of Complex Organisations*, New York: Free Press.

Evans, M. G. (1970) 'The effects of supervisory behavior on the path–goal relationship', *Organizational Behavior and Human Performance* 5(3): 277–98.

Fiedler, F. E. (1964) 'A contingency model of leadership effectiveness', in L. Berkowitz (ed.) *Advances in Experimental Social Psychology, Vol. 1*, New York: Academic Press.

—— (1967) *A Theory of Leadership Effectiveness*, New York: McGraw-Hill.

—— (1972) 'Personality, motivational systems and behavior of high and low LPC persons', *Human Relations* 25(5): 391–412.

—— (1982) 'Are leaders an intelligent form of life? A long neglected question of leadership theory', 20th International Congress of Applied Psychology, Edinburgh, July.

Fiedler, F. E. and Chemers, M. M. (1984) *Improving Leadership Effectiveness: The Leader Match Concept*, 2nd edn, New York: Wiley.

Fiedler, F. E. and Garcia, J. E. (1987) *New Approaches to Effective Leadership: Cognitive Resources and Organizational Performance*, New York: Wiley.

Fiedler, F. E. and House, R. J. (1988) 'Leadership theory and research: A report of progress', in C. L. Cooper and I. Robertson (eds) *International Review of Industrial and Organizational Psychology 1988*, Chichester, Sussex: Wiley.

Filley, A. C., House, R. J. and Kerr, S. (1976) *Managerial Process and Organizational Behavior*, Glenview, IL: Scott, Foresman.

Fineman, S. (1991) 'Organizing and emotion', paper presented at conference 'Towards a New Theory of Organization', University of Keele, April.

—— (1993) *Emotion in Organizations*, London: Sage.

Fisher, B. M. and Edwards, J. E. (1988) 'Consideration and initiating structure and their relationships with leadership effectiveness: A meta-analysis', *Best Papers Proceedings, Academy of Management*, Anheim, CA: 201–5.

Fleishman, E. A. (1953) 'The description of supervisory behaviour', *Journal of Applied Psychology* 37(1): 1–6.

Fleishman, E. A. and Harris, E. F. (1962) 'Patterns of leadership behavior related to employee grievances and turnover', *Personnel Psychology* 15(1): 43–56.

Folger, J. P. (1980) 'The effects of vocal participation and questioning behavior on perceptions of dominance', *Social Behavior and Personality* 8(2): 203–7.

French, J. R. P., Israel, J. and Ås, D. (1960) 'An experiment on participation in a Norwegian factory: Interpersonal dimensions of decision making', *Human Relations* 13(1): 3–19.

Fried, Y. and Ferris, G. R. (1987) 'The validity of the job characteristics model: A review and meta-analysis', *Personnel Psychology* 40(2): 287–322.

Gantz, B. S., Erickson, C. O. and Stephenson, R. W. (1977) 'Measuring the motivation to manage in a research and development population', in J. B. Miner (ed.) *Motivation to Manage: A Ten-year Update on the 'Studies in Management Education' Research*, Buffalo, NY: Organizational Measurement Systems Press.

Garcia Saiz, M. and Gil, F. (1993a) 'Skills of leadership and supervision in organizations'. Paper presented at 6th European Congress on Work and Organizational Psychology, Alicante, April.

Garcia Saiz, M. and Gil, F. (1993b) 'Habilidades sociales y liderazgo politico', *Interaccion Social* 3: 215–45.

Georgopoulos, B. S., Mahoney, G. M. and Jones, N. W. (1957) 'A path–goal approach to productivity', *Journal of Applied Psychology* 41(6): 345–53.

Gibson, F. W. (1992) 'Leader abilities and group performance as a function of stress', in K. E. Clark, M. B. Clark and D. P. Campbell (eds) *Impact of Leadership*, Greensboro, NC: Center for Creative Leadership.

Gibson, F. W., Fiedler, F. E. and Barrett, K. M. (1993) 'Stress, babble, and the utilization of the leader's intellectual abilities', *Leadership Quarterly* 4(2): 189–208.

Gil, F. and Garcia Saiz, M. (1993) *Habilidades de direccion en las organizaciones*. Madrid: Eudema.

Gil. F., Rodriguez Mazo, F. and Garcia Saiz, M. (1995) 'Skills training for future European managers'. Paper presented at 7th European Congress on Work and Organizational Psychology, Gyor, April.

Gill, R. W. T. and Taylor, D. S. (1976) 'Training managers to handle discipline and grievance interviews', *Journal of European Training* 5(5): 217–27.

Gioia, D. A., Donnellon, A. and Sims, H. P. (1989) 'Communication and cognition in appraisal: A tale of two paradigms', *Organization Studies* 10(4): 503–30.

Gioia, D. A. and Sims, H. P. (1986) 'Cognition–behavior connections: Attribution and verbal behavior in leader–subordinate interactions', *Organizational Behavior and Human Decision Processes* 32(2): 197–229.

Goodman, P. S., Devadas, R. and Griffith Hughson, T. L. (1988) 'Groups and productivity: Analysing the effectiveness of self-managing teams', in J. P. Campbell and R. J. Campbell (eds) *Productivity in Organizations: New Perspectives from Industrial and Organizational Psychology*, San Francisco: Jossey-Bass.

Graeff, C. L. (1983) 'The situational leadership theory: A critical review', *Academy of Management Review* 8(2): 285–91.

Graen, G. B. (1990) 'Designing productive leadership systems to improve both work motivation and organizational effectiveness', in U. Kleinbeck *et al.* (eds) *Work Motivation*, Hillsdale, NJ: Erlbaum.

Graen, G. and Cashman, J. F. (1975) 'A role-making model of leadership in formal organizations: A developmental approach', in J. G. Hunt and L. L. Larson (eds) *Leadership Frontiers*, Kent, OH: Kent State University Press.

Graen, G. B., Novak, M. A. and Sommerkamp, P. (1982) 'The effects of leader–member exchange and job design on productivity and satisfaction: Testing a dual attachment model', *Organizational Behavior and Human Performance* 30(1): 109–13.

Graen, G. B. and Scandura, T. A. (1987) 'Toward a psychology of dyadic organizing', in L. L. Cummings and B. M. Staw (eds) *Research in Organizational Behavior, Volume 9*, Greenwich, CT: JAI Press.

Graen, G. B., Scandura, T. A. and Graen, M. R. (1986) 'A field experimental test of the moderating effects of growth need strength on productivity', *Journal of Applied Psychology* 71(3): 384–91.

Green, S. G. and Mitchell, T. R. (1979) 'Attributional processes of leaders in leader–member interactions', *Organizational Behavior and Human Performance* 23(3): 429–58.

Guest, R. H. (1956) 'Of time and the foreman', *Personnel* 32: 478–86.

Guthrie, G. M. (1966) 'Cultural preparation for the Philippines', in R. B. Textor (ed.) *Cultural Frontiers of the Peace Corps*, Cambridge, MA: MIT Press.

Gyllenhammer, P. G. (1977) 'How Volvo adapts work to people', *Harvard Business Review* 55(4), July–August: 102–13.

Hackman, J. R. (1986) 'The psychology of self-management in organizations', in M. S. Pallak and R. Perloff (eds) *Psychology and Work: Productivity, Change and Employment*, Washington, DC: American Psychological Association.

—— (ed.)(1990) *Groups that Work (and those that don't): Creating Conditions for Effective Teamwork*, San Francisco: Jossey-Bass.

Hackman, J. R. and Oldham, G. R. (1975) 'Development of the job diagnostic survey', *Journal of Applied Psychology* 60(2): 159–70.

—— (1976) 'Motivation through the design of work: Test of a theory', *Organizational Behaviour and Human Performance* 16(2): 250–79.

—— (1980) *Work Redesign*, Reading, MA: Addison-Wesley.

Hackman, J. R. and Walton, R. E. (1986) 'Leading groups in organizations', in P. S. Goodman (ed.) *Designing Effective Work Groups*, San Francisco: Jossey-Bass.

Halpin, A. W. and Winer, B. J. (1957) 'A factorial study of the leader behavior descriptions', in R. M. Stogdill and A. E. Coons (eds) *Leader Behavior: Its Description and Measurement*, Columbus, OH: Bureau of Business Research, Ohio State University.

Hartanto, F. M. (1994) 'The effects of the shame culture and respect to elders towards the effectiveness of transformational leadership in the change process: The Indonesian case', paper presented at 23rd International Congress of Applied Psychology, Madrid, July.

Hersey, P. and Blanchard, K. H. (1969) 'Life cycle theory of leadership', *Training and Development Journal* 23(5): 26–34.

—— (1977) *The Management of Organizational Behavior: Utilizing Human Resources*, 3rd edn, Englewood Cliffs, NJ: Prentice-Hall.

—— (1982) *The Management of Organizational Behavior: Utilizing Human Resources*, 4th edn, Englewood Cliffs, NJ: Prentice-Hall.

Herzberg, F. (1968) 'One more time: How do you motivate employees?', *Harvard Business Review* 46(1), January–February: 53–62.

Heslin, R. (1964) 'Predicting group task effectiveness from member characteristics', *Psychological Bulletin* 62(4): 248–56.

Hill, W. (1969) 'The validation and extension of Fiedler's theory of leadership effectiveness', *Academy of Management Journal* 12: 33–47.

Hofstede, G. (1980) *Culture's Consequences: International Differences in Work-related Values*, Beverly Hills, CA: Sage.

—— (1991) *Cultures and Organizations: Software of the Mind*, London: McGraw-Hill.

Hogan, R., Raskin, R. and Fazzini, D. (1990) 'The dark side of charisma', in K. E. Clark and M. B. Clark (eds) *Measures of Leadership*, West Orange, NJ: Leadership Library of America.

Hollander, E. P. and Offermann, L. R. (1990) 'Power and leadership in organizations: Relationships in transition', *American Psychologist* 45(2): 179–89.

Hosking, D. M. and Fineman, S. (1990) 'Organizing processes', *Journal of Management Studies* 27(6): 583–604.

Hosking, D. M. and Morley, I. E. (1988) 'The skills of leadership', in J. G. Hunt, B. R. Balgia, H. P. Dachler and C. A. Schriesheim (eds) *Emerging Leadership Vistas*, Lexington, MA: Lexington Books.

House, R. J. (1971) 'A path goal theory of leadership effectiveness', *Administrative Science Quarterly* 16(3): 321–38.

—— (1977) 'A 1976 theory of charismatic leadership', in J. G. Hunt and L. L. Larson (eds) *Leadership: The Cutting Edge*, Carbondale, IL: Southern Illinois University Press.

House, R. J. and Mitchell, T. R. (1974) 'Path–goal theory of leadership', *Journal of Contemporary Business* 3, Autumn: 81–97.

House, R. J. and Singh, J. V. (1987) 'Organizational behavior: Some new directions in I/O psychology', in M. R. Rosenzweig and L. W. Porter (eds) *Annual Review of Psychology, Volume 38*, Palo Alto, CA: Annual Reviews Inc.

House, R. J., Woycke, J. and Fodor, E. M. (1988) 'Charismatic and noncharismatic leaders: Differences in behavior and effectiveness', in J. A. Conger and R. N. Kanungo (eds) *Charismatic Leadership: The Elusive Factor in Organizational Effectiveness*, San Francisco: Jossey-Bass.

Howell, J. M. (1988) 'Two faces of charisma: Socialized and personalized leadership in organizations', in J. A. Conger and R. N. Kanungo (eds) *Charismatic Leadership: The Elusive Factor in Organizational Effectiveness*, San Francisco: Jossey-Bass.

Howell, J. M. and Avolio, B. J. (1993) 'Transformational leadership, transactional leadership, locus of control, and support for innovation: Key predictors of consolidated-business-unit performance', *Journal of Applied Psychology* 78(6): 891–902.

Howell, J. M. and Frost, P. J. (1989) 'A laboratory study of charismatic leadership', *Organizational Behavior and Human Decision Processes*, 43(2): 243–69.

Howell, J. M. and Higgins, C. A. (1990) 'Champions of change: Identifying, understanding, and supporting champions of technological innovations', *Organizational Dynamics* 19(1): 40–55.

Howell, J. P. and Dorfman, P. W. (1981) 'Substitutes for leadership: Test of a construct', *Academy of Management Journal* 24(4): 714–28.

—— (1986) 'Leadership and substitutes for leadership among professional and non-professional workers', *Journal of Applied Behavioral Science* 22(1): 29–46.

Howell, W. C. (1976) *Essentials of Industrial and Organizational Psychology*, Homewood, IL: Dorsey Press.

Howell, W. C. and Dipboye, R. L. (1982) *Essentials of Industrial and Organizational Psychology*, Homewood, IL: Dorsey Press.

Huber, J. P. (1975) 'How to decide how to decide', *Contemporary Psychology* 20(2): 110–12.

Hulin, C. L. (1971) 'Individual differences and job enrichment: The case against general treatments', in J. R. Maher (ed.) *New Perspectives in Job Enrichment*, New York: Van Nostrand Reinhold.

Hunt, J. G. (1991) *Leadership: A New Synthesis*, Newbury Park, CA: Sage.

Hunt, J. G. and Boal, K. B. (1992) 'Review of *SuperLeadership: Leading others to lead themselves*', by C. C. Manz and H. P. Sims, *Leadership Quarterly* 3(2): 159–63.

Hunt, J. G., Sekaran, U. and Schriesheim, C. A. (eds) (1982) *Leadership: Beyond Establishment Views*, Carbondale, IL: Southern Illinois University Press.

Indvik, J. (1986) 'Path–goal theory of leadership: A meta-analysis', proceedings, Academy of Management, Chicago: 189–92.

—— (1988) *A More Complete Testing of Path–Goal Theory*, paper, Academy of Management, Anaheim, CA.

Ivey, A. E. and Galvin, M. (1984) 'Microcounselling: A metamodel for counselling, therapy, business and medical interviews', in D. Larson, *Teaching Psychological Skills: Models for Giving Psychology Away*, Belmont, CA: Wadsworth.

Jago, A. G. and Vroom, V. H. (1982) 'Sex differences in the incidence and evaluation of participative leader behaviour', *Journal of Applied Psychology* 67(6): 776–83.

Jermier, J. M. and Berkes, L. J. (1979) 'Leader behavior in a police command bureaucracy: A closer look at the quasi-military model', *Administrative Science Quarterly* 24(1): 1–23.

Johns, G. (1978) 'Task moderators of the relationship between leadership style and subordinate responses', *Academy of Management Journal* 21(2): 319–25.

Johnston, T. (1990) 'Leadership skills in work teams', unpublished PhD thesis, University of Bradford Management Centre.

Kahn, R. L. and Cannel, C. F. (1957) *The Dynamics of Interviewing: Theory, Technique and Cases*, New York: Wiley.

Kanter, R. M. (1989) 'The new managerial work', *Harvard Business Review* 89(6), November–December: 85–92.

Katz, D. and Kahn, R. L. (1978) *The Social Psychology of Organizations*, 2nd edn, New York: Wiley.

Katz, D., Maccoby, N., Gurin, G. and Floor, L. (1951) *Productivity, Supervision and Morale among Railroad Workers*, Ann Arbor, MI: University of Michigan, Institute for Social Research.

Katz, D., Maccoby, N. and Morse, N. C. (1950) *Productivity, Supervision and Morale in an Office Situation*, Ann Arbor, MI: University of Michigan, Institute for Social Research.

Kelly, J. E. (1978) 'A reappraisal of sociotechnical systems theory', *Human Relations* 31(12): 1069–99.

Kennedy, J. K. (1982) 'Middle LPC leaders and the contingency model of leadership effectiveness', *Organizational Behavior and Human Performance* 30(1): 1–14.

Kennedy, M. M. (1994) 'Empowered or overpowered', *Across the Board*, April: 11–12.

Kenny, D. A. and Zaccaro, S. J. (1983) 'An estimate of variance due to traits in leadership', *Journal of Applied Psychology* 68(4): 678–85.

Kerr, S. and Jermier, J. M. (1978) 'Substitutes for leadership: Their meaning and measurement', *Organizational Behavior and Human Performance* 22(3): 375–403.

Kerr, S. and Schriesheim, C. (1974) 'Consideration, initiating structure and organizational criteria – An update of Korman's 1966 review', *Personnel Psychology* 27(4): 555–68.

King, D. C. and Bass, B. M. (1974) 'Leadership, power, and influence', in H. L. Fromkin and J. J. Sherwood (eds) *Integrating the Organization*, New York: Free Press.

Kirkpatrick, S. A. (1992) 'Decomposing charismatic leadership: The effects of leader content and process on follower performance, attitudes, and perceptions', unpublished doctoral dissertation, University of Maryland.

Komaki, J. L. (1986) 'Toward effective supervision: An operant analysis and comparison of managers at work', *Journal of Applied Psychology* 71(2): 270–79.

Komaki, J. L. and Citera, M. (1990) 'Beyond effective supervision: Identifying key interactions between superior and subordinate', *Leadership Quarterly* 1(2): 91–105.

Komaki, J. L., Desselles, M. L. and Bowman, E. D. (1989) 'Definitely not a breeze: Extending an operant model of effective supervision to teams', *Journal of Applied Psychology* 74(3): 522–9.

Komaki, J. L., Zlotnick, S. and Jensen, M. (1986) 'Development of an operant-based taxonomy and observational index of supervisory behavior', *Journal of Applied Psychology* 71(2): 260–69.

Korman, A. K. (1966) ' "Consideration", "initiating structure", and organizational criteria: A review', *Personnel Psychology* 19(4): 349–61.

—— (1968) 'The prediction of managerial performance: A review', *Personnel Psychology* 21(3): 295–322.

Kotter, J. P. (1982) *The General Managers*, New York: Free Press.

Kraut, A. I., Pedigo, P. R., McKenna, D. D. and Dunnette, M. D. (1989) 'The role of the manager: What's really important in different managerial jobs', *Academy of Management Executive* 3(4): 286–93.

Kurke, L. B. and Aldrich, H. E. (1983) 'Mintzberg was right!: A replication and extension of *The Nature of Managerial Work*', *Management Science* 29(8): 975–84.

Larson, L. L., Hunt, J. G. and Osborn, R. N. (1976) 'The great hi-hi leader behavior myth: A lesson from Occam's razor', *Academy of Management Journal* 19: 628–41.

Lawler, E. E. (1977) 'Reward systems', in J. R. Hackman and J. L. Suttle (eds) *Improving Life at Work: Behavioral Approaches to Organizational Change*, Santa Monica, CA: Goodyear.

—— (1986) *High-involvement Management: Participative Strategies for Improving Organizational Performance*, San Francisco: Jossey-Bass.

—— (1992) *The Ultimate Advantage: Creating the High-involvement Organization*, San Francisco: Jossey-Bass.

Lawler, E. E. and Suttle, J. L. (1973) 'Expectancy theory and job behavior', *Organizational Behavior and Human Performance* 9(3): 482–503.

Lawrence, P. (1984) *Management in Action*, London: Routledge & Kegan Paul.

Lepsius, M. R. (1986) 'Charismatic leadership: Max Weber's model and its applicability to the rule of Hitler', in C. F. Graumann and S. Muscovici (eds) *Changing Conceptions of Leadership*, New York: Springer-Verlag.

Lewin, K., Lippitt, R. and White, R. K. (1939) 'Patterns of aggressive behaviour in experimentally created "social climates" ', *Journal of Social Psychology* 10: 271–99.

Liden, R. C. and Graen, G. (1980) 'Generalizability of the vertical dyad linkage model of leadership', *Academy of Management Journal* 23(3): 451–65.

Likert, R. (1961) *New Patterns of Management*, New York: McGraw-Hill.

—— (1967) *The Human Organization*, New York: Wiley.

Lindell, M. and Rosenqvist, G. (1992) 'Management behavior dimensions and development orientation', *Leadership Quarterly* 3(4): 355–77.

Litwin, G. H. and Siebrecht, A. (1967) 'Integrators and entrepreneurs: Their motivation and effect on management', *Hospital Progress*, St Louis, MO.

Locke, E. A. and Schweiger, D. M. (1979) 'Participation in decision-making: One more look', in B. Staw (ed.) *Research in Organizational Behavior, Vol 1*, Greenwich, CT: JAI Press.

Locke, E. A., Feren, D. B., McCaleb, V. M., Shaw, K. N. and Denny, A. T. (1980) 'The relative effectiveness of four methods of motivating employee performance', in K. D. Duncan, M. M. Greenberg and D. Wallis (eds) *Changes in Working Life*, New York: Wiley.

Lord, R. G., De Vader, C. L. and Alliger, G. M. (1986) 'A meta-analysis of the relation between personality traits and leadership perceptions: An application of validity generalization procedures', *Journal of Applied Psychology* 71(3): 402–10.

Lord, R. G., Foti, R. J. and De Vader, C. L. (1984) 'A test of leadership categorization theory: Internal structure, information processing, and leadership perceptions', *Organizational Behavior and Human Performance* 34(3): 343–78.

Lord, R. G., Foti, R. J. and Phillips, J. S. (1982) 'A theory of leadership categorization', in J. G. Hunt, U. Sekaran and C. Schriesheim (eds) *Leadership: Beyond Establishment Views*, Carbondale, IL: Southern Illinois University Press.

Lord, R. G. and Maher, K. J. (1993) *Leadership and Information Processing: Linking Perceptions and Performance*, London: Routledge.

Luthans, F. (1992) *Organizational Behavior*, 6th edn, New York: McGraw-Hill.

Luthans, F. and Davis, T. V. R. (1979) 'Behavioral self-management: The missing link in managerial effectiveness', *Organizational Dynamics* 8(1): 42–60.

Luthans, F. and Kreitner, R. (1975) *Organizational Behavior Modification*, Glenview, IL: Scott, Foresman.

Luthans, F. and Lockwood, D. L. (1984) 'Toward an observation system for measuring leader behavior in natural settings', in J. G. Hunt, D. M Hosking, C. A. Schriesheim and R. Stewart (eds) *Leaders and Managers: International Perspectives on Managerial Behavior and Leadership*. New York: Pergamon.

Luthans, F., Hodgetts, R. M. and Rosenkrantz, S. A. (1988) *Real Managers*, Cambridge, MA: Ballinger.

McCall, M. W. and Lombardo, M. M. (1978) 'Leadership', in M. W. McCall and M. M. Lombardo (eds) *Leadership: Where Else Can We Go?*, Durham, NC: Duke University Press.

McCall, M. W., Morrison, A. M. and Hannan, R. L. (1978) *Studies of Managerial Work: Results and Methods*, Technical Report No. 9, Greensboro, NC: Center for Creative Leadership.

McClelland, D. C. (1958) 'The use of measures of human motivation in the study of society', in J. W. Atkinson (ed.) *Motives in Fantasy, Action and Society*, Princeton, NJ: Van Nostrand.

—— (1975) *Power: The Inner Experience*, New York: Irvington.

McClelland, D. C. and Boyatzis, R. E. (1982) 'Leadership motive pattern and long-term success in management', *Journal of Applied Psychology* 67(6): 737–43.

McClelland, D. C. and Burnham, D. H. (1976) 'Power is the great motivator', *Harvard Business Review* 54(2), March–April: 100–110.

McClelland, D. C. and Winter, D. G. (1969) *Motivating Economic Achievement*, New York: Free Press.

McGregor, D. M. (1957) 'The human side of enterprise', in 'Adventures in thought and action', proceedings of the Fifth Anniversary Convocation of the School of Industrial Management, Massachusetts Institute of Science and Technology: 23–30, reprinted in V. H. Vroom and E. L. Deci (eds) (1992) *Management and Motivation*, 2nd edn, London: Penguin.

Maier, N. R. F. (1952) *Principles of Human Relationships: Applications to Management*, New York: Wiley.

—— (1955) *Psychology in Industry*, 2nd edn, London: Harrap.

—— (1958) 'Three types of appraisal interview', *Personnel* 54(5): 27–40.

Mann, R. D. (1959) 'A review of the relationships between personality and performance in small groups', *Psychological Bulletin* 56(4): 241–70.

Manz, C. C. (1986) 'Self-leadership: Toward an expanded theory of self-influence processes in organizations', *Academy of Management Review* 11(3): 585–600.

Manz, C. C. and Angle, H. L. (1993) 'The illusion of self-management: Using teams to disempower', in C. C. Manz and H. P. Sims, *Business Without Bosses*, New York: Wiley.

Manz, C. C., Keating, D. and Donnellon, A. (1993) 'On the road to teams: Overcoming the middle management brick wall', in C. C. Manz and H. P. Sims, *Business Without Bosses*, New York: Wiley.

Manz, C. C. and Newstrom, J. W. (1990) 'Self-managing teams in a paper mill: Success factors, problems and lessons learned', in A. Nedd (ed.) *International Human Resource Management Review, Vol 1*, Singapore: McGraw-Hill.

—— (1993) 'The good and bad of teams: A practical look at successes and challenges', in C. C. Manz and H. P. Sims, *Business Without Bosses*, New York: Wiley.

Manz, C. C. and Sims, H. P. (1980) 'Self-management as a substitute for leadership: A social learning theory perspective', *Academy of Management Review* 5(3): 361–7.

—— (1984) 'Searching for the "unleader": Organizational member views on leading self-managed groups', *Human Relations* 37(5): 409–24.

—— (1989) *SuperLeadership: Leading Others to Lead Themselves*, New York: Prentice-Hall.

—— (1993) *Business Without Bosses*, New York: Wiley.

Margerison, C. and Glube, R. (1979) 'Leadership decision-making: An empirical test of the Vroom and Yetton model', *Journal of Management Studies* 16(1): 45–55.

Martinko, M. J. and Gardner, W. L. (1984a) 'The behavior of high performing managers: An observational study', unpublished manuscript, Department of Management, College of Business, Florida State University, Tallahassee.

—— (1984b) 'The observation of high performing educational managers: Methodological issues and managerial implications', in J. G. Hunt, D. M. Hosking, C. A. Schriesheim and R. Stewart (eds) *Leaders and Managers: International Perspectives on Managerial Behavior and Leadership*, New York: Pergamon.

—— (1985) 'Beyond structured observation: Methodological issues and new directions', *Academy of Management Review* 10(4): 676–95.

—— (1990) 'Structured observation of managerial work: A replication and synthesis', *Journal of Management Studies* 27(3): 329–57.

Maslow, A. H. (1943) 'A theory of human motivation', *Psychological Review* 50: 370–96.

Mayhand, E. and Grusky, O. (1972) 'A preliminary experiment on the effects of black supervision on white and black subordinates', *Journal of Black Studies* 2: 461–70.

Meade, R. D. (1967) 'An experimental study of leadership in India', *Journal of Social Psychology* 72(1): 35–43.

Meindl, J. R. (1988) 'On the romanticized perception of charisma', unpublished manuscript, School of Management, State University of New York at Buffalo, Buffalo, New York (quoted Meindl 1990).

—— (1990) 'On leadership: An alternative to the conventional wisdom', in B. M. Staw and L. L. Cummings (eds) *Research in Organizational Behavior, Volume 12*, Greenwich, CT: JAI Press.

Meindl, J. R. and Ehrlich, S. B. (1988) 'Developing a "romance of leadership scale"', proceedings of the Eastern Academy of Management: 133–5 (quoted Meindl 1990).

Miller, K. I. and Monge, P. R. (1986) 'Participation, satisfaction and productivity: A meta-analytic review', *Academy of Management Journal* 29(4): 727–53.

Miner, J. B. (1960) 'The effects of a course in psychology on the attitudes of research and development supervisors', *Journal of Applied Psychology* 44(3): 224–32.

—— (1965) *Studies in Management Education*, New York: Springer-Verlag.

—— (1993) *Role Motivation Theories*, London: Routledge.

Mintzberg, H. (1973) *The Nature of Managerial Work*, New York: Harper & Row.

—— (1975) 'The manager's job: Folklore and fact', *Harvard Business Review* 53(4), July–August: 49–61.

—— (1982) 'If you're not serving Bill and Barbara, then you're not serving leadership', in J. G. Hunt, U. Sekaran and C. A. Schriesheim (eds) *Leadership: Beyond Establishment Views*, Carbondale, IL: Southern Illinois University Press.

Misumi, J. (1985) *The Behavioral Science of Leadership: An Interdisciplinary Japanese Research Program*, Ann Arbor, MI: University of Michigan Press.

Misumi, J. and Peterson, M. F. (1985) 'The Performance–Maintenance (PM) theory of leadership: Review of a Japanese research program', *Administrative Science Quarterly* 30(2): 198–223.

Mitchell, T. R. and Wood, R. E. (1980) 'Supervisor's responses to subordinate poor performance: A test of an attributional model', *Organizational Behavior and Human Performance* 25(1): 123–38.

Morse, N. C. and Reimer, E. (1956) 'The experimental change of a major organizational variable', *Journal of Abnormal and Social Psychology* 52: 120–29.

Mowday, R. T. (1987) 'Equity theory predictions of behavior in organizations', in R. M. Steers and L. W. Porter (eds) *Motivation and Work Behavior*, 4th edn, New York: McGraw-Hill.

Murphy, S. E., Blyth, D. and Fiedler, F. E. (1992) 'Cognitive resources theory and the utilization of the leader's and group members' technical competence', *Leadership Quarterly* 3(3): 237–55.

Nathan, B. R., Hass, M. A. and Nathan, M. L. (1986) 'Meta-analysis of Fiedler's leadership theory: A figure is worth a thousand words', paper, American Psychological Association, Washington, DC.

Nystrom, P. C. (1978) 'Managers and the hi-hi leader myth', *Academy of Management Journal* 21(2) 325–31.

O'Connell, M. S., Lord, R. G. and O'Connell, M. K. (1990) 'An empirical comparison of Japanese and American leadership prototypes: Implications for overseas assignment of managers', unpublished manuscript (quoted Lord and Maher 1993).

Oldham, G. R. (1976) 'The motivational strategies used by supervisors: Relationships to effectiveness indicators', *Organizational Behavior and Human Performance* 15(1): 66–86.

Oshagbemi, T. A. (1988) *Leadership and Management in Universities*, Berlin/New York: Walter de Gruyter.

Ostell, A. O. (under review) 'Managing disfunctional emotions in organizations'.

Parker, M. and Slaughter, J. (1988) *'Choosing Sides': Unions and the Team Concept*, Boston: South End Press.

Pasmore, W., Francis, C., Haldeman, J. and Shani, A. (1982) 'Sociotechnical systems: A North American reflection on empirical studies of the seventies', *Human Relations* 35(12): 1179–204.

Paul, R. J. and Ebadi, Y. M. (1989) 'Leadership decision making in a service organization: A field test of the Vroom–Yetton model', *Journal of Occupational Psychology* 62(3): 201–11.

Pelz, D. C. and Andrews, F. M. (1966) *Scientists in Organizations*, New York: Wiley.

Peters, L. H., Hartke, D. D. and Pohlmann, J. T. (1985) 'Fiedler's Contingency Theory of leadership: An application of the meta-analysis procedures of Schmidt and Hunter', *Psychological Bulletin* 97(2): 274–85.

Peterson, M. F. (1979) 'Problem-appropriate leadership in hospital emergency units', unpublished doctoral dissertation, University of Michigan.

—— (1985) 'Experienced acceptability: Measuring perceptions of dysfunctional leadership', *Group and Organization Studies* 10: 447–77.

—— (1988) 'PM Theory in Japan and China: What's in it for the United States?', *Organizational Dynamics* 16(4): 22–38.

Phillips, J. S. (1984) 'The accuracy of leadership ratings: A cognitive categorization perspective', *Organizational Behavior and Human Performance* 33(1): 125–38.

Phillips, J. S. and Lord, R. G. (1981) 'Causal attributions and perceptions of leadership', *Organizational Behavior and Human Performance* 28(2): 143–63.

Podsakoff, P. M., Todor, W. D. and Skov, R. (1982) 'Effects of leader contingent reward and punishment behaviors on subordinate performance and satisfaction', *Academy of Management Journal* 25(4): 810–21.

Potter, E. H. and Fiedler, F. E. (1981) 'The utilization of staff member intelligence and experience under conditions of high and low stress', *Academy and Management Journal* 24(2): 361–76.

Puffer, S. M. (1990) 'Attributions of charismatic leadership: The impact of decision style, outcome and observer characteristics', *Leadership Quarterly* 1(3): 177–92.

Quinn, R. E. (1984) 'Applying the competing values approach to leadership: Toward an integrative framework', in J. G. Hunt, D. M. Hosking, C. A. Schriesheim and R. Stewart (eds) *Leaders and Managers: International Perspectives on Managerial Behavior and Leadership*, Pergamon: New York.

Rackham, N. and Carlisle, J. (1978) 'The effective negotiator, part 1: The behaviour of successful negotiators', *Journal of European Industrial Training* 2(6): 6–11.

Rackham, N. and Morgan, T. (1977) *Behaviour Analysis in Training*, Maidenhead, Berks: McGraw-Hill.

Randell, G. A. R. (1981) 'Management education and training', in W. T. Singleton (ed.) *Management Skills*, Lancaster: MTP Press.

Randell, G. A., Packard, P. M. A. Shaw, R. L. and Slater, A. J. (1972) *Staff Appraisal*, London: Institute of Personnel Management.

Randell, G. A., Packard, P. M. A. and Slater, J. (1984) *Staff Appraisal: A First Step to Effective Leadership*, London: IPM.

Rasmussen, R. V. (1991) 'Issues in communication skills training', in J. D. Bigelow (ed.) *Managerial Skills: Explorations in Practical Knowledge*, Newbury, CA: Sage.

Reddin, W. J. (1966) 'The tri-dimensional grid', *The Canadian Personnel and Industrial Relations Journal*, January: 13–20.

—— (1970) *Managerial Effectiveness*, New York: McGraw-Hill.

—— (1987) *How to Make Your Management Style More Effective*. Maidenhead, Berks: McGraw-Hill.

Redding, S. G. and Casey, T. W. (1976) 'Managerial beliefs among Asian managers', proceedings, Academy of Management, Kansas City: 351–5.

Rehder, R. R. (1994) 'Is Saturn competitive?', *Business Horizons* 37(2): 7–15.

Rice, A. (1958) *Productivity and Social Organization: The Ahmedabad Experiment*, London: Tavistock.

Rice, R. W. (1978) 'Construct validity of the least preferred co-worker score', *Psychological Bulletin* 85(6): 1199–237.

Rice, R. W., Bender, L. R. and Vitters, A. G. (1980) 'Leader sex, follower attitudes toward women and leadership effectiveness: A laboratory experiment', *Organizational Behavior and Human Performance* 25(1): 46–78.

—— (1982) 'Validity tests of the contingency model for male and female leaders', unpublished manuscript, quoted Adams and Yoder (1985).

Richards, S. A. and Jaffee, C. L. (1972) 'Blacks supervising whites: A study of interracial difficulties in working together in a simulated organization', *Journal of Applied Psychology* 56(3): 234–40.

Ripley, R. E. and Ripley, M. J. (1993) 'Empowering management in innovative organizations in the 1990s', *Empowerment in Organizations* 1(1): 29–40.

Roberts, N. C. and Bradley, R. T. (1988) 'Limits of charisma', in J. A. Conger and R. N. Kanungo (eds) *Charismatic Leadership: The Elusive Factor in Organizational Effectiveness*, San Francisco: Jossey-Bass.

Rogers, C. R. (1951) *Client-centered Therapy*, Boston, MA: Houghton Mifflin.

Rousseau, D. M. (1977) 'Technological differences in job characteristics, employee satisfaction, and motivation: A synthesis of job design research and sociotechnical systems theory', *Organizational Behavior and Human Performance* 19(1): 18–42.

Rush, M. C., Phillips, J. S. and Lord, R. G. (1981) 'Effects of temporal delay in rating on leader behavior descriptions: A laboratory investigation', *Journal of Applied Psychology* 66(4): 442–50.

Sadler, P. J. (1970) 'Leadership style, confidence in management, and job satisfaction', *Journal of Applied Behavioral Science* 6(1): 3–19.

Sashkin, M. (1988) 'The visionary leader', in J. A. Conger and R. N. Kanungo (eds) *Charismatic Leadership: The Elusive Factor in Organizational Effectiveness*, San Francisco: Jossey-Bass.

Sayles, L. R. (1979) *Leadership: What Effective Managers Really Do ... and How They Do It*, New York: McGraw-Hill.

Scandura, T. A. and Graen, G. B. (1984) 'Moderating effects of initial leader–member exchange status on the effects of a leadership intervention', *Journal of Applied Psychology* 69(3): 428–36.

Schein, E. H. (1965) *Organizational Psychology*, Englewood Cliffs, NJ: Prentice-Hall.

—— (1987) *Process Consultation, Volume 2: Some Lessons for Managers and Consultants*, Reading, MA: Addison Wesley.

Schermerhorn, J. R., Hunt, J. G. and Osborn, R. N. (1994) *Managing Organizational Behavior*, 5th edn, New York: Wiley.

Schriesheim, C. A. (1979) 'The similarity of individual directed and group directed leader behavior descriptions', *Academy of Management Journal* 22(2): 345–55.

Schriesheim, C. A. and DeNisi, A. S. (1981) 'Task dimensions as moderators of the effects of instrumental leadership: A two-sample replicated test of Path–Goal leadership theory', *Journal of Applied Psychology* 66(5): 589–97.

Schriesheim, C. A. and Kerr, S. (1974) 'Psychometric properties of the Ohio State leadership scales', *Psychological Bulletin* 81(11): 756–65.

—— (1977) 'Theories and measures of leadership: A critical appraisal of current and future directions', in J. G. Hunt and L. L. Larson (eds) *Leadership: The Cutting Edge*, Carbondale, IL: Southern Illinois University Press.

Shamir, B., House, R. J. and Arthur, M. B. (1993) 'The motivational effects of charismatic leadership: A self-concept based theory', *Organization Science* 4(4): 577–94.

Sims, H. P. (1977) 'The leader as a manager of reinforcement contingencies: An empirical example and a model', in J. G. Hunt and L. L. Larson (eds) *Leadership: The Cutting Edge*, Carbondale, IL: Southern Illinois University Press.

—— (1980) 'Further thoughts on punishment in organizations', *Academy of Management Review* 5: 133–8.

Sims, H. P. and Lorenzi, P. (1992) *The New Leadership Paradigm: Social Learning and Cognitions in Organizations*, Newbury Park, CA: Sage.

Sims, H. P. and Manz, C. C. (1984) 'Observing leader verbal behavior: Toward reciprocal determinism in leadership theory', *Journal of Applied Psychology* 69(2): 222–32.

Sims, H. P., Manz, C. C. and Bateman, B. (1993) 'The early implementation stage: Getting teams started in the office', in C. C. Manz and H. P. Sims, *Business Without Bosses*, New York: Wiley.

Skinner, B. F. (1953) *Science and Human Behavior*, New York: Macmillan.

Smith, B. J. (1982) 'An initial test of charismatic leadership based on the responses of subordinates', unpublished doctoral dissertation, University of Toronto.

Smith, P. B. and Peterson, M. F. (1988) *Leadership, Organizations and Culture: An Event Management Model*, London: Sage.

Stahl, M. S. (1983) 'Achievement, power and managerial motivation: Selecting managerial talent with the job choice exercise', *Personnel Psychology* 36(4): 775–89.

Stewart, R. (1967) *Managers and Their Jobs*, London: Macmillan.

—— (1982) *Choices for the Manager: A Guide to Managerial Work and Behaviour*, London: McGraw-Hill.

Stiles, W. B. (1992) *Describing Talk: A Taxonomy of Verbal Response Modes*, Newbury Park, CA: Sage.

Stogdill, R. M. (1948) 'Personal factors associated with leadership: A survey of the literature', *Journal of Psychology* 25: 35–71.

—— (1974) *Handbook of Leadership: A Survey of Theory and Research*, New York: Free Press.

Strauss, G. (1977) 'Managerial practices', in J. R. Hackman and J. L. Suttle (eds) *Improving Life at Work: Behavioral Science Approaches to Organizational Change*, Santa Monica, CA: Goodyear.

Strube, M. and Garcia, J. E. (1981) 'A meta-analytic investigation of Fiedler's Contingency Model of leadership effectiveness', *Psychological Bulletin* 90(2): 307–21.

Szanton, D. L. (1966) 'Cultural confrontation in the Philippines', in R. B. Textor (ed.) *Cultural Frontiers of the Peace Corps*, Cambridge, MA: MIT Press.

Szilagyi, A. D. (1980) 'Causal inferences between leader reward behaviour and subordinate performance, absenteeism and work satisfaction', *Journal of Occupational Psychology* 53(3): 195–204.

Tannenbaum, R. and Schmidt, W. H. (1958) 'How to choose a leadership pattern', *Harvard Business Review* 36(2), March–April: 95–101.

Taylor, D. S. and Wright, P. L. (1977) 'Training auditors in interviewing skills', *Journal of European Industrial Training* 1(5): 8–10, 16.

—— (1988) *Developing Interpersonal Skills through Tutored Practice*, Hemel Hempstead, Herts: Prentice-Hall.

Tengler, C. D. and Jablin, F. M. (1983) 'Effects of question type, orientation and sequencing in the employment screening interview', *Communication Monographs* 50, September: 245–63.

Trice, H. M. and Beyer, J. M. (1986) 'Charisma and its routinization in two social movement organizations', in B. M. Staw and L. L. Cummings (eds) *Research in Organizational Behavior, Volume 8*, Greenwich, CT: JAI Press.

—— (1993) *The Cultures of Work Organizations*, Englewood Cliffs, NJ: Prentice-Hall.

Trist, E. L. (1977) 'Collaboration in work settings: A personal perspective', *Journal of Applied Behavioral Science* 13(3): 268–78.

Trist, E. L. and Bamforth, K. W. (1951) 'Some social and psychological consequences of the longwall method of coal-getting', *Human Relations* 4(1): 6–24, 37–8.

Trist, E. L., Susman, G. I. and Brown, G. R. (1977) 'An experiment in autonomous working in an American underground coal mine', *Human Relations* 30(3): 201–36.

Uhl-Bien, M. and Graen, G. B. (1992) An empirical test of the leadership-making model in professional project teams', in K. E. Clark, M. B. Clark and D. P. Campbell (eds) *Impact of Leadership*, Greensboro, NC: Center for Creative Leadership.

Van Oudtshoorn, M. and Thomas, L. (1993) 'A management synopsis of empowerment', *Empowerment in Organizations* 1(1): 4–12.

Varga, K. (1975) 'n Achievement, n Power and effectiveness of research and development', *Human Relations* 28(6): 571–90.

Vecchio, R. P. (1987) 'Situational Leadership Theory: An examination of a prescriptive theory', *Journal of Applied Psychology* 72(3): 444–541.

—— (1990) 'Theoretical and empirical examination of cognitive resource theory', *Journal of Applied Psychology* 75(2): 141–7.

Vecchio, R. P. and Godbel, B. C. (1984) 'The vertical dyad linkage model of leadership: Problems and prospects', *Organizational Behavior and Human Performance* 34(1): 5–20.

Vroom, V. H. (1964) *Work and Motivation*, New York: Wiley.

—— (1984) 'Reflections on leadership and decision-making', *Journal of General Management* 9(3): 18–36.

Vroom, V. H. and Jago, A. G. (1988) *The New Leadership: Managing Participation in Organizations*, Englewood Cliffs, NJ: Prentice-Hall.

—— and Yetton, P. W. (1973) *Leadership and Decision-making*, Pittsburgh: University of Pittsburgh Press.

Wainer, H. A. and Rubin, I. M. (1969) 'Motivation of research and development entrepreneurs: Determinants of company success', *Journal of Applied Psychology* 53(3): 178–84.

Walker, C. R. (1950) 'The problem of the repetitive job', *Harvard Business Review* 28(3), May: 54–8.

Wall, T. D., Kemp, N. J., Jackson, P. R. and Clegg, C. W. (1986) 'Outcomes of autonomous workgroups: A long-term field experiment', *Academy of Management Journal* 29(2) 280–304.

Walton, R. E. and Schlesinger, L. A. (1979) 'Do supervisors thrive in participative work systems?', *Organizational Dynamics* 7(3): 25–38.

Weber, M. (1947) *The Theory of Social and Economic Organization*, New York: Free Press [translated and edited by A. M. Henderson and T. Parsons].

White, R. K. and Lippitt, R. (1960) *Autocracy and Democracy*, New York: Harper.

Wilson, H. J., Callaghan, C. A. and Wright, P. L. (under review) 'A comparison of the observed leadership skills of British and Philippine managers in appraisal interviews'.

Winter, D. G. (1979) *Navy Leadership and Management Competencies: Convergence Among Tests, Interviews and Performance Ratings*, Boston, MA: McBer and Company.

Wolfgang, A. (ed.) (1979) *Nonverbal Behaviour: Applications and Cultural Implications*, New York: Academic Press.

Wright, P. L. (1993) 'Interpersonal skills training: Interactions between research and practice', paper presented at 6th European Congress on Work and Organizational Psychology, Alicante, April.

—— (1994) 'Intercultural communication: The case for the systematic study of verbal behaviour', paper presented at the 23rd International Congress of Applied Psychology, Madrid, July.

Wright, P. L. and Taylor, D. S. (1984) *Improving Leadership Performance*, Hemel Hempstead, Herts: Prentice-Hall.

—— (1985) 'The implications of a skills approach to leadership', *Journal of Management Development* 4(3): 15–28.

—— (1994) *Improving Leadership Performance: Interpersonal Skills for Effective Leadership*, 2nd edn, Hemel Hempstead, Herts: Prentice-Hall.

Yeatts, D. E., Hipskind, M. and Barnes, D. (1994) 'Lessons learned from self-managed work teams', *Business Horizons* 37(4): 11–18.

Yukl, G. A. (1981) *Leadership in Organizations*, Englewood Cliffs, NJ: Prentice-Hall.

—— (1989) *Leadership in Organizations*, 2nd edn, Englewood Cliffs, NJ: Prentice-Hall.

—— (1994) *Leadership in Organizations*, 3rd edn, Englewood Cliffs, NJ: Prentice-Hall.

Yukl, G. and Nemeroff, W. F. (1979) 'Identification and measurement of specific categories of leadership behaviour: A progress report', in J. G. Hunt and L. L. Larson (eds) *Crosscurrents in Leadership*, Carbondale, IL: Southern Illinois University Press.

Yukl, G., Wall, S. and Lepsinger, R. (1990) 'Preliminary report on validation of the Managerial Practices Survey', in K. E. Clark and M. B. Clark (eds) *Measures of Leadership*, West Orange, NJ: Leadership Library of America.

Zaccaro, S. J., Foti, R. J. and Kenny, D. A. (1991) 'Self-monitoring and trait-based variance in leadership: An investigation of leader flexibility across multiple group situations', *Journal of Applied Psychology* 76(2): 308–15.

Name index

Subject index